D0752286

Build a Program

Microsoft®
Visual C#® 2008
Express Edition

Patrice Pelland

PUBLISHED BY
Microsoft Press
A Division of Microsoft Corporation
One Microsoft Way
Redmond, Washington 98052-6399

Library of Congress Control Number: 2008920573

Printed and bound in the United States of America.

1 2 3 4 5 6 7 8 9   QWT   3 2 1 0 9 8

Distributed in Canada by H.B. Fenn and Company Ltd.

A CIP catalogue record for this book is available from the British Library.

Microsoft Press books are available through booksellers and distributors worldwide. For further information about international editions, contact your local Microsoft Corporation office or contact Microsoft Press International directly at fax (425) 936-7329. Visit our Web site at www.microsoft.com/mspress. Send comments to mspinput@microsoft.com.

Microsoft, Microsoft Press, DirectX, Excel, Expression, Expression Blend, IntelliSense, Internet Explorer, JScript, MSDN, MSN, Outlook, Silverlight, SQL Server, Visual Basic, Visual C#, Visual C++, Visual Studio, Visual Web Developer, Windows, Windows Live, Windows Mobile, Windows Server, Windows Vista, Xbox and Xbox 360 are either registered trademarks or trademarks of Microsoft Corporation in the United States and/or other countries. Other product and company names mentioned herein may be the trademarks of their respective owners.

The example companies, organizations, products, domain names, e-mail addresses, logos, people, places, and events depicted herein are fictitious. No association with any real company, organization, product, domain name, e-mail address, logo, person, place, or event is intended or should be inferred.

This book expresses the author's views and opinions. The information contained in this book is provided without any express, statutory, or implied warranties. Neither the authors, Microsoft Corporation, nor its resellers, or distributors will be held liable for any damages caused or alleged to be caused either directly or indirectly by this book.

Acquisitions Editor: Ben Ryan
Developmental Editor: Sandra Haynes
Project Manager: John Pierce

Editorial Production: Happenstance Type O Rama
Technical Reviewer: Dan Maharry

Body Part No. X14-55517

Contents

Chapter 1

Introducing Microsoft Visual C# 2008 Express Edition — 1

What Is .NET? — 2
What Is C#? — 4
Is C# an Object-Oriented Programming Language? — 4
What Is Visual C# 2008 Express Edition? — 10
What Kinds of Applications Can You Build with Visual C# 2008 Express Edition? — 10
What Are the Key Features You Need to Know About? — 11

Chapter 2

Installing Visual C# 2008 Express Edition — 17

Preparing to Install Visual C# 2008 Express Edition — 18
Side-by-Side Installation — 18
Prerelease Versions of Visual C# 2008 Express Edition — 19
Installing Visual C# 2008 Express Edition — 19

Chapter 3

Creating Your First Applications — 27

Three Types of Applications: What's the Difference? — 28
Getting Started with the IDE — 30
Building the Projects — 33
Building a Console Application — 33
Getting to Know Solution Explorer — 35

Getting Help: Microsoft Visual Studio 2008 Express Edition Documentation — 36
Coding Your Console Application — 40
Customizing the IDE — 42
Creating a Windows Application — 44

Chapter 4

Creating Your Own Web Browser in Less Than Five Minutes — 51

What Is a Project? — 52
What Is the Design Layout? — 53
Putting It All Together — 60

Chapter 5

Using Rapid Application Development Tools with Visual C# 2008 — 63

Snapping and Aligning Controls Using Snap Lines — 64
Using IntelliSense—Your New Best Friend! — 66
Opening IntelliSense: Pressing Ctrl+Spacebar — 66
Opening IntelliSense: Typing a Period or Left Parenthesis — 67
IntelliSense Filtering: Preselecting the "Most Recently Used" — 69
Using IntelliSense Code Snippets: The Time-Saver — 69
Invoking Code Snippets — 70
Using IntelliSense Automatic *Using* Statements — 72

What do you think of this book? We want to hear from you!

Microsoft is interested in hearing your feedback so we can continually improve our books and learning resources for you. To participate in a brief online survey, please visit:

www.microsoft.com/learning/booksurvey/

Organizing *Using* Statements 73
Automatically Generating a Method Stub 73
Renaming and Refactoring **74**
Why Should You Rename? 75
Using the Rename Feature 75
Refactoring: Using the Extract Method Command 79
Exploring Common Windows Controls **80**
What Happens When an Event Is Triggered? **83**

Chapter 6
Modifying Your Web Browser *89*
Opening Your Application **90**
Interacting Through Dialog Boxes **100**
Adding an About Dialog Box 100
Adding a Navigate Dialog Box 102
Having a Professional Look and Feel at Your Fingertips **106**
Adding a Tool Strip Container and Some Tools 106
Adding a Status Bar to Your Browser 108
Personalizing Your Application with Windows Icons 111
Redoing the Browser **118**
Using Windows Presentation Foundation 119
WPF and XAML 119

Chapter 7
Fixing the Broken Blocks *133*
Debugging an Application **134**
Using a DLL in an Application 134
Using Breakpoints, Locals, Edit and Continue, and
Visualizers 136

Chapter 8
Managing the Data *149*
What Is a Database? **150**
What's in a Database? 150
What Are Data Normalization and Data Integrity? 151

What Is Null? 154
What Are Primary Keys and Foreign Keys? 154
Interacting with a Relational Database 157
**Using SQL Server 2005 Express in Visual C#
Express Edition** **158**
Creating a Database Using Visual C# 2008
Express Edition 159
Creating Tables in Your Database 161
Creating Relationships Between the Tables 163
Entering Data in SQL Server Tables Using Visual Studio 167
What Are ADO.NET, Data Binding, and LINQ? **171**
Developing the CarTracker Application 173
Using the Component Tray 180
Getting More Meaningful Information on the Form 181
Using LINQ 190

Chapter 9
Building Your Own Weather Tracker Application *195*
**Exploring the Features of the Weather Tracker
Application** **196**
Creating the Application User Interface **197**
Adding Notification Area Capabilities 199
Adding the Splash Screen and About Dialog Box 207
Adding the Options Dialog Box 210
Using the MSN Weather Web Service **213**
Connecting to MSN Weather Web Services 214
Setting User and Application Preferences 219
Working in the Background 220
Completing the Core Weather Tracker Functionality 229
Testing Weather Tracker 235
Working with the Options Dialog Box 236
Testing Weather Tracker Options 240
And Now, Just ClickOnce **241**

Glossary *247*
Index *249*

Introduction

Microsoft Visual C# 2008 Express Edition (and the other Visual Studio 2008 Express Edition products) is, in my opinion, one of the best and most intelligent ideas to come from the Developer Division at Microsoft. I'm applauding and cheering for the people who had this brilliant idea because I believe there is a real need and demand for a world-class, powerful product for hobbyist programmers, students, and professional developers. And Visual C# 2008 Express Edition provides all of that and more.

Visual C# 2008 Express Edition is a fully functional subset of Visual Studio 2008, suitable for creating and maintaining Windows applications and libraries. It's not a timed-bomb edition, a demo, or a feature-limited version—no, it's a key Microsoft initiative to reach more people and give them the ability to have fun while creating cool software.

Who Is This Book For?

This book is for everybody: students, hobbyist programmers, and people who always thought programming was a tough task. It's for people who have ideas like "I wish I could build a tool to store all my recipes and then print them and send them to my friends," "I wish I could build this cool card game that I have never found anywhere else," "I wish I could build this cool software to store my DVD and CD collection," "I wish I could build this software to help me work with matrices and plot graphics for my math class," and many more projects that you can imagine!

This book is for people who have ideas but don't know how to bring them to reality. And it's a good introduction to the art and science of developing software.

How This Book Is Organized

This book consists of nine chapters, each covering a particular feature or technology about Visual C# 2008 Express Edition. Most chapters build on previous chapters, so you should plan on reading the material sequentially.

Conventions and Features in This Book

This book presents information using conventions designed to make the information readable and easy to follow. Before you start the book, read the following list, which explains conventions you'll see throughout the book and points out helpful features in the book that you might want to use:

- Each exercise is a series of tasks. Each task is presented as a series of numbered steps (step 1, 2, and so on). Each exercise is preceded by a procedural heading that lets you know what you will accomplish in the exercise.

- Boxes labeled *TIP, NOTE, MORE INFO,* and so on provide additional information or alternative methods for completing a step successfully.

- Boxes labeled *CAUTION* alert you to information you need to verify before continuing.

- Text that you type appears in bold.

- Menu commands, dialog box titles, and other user interface elements appear with each word capitalized, such as in "click Save As."

- A plus sign (+) between two key names means that you must press those keys at the same time. For example, "Press Alt+Tab" means that you hold down the Alt key while you press the Tab key.

- Code listings appear in a monospaced font in this book.

- Sidebars throughout the book provide more in-depth information about the content. The sidebars might contain background information, design tips, or features related to the information being discussed.

- Each chapter ends with an "In Summary..." section that briefly reviews what you learned in the current chapter and previews what the next chapter will present.

System Requirements

You'll need the following hardware and software to complete the exercises in this book:

- Windows Vista, Microsoft Windows XP with Service Pack 2, or Microsoft Windows Server 2003 with Service Pack 2

- Visual C# 2008 Express Edition

- 1 GHz 32-bit (x86) processor

- 1 GB MB RAM (512 MB minimum)

- 40 GB hard drive with at least 15 GB of available space

- Support for Super VGA graphics (for support for DirectX 9 graphics, see the recommended requirements at *www.microsoft.com/windows/products/windowsvista/editions/systemrequirements.mspx*)

- CD-ROM or DVD-ROM drive

- Microsoft mouse or compatible pointing device

You'll also need administrator access to your computer to configure SQL Server 2005 Express Edition.

NOTE

The companion DVD contains the Visual C# 2008 Express Edition software needed to complete the exercises in this book. The DVD also includes the other Visual Studio 2008 Express Editions—for Visual Basic, Visual C++, and Web development. You can install any of the Express Edition products included on the DVD. See Chapter 2, "Installing Visual C# 2008 Express Edition" for detailed installation instructions.

Code Samples

You can download the code samples for the examples in this book from the book's companion content page at the following address: *http://www.microsoft.com/mspress/companion/9780735625426*.

You'll use the code samples and starter solutions as you perform the exercises in the book. By using the code samples, you won't waste time creating files that aren't relevant to the exercise. The files and step-by-step instructions in the lessons also let you learn by doing, which is an easy and effective way to acquire and remember new skills. You'll also find the complete solutions if you want to verify your work or if you simply want to look at it.

Installing the Code Samples

Follow these steps to install the code samples on your computer.

1. Download the code samples from *http://www.microsoft.com/mspress/companion/9780735625426*.

2. After you download the code samples file, run the installer.

3. Follow the instructions that appear.

   The code samples are installed in the Documents\Microsoft Press\VCS 2008 Express folder on your computer.

Using the Code Samples

Each chapter in this book explains when and how to use any code samples for that chapter. When it's time to use a code sample, the book will list the instructions for how to open the files. The chapters are built around scenarios that simulate real programming projects so you can easily apply the skills you learn to your own work.

For those of you who like to know all the details, a list of the code sample projects appears in the following table. Almost all projects have solutions available for the practice exercises. The solutions for each project are included in the folder for each chapter and are labeled "Complete."

Project	Description
Chapters 1 and 2	No sample projects.
Chapter 3	
MyFirstConsoleApplication	Application that takes two numbers, adds them together, and then displays the sum in a console window.
MyFirstWindowsApplication	Same application as MyFirstConsoleApplication, but this one displays the result in a message box.
Chapter 4	Simple Web browser application that enables the user to browse on the Internet.
MyOwnBrowser	
Chapter 5	Application that teaches you to use the most important features in Visual C# 2008 Express Edition.
TestProject	
Chapter 6	This is the same application you developed in Chapter 4, enhanced with additional features. You'll add menus, toolbars, status and progress bars, and a navigation window with autocomplete. You'll also build a simple browser using Windows Presentation Foundation (WPF).
MyOwnBrowser	

Project	Description
Chapter 7 Debugger	An application full of problems to help you learn how to debug an application by using features of Visual C# 2008 Express Edition.
Chapter 8 CarTracker	An application enabling the user to track car ads from the Internet using a SQL Server 2005 Express database to store the information. You'll also be introduced to Language Integrated Query (LINQ).
Chapter 9 Weather Tracker	An application that runs in the system tray and has a nice user interface to display weather data collected by your application from the MSN Weather service. You'll also create a deployment package for the distribution of your application.

Uninstalling the Code Samples

Follow these steps to remove the code samples from your computer.

ON WINDOWS VISTA

1. In Control Panel, click Programs.

2. Under Programs and Features, click Uninstall a Program.

3. In the list of programs, select Microsoft Visual C# 2008 Express Edition: Build a Program Now!, and then click Uninstall.

4. Follow the instructions on the screen to remove the code samples.

ON WINDOWS XP

1. In Control Panel, open Add or Remove Programs.

2. From the Currently Installed Programs list, select Microsoft Visual C# 2008 Express Edition: Build a Program Now!, and click Remove.

3. Follow the instructions on the screen to remove the code samples.

Prerelease Software

This book was reviewed and tested against the November 2007 release candidate for Visual Studio 2008. This book is expected to be fully compatible with the final release of Visual Studio 2008. If there are any changes or corrections for this book, they'll be collected and added to a Microsoft Knowledge Base article. See the "Support for This Book" section later in this introduction for more information.

Technology Updates

As technologies related to this book are updated, links to additional information will be added to the Microsoft Press

Technology Updates Web page (*http://www.microsoft.com/mspress/updates/*). Visit this page periodically for updates on Visual Studio 2008 and other technologies.

Support for This Book

Every effort has been made to ensure the accuracy of this book and the companion content. As corrections or changes are collected, they'll be added to a Microsoft Knowledge Base article. To view the list of known corrections for this book, visit *http://support.microsoft.com/* and in the Search box, enter the book title.

Microsoft Press provides support for books and companion content at *http://www.microsoft.com/learning/support/books/*.

Questions and Comments

If you have comments, questions, or ideas regarding the book or the companion content or have questions that are not answered by visiting the sites listed earlier, please send them to Microsoft Press via e-mail to *mspinput@microsoft.com*.

Or you can send them via postal mail to the following address:

Microsoft Press
Attn: Visual C# 2008 Express Edition: Build a Program Now! Editor
One Microsoft Way
Redmond, WA 98052-6399

Please note that Microsoft offers no software product support through these addresses.

About the Author

Patrice Pelland is a development manager at Microsoft working in the Online Services Group. He has a passion for Web 2.0 technologies, Silverlight, WCF, and ASP.NET. For the past four years, he has been working, teaching, evangelizing, and talking about these technologies to everyone.

For the past 14 years, he has been working in software development in various roles: developer, project lead, manager and mentor, and software engineer in QA organizations. He has vast experience spanning multiple technologies and fields, including Web development, developer tools, fiber optics telecommunication, aviation, and coffee and dairy companies. He also spent three years teaching computer science and software development at a college in Canada.

When not developing great tools for developers and helping customers throughout the world, he enjoys spending time with his family and friends, playing games on Xbox 360 and his PC, reading books, reading about cars, playing hockey, watching NHL hockey and NFL football, and having great dinners with good food and fine drinks with friends and family. He resides with his family in Sammamish, Washington.

Dedication

This book is dedicated to my family. My wife, Hélène, is my strength; because of her love and her respect, I am a better human being. She's beautiful—my idol, my inspiration, my sunshine, my best friend, my love, and an awesome mother! *Mon amour*, thanks for being who you are and for being there for me. I love you! Thanks to her for letting me repeat this crazy adventure of writing a book.

Thanks

First of all, thanks to my parents. Mom and Dad, you gave me all the chances to be what I am in life and you gave me the values to be the man I am. Thanks, and I love you!

A book is a huge adventure in somebody's life (imagine two ☺), and it would not be possible without the help of many people. I've always read the "thank you" sections in other people's books, and I was always amazed at how many people are needed to make a book what it is. Now I really understand why!

Although writing a book is tough—real tough—it's really satisfying at the same time. During the writing process, you sometimes have doubts, and I had my share of them, especially those nights at 3 A.M. when all other souls in the house were asleep, even my dog; when I was in front of my laptop with an exception and a white page in Microsoft Word. I can't remember how many times I said to my friends, "No, I won't be able to be there. I need to work on my book." But it's an awesome experience to write a book; everybody who has the chance should take the challenge!

That said, I first need to thank my lovely family for letting me do this to them again. My kids (Laura, 13, and Antoine, 11) and my wife, Hélène, were so great and *patient*. This time they said, "You're writing another book! Oh, no...we'll see you after Thanksgiving." But at the same time, they were respecting the space I needed and the time alone! You guys are great, and I love you!

I have to thank all the people at Microsoft Learning and the publishing team. I would especially like to thank Ben Ryan for offering me the chance to work with him again;

Sandra for her constant motivation, help, and suggestions and also for helping me through all the hurdles of writing a book; and all the folks on the publishing team for all their help getting the job done and producing a real, tangible product. You guys have my respect for working day in, day out in the crazy world of publishing.

I would also like to thank all the people in the Visual Basic, C#, Windows Forms, MSDN, and setup teams who helped me by answering all my questions in a dynamic and constantly changing product life cycle. I would like to thank more specifically Dan Fernandez, Joe Binder, Brian Keller, Brian Johnson, Hong Gao, Jay Roxe, Kavitha Radhakrishnan, Kent Sharkey, Lisa Feigenbaum, Shamez Rajan, Steve Lasker, Aaron Stebner, and Habib Heydarian.

Thanks also to my colleagues at MSN for always giving me good words of encouragement and to my friends Pascal, Simon, Nicolas, John, and Patrice for reviewing the samples and some chapters.

Thanks to my good friends here in the Puget Sound area for the kind words of encouragement and to my family and friends in Canada for understanding why I'm not calling or giving any news. Sorry, Mom and Dad!

Thanks to everybody I might have forgotten!

Patrice Pelland
November 2007
Sammamish, WA

Chapter 1
Introducing Microsoft Visual C# 2008 Express Edition

What Is .NET?, 2

What Is C#?, 4

What Is Visual C# 2008 Express Edition?, 10

Maybe you've decided to try programming and find yourself with this book. If that's the case, you've come to the right place. This book is all about introducing you to the art, science, and joys of creating software for Microsoft Windows—yes, the same Microsoft Windows you probably use every day. Throughout the book, I'll show you how to build applications that are similar to many of the applications you use on a regular basis, such as your Internet browser, your word processor, your e-mail software, and your personal finance application. You're probably wondering how you could possibly do this with no programming experience. Don't worry. By the time you finish this book, you'll be a believer. We'll have a blast, and because you'll actually be building applications as you follow along with each exercise, you'll see for yourself just how easy it can be.

What is this .NET thing everybody is talking about? Maybe you've seen the term somewhere online or come across it in the jobs section of your Sunday newspaper. A good analogy is that .NET—also called the .NET Framework—is to a software developer what tools and manuals are to an auto mechanic.

Here is a formal definition of the .NET Framework:

The .NET Framework is a platform with which you can develop software applications and libraries called managed applications; *it provides you with the compiler and tools you need to build, debug, and execute managed applications.*

For our purposes, you could say that .NET is the platform that gives you everything you need to develop and run managed applications that run on Windows.

We say that applications are *managed* because their execution is managed by the .NET Framework. In fact, the .NET Framework manages the execution by providing a controlled runtime environment that offers a wide variety of services, such as loading your applications, managing memory, and monitoring and maintaining security and integrity while the application runs. Before .NET (and Java), applications were unmanaged because they were not executed by a controlled runtime environment. No other component of the operating system provides the services .NET offers. The applications had to manage their own services, which sometimes led to erroneous code, security holes, and data corruption. Because of these problems, applications were tough to maintain and debug.

The .NET Framework provides you with a wide variety of tools, such as compilers, debuggers, programming languages, an execution engine (named the Common Language Runtime [CLR]), developer tools, and a large number of predefined "building block" libraries. These libraries are named Framework Class Libraries (FCLs). You can think of each .NET component as a building block in a house and each version of .NET as an insulation layer in the walls of the house. Figure 1-1 illustrates how many versions of .NET are out in the market, what components have been added, in which version they belong.

NOTE

Throughout this book, I'll use the terms *framework* and *.NET Framework* synonymously.

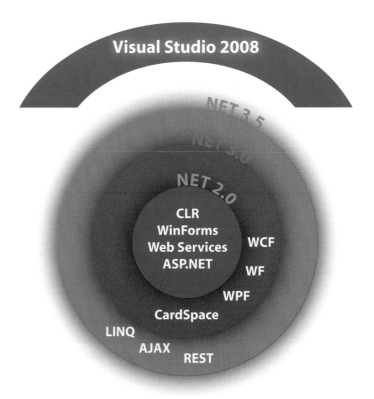

Visual Studio 2008

NET 3.5
NET 3.0
NET 2.0

CLR
WinForms
Web Services
ASP.NET

WCF

WF

WPF

CardSpace

LINQ

AJAX

REST

Figure 1-1
Additive versions of the .NET Framework

NOTE

What do the other abbreviations and names in Figure 1-1 mean? WF is the Windows Workflow Foundation, another building block that developers can use to help automate business processes through programs. CardSpace is a technology related to managing online identities—something like using a credit card. AJAX (Asynchronous JavaScript And XML) is used to develop Web applications, and REST (Representational State Transfer) is a programming architecture used for transferring data on the Web.

Some of these building blocks ship with the Windows Vista operating system. Two popular ones are Windows Presentation Foundation (WPF) and Windows Communication Foundation (WCF). WPF is a library that helps you build richer user interfaces and Windows Vista–like applications for Windows. WCF, as its name implies, is a library that helps two applications talk to each other using messages. To understand the relationship between .NET 3.0 and .NET 3.5, remember that .NET 3.0 comes with Windows Vista and .NET 3.5 comes with Visual Studio 2008. Language Integrated Query (LINQ), which simplifies writing code that manipulates data from various data sources (SQL Server databases, XML files, and so on), is one of the features in .NET 3.5 that we'll cover in this book.

I won't put you to sleep with all the definitions for each building block. We're going to use or talk about most of them in our projects in this book, and I'll introduce the blocks when appropriate. Just consider Figure 1-1, and return to it when you need to do so.

Two notes about this image are worth mentioning.

First, look at the blue component on top of the concentric circles. Microsoft Visual Studio 2008 is not part of the .NET Framework, but it touches the .NET Framework at all levels. With Visual Studio 2008, you can develop applications that take advantage of all the components of the .NET Framework.

Second, notice that the CLR, among other components, is at the center of the circles. The CLR is a crucial part of the foundation because it's the engine that loads and manages the execution of source code.

What Is C#?

C# is one of the programming languages that targets the .NET Framework. Like any spoken or written language, C# has syntax rules and a series of valid words you can use to create your applications. C# is a popular choice for beginners because some people find the syntax simpler than the syntax of many other programming languages.

Is C# an Object-Oriented Programming Language?

C# is a fully fledged object-oriented programming language. Let's talk about what this means.

Object-oriented programming (OOP) is a programming style (or programming paradigm). There are other programming paradigms, such as functional or procedural programming. Languages such as C, Fortran, and Pascal all use functional or procedural programming paradigms. These paradigms focus more on actions, while OOP focuses more on the data itself.

Applications that use the OOP paradigm are developed using OOP languages (OOPLs). The first OOPLs were introduced in the late 1960s, but they really became popular in the late

1970s. They are widely used today because most people agree that they're easy to learn, use, debug, and maintain. For instance, OOPLs easily represent real-world objects. C# is an OOPL, as are Visual Basic .NET, C++, Java, Smalltalk, Lisp, and others.

Programmers use OOP to write programs that contain representations of real-world objects that are known as *classes* or *types*. You can think of an OOP program as a collection of objects interacting with each other. Using OOP, a programmer defines new types to represent real-world objects, such as a plane, a person, a customer, a dog, or a car. Those types or classes have constructors that developers use to create objects or instances. An *object* is a unit that represents one instance of a real-world object. It's a self-contained unit because it includes all the data and functionality associated with that object. This means each object created in an application contains all the information that characterizes it (*data members* or *fields*) and all the actions (*methods*) that can access or modify that information.

Here is a simple example in C# that defines a *Person* class:

```
1   using System;
2
3   public class Person
4   {
5       //Data members
6       private string Name;
7       private string Address;
8       private string City;
9       private string State;
10      private string ZIP;
11      private string Country;
12
13      // Methods
14      public virtual void Display()
15      {
16          Console.WriteLine(Name);
17          Console.WriteLine(Address);
18          Console.WriteLine(City);
19          Console.WriteLine(State);
20          Console.WriteLine(ZIP);
21          Console.WriteLine(Country);
22      }
23  }
```

This class includes private data members and a *Display* method to print the object's content to the console. The *virtual* keyword used in the definition of the *Display* method means that a class derived from this class will be able to write its own implementation of the *Display* method.

Let's use a different example to go over these concepts some more. My dog, Chopin, is an instance of the class *Dog*, and the class *Dog* is a subclass of the *Animal* class. Because Chopin is a dog, he has some behaviors and data that are proper for a dog. But because a dog is also an animal, Chopin also inherits some data and behaviors from the *Animal* class.

This means that the instance *Chopin* of the *Dog* class has data members that characterize him and methods that I can call on that little furry ball. For example, here is the instance information for the *Chopin* object:

Data

- **Breed**　He's a Maltese.

- **Gender**　He's male.

- **Weight**　His weight is 5.5 pounds (2.5 kilograms).

- **Color**　He's white.

- **Name**　His name is Chopin Chabispel.

- **Age**　He's 1.5 years old.

Actions

- He speaks (barks).

- He eats.

- He moves.

- He sleeps.

All these data items (breed, gender, weight, color, name, and age) and actions (speak, eat, move, and sleep) characterize him, but they can also characterize any other dog, such as my neighbor's dog, Molly. And if you think about it, those items can characterize any animal. This means that the class *Dog* inherits data members and methods from the class *Animal*.

Let's say you want to develop an application for a veterinary clinic. To cover the cats who come to your clinic, all you must do is create a *Cat* class that also inherits from the class *Animal*. Then each class (*Cat* or *Dog*) could override functionality from the *Animal* class as needed. For instance, for the *Cat* class, the *Speak* method would be *meow* instead of *bark*. This means that the *Speak* methods for *Cat* and *Dog* are specializations of the regular animal *Speak* method.

Let's look at the *Person* class example again. This time, I'll also show an *Employee* class that derives from the *Person* class. The *Employee* class derives from the *Person* class by using a colon (:) followed by the *Person* element. The keyword *override* changes the implementation of the *Display* method.

```
52  public class Employee : Person
53
54  {
55      public int Level;
56      public int Salary;
57
58      public override void Display()
59      {
60          Console.WriteLine(Name + " is at level " + Level.ToString() + "
              and has a salary of : " + Salary.ToString() + "$");
61          Console.WriteLine("His address is:");
62          Console.WriteLine(Address);
63          Console.WriteLine(City + "," + State + " " + ZIP);
64          Console.WriteLine(Country);
65      }
66  }
```

TIP
In this book, you'll notice that some code listings include line numbers. If a line does not include a number, it indicates that the code is a continuation from the previous line. Some code lines can get rather long and must be wrapped to be displayed on the printed page. If you need to type in the code in Visual C#, be sure to put continued lines on a single line.

In this case, the *Employee* class inherits from the *Person* class and therefore gets all the data fields from that base class. The *Employee* class doesn't have to redefine any of the fields in its definition because it gets them automatically from *Person*. So, for the *Employee* class, you must specify only what is different from an instance of the *Person* class. For example, an instance of the *Employee* class would have *Level* and *Salary*, whereas none of the instances of the *Person* class would have these. Plus, the *Display* method for *Employee* could thus add *Level* and *Salary* information to the displayed message when it is called.

This was just a brief introduction to OOP and some of its concepts. C# supports all of these concepts and many more. Throughout this book you'll see more OOP concepts, and when you do, I'll highlight them in a "reader aid" information box, as shown in the left margin.

Here's the complete listing used in this section with the addition of the *Customer* class:

```csharp
1   using System;
2
3   public class Person
4   {
5       //Data members
6       public string Name;
7       public string Address;
8       public string City;
9       public string State;
10      public string ZIP;
11      public string Country;
12
13       // Methods
14       public virtual void Display()
15       {
16           Console.WriteLine(Name);
17           Console.WriteLine(Address);
18           Console.WriteLine(City);
19           Console.WriteLine(State);
20           Console.WriteLine(ZIP);
21           Console.WriteLine(Country);
22       }
23   }
24
25   public class Customer : Person
26
27   {
28       public int ID;
29       public bool IsPartner;
30
31       public override void Display()
32       {
33           string partnerMessage;
```

```
34
35          if (IsPartner)
36          {
37              partnerMessage = " is a partner";
38          }
39          else
40          {
41              partnerMessage = " is not a partner";
42          }
43
44          Console.WriteLine("Customer ID: " + ID.ToString());
45          Console.WriteLine(Name + partnerMessage);
46          Console.WriteLine(Address);
47          Console.WriteLine(City + "," + State + " " + ZIP);
48          Console.WriteLine(Country);
49      }
50  }
51
52  public class Employee : Person
53
54  {
55      public int Level;
56      public int Salary;
57
58      public override void Display()
59      {
60          Console.WriteLine(Name + " is at level " + Level.ToString() +
                  " and has a salary of : " + Salary.ToString() + "$");
61          Console.WriteLine("His address is:");
62          Console.WriteLine(Address);
63          Console.WriteLine(City + "," + State + " " + ZIP);
64          Console.WriteLine(Country);
65      }
66  }
```

This is a simple case, but it illustrates some of the basic concepts of OOP.

Visual C# 2008 Express Edition is the tool we will use throughout this book to develop applications that run on Windows.

The Express editions of Visual Studio 2008 were designed to focus on productivity. As with their high-end version counterparts, the Express editions of Visual Studio 2008 are also what we call *rapid application development* (RAD) tools because their philosophy is geared toward productivity. The Express editions of Visual Studio are easy to use, easy to learn, and streamlined because although they contain mostly the same components, they lack the full breadth of features found in the higher-end versions of Visual Studio. Most features and components in the Express editions were simplified to make the learning curve less steep and to fit the needs of the nonprofessional developer.

The Visual Studio 2008 Express Edition family is designed with beginner programmers in mind—people like you who are curious about programming and who are looking for an easy way to build Windows applications while learning how to program. Visual C# 2008 Express Edition is the ideal tool to use to rapidly develop applications for topics you really love or for hobbies you enjoy. You can also use it to help ease your day-to-day job or school tasks. Most important, you can have fun with the tool while you're learning to program.

What Kinds of Applications Can You Build with Visual C# 2008 Express Edition?

With this version of Visual Studio 2008, you'll be able to create the following types of applications:

■ **Windows applications**   These are the applications that have a graphical interface with buttons, windows, menus, toolbars, and so on, as in Microsoft Word or Windows Internet Explorer. With this book you'll learn how to take advantage of WPF, which lets you build applications that create a rich user experience while exploiting all the power of your computer. You can also build applications that look like Windows Vista–based applications.

- **Console applications**   These are the applications that have no graphical interface and that simply use text to communicate with the user. (Typically, these applications run in a command window or DOS window.)

- **Reusable components or class libraries**   These are groups of tools created to help build other applications.

What you won't be able to build are Web sites and Web services. To create any type of Web application, you will need to get Microsoft Visual Web Developer 2008 Express Edition.

NOTE
We will look into the details of what types of applications fall into these categories in Chapter 3, "Creating Your First Applications."

What Are the Key Features You Need to Know About?

The following list, although not complete, describes the essential features of Visual C# 2008 Express Edition. At this point, don't worry if you don't understand every feature listed. I'm presenting the features in the list because you'll come across all of them in some way in the fun sample applications you will be creating as you read this book.

Most of the features listed here emphasize the RAD philosophy. Although the idea is to give you an overview of the interesting features that can make your life easier, the names of the features alone are not sufficient to understand what they mean. I've included a brief description giving you the essentials and explaining how they will help you develop applications.

- **Built-in Starter Kits**   The Starter Kits are fully developed applications with best prac- tices and examples to follow. These applications will give you another example on which to base your learning. They will be a good complement to what we are doing with this book. You can find them at *http://msdn2.microsoft.com/en-us/vcsharp/aa336742.aspx*, and you can find a few others at *http://www.microsoft.com/express/vcsharp/Default.aspx*.

- **Beginner's targeted documentation and tutorials**   These are a fast and easy way to get information. They also provide samples.

- **IntelliSense**   This feature provides real-time syntax suggestions and even finishes your typing for you. In Visual Studio 2008, IntelliSense, as you will see, is everywhere, and it provides a more complete and contextual set of suggestions than in earlier versions of Visual Studio.

- **Code snippets**   Snippets provide code for various programming tasks to help you complete many common tasks automatically. In addition, code snippets show the recommended way of performing a task. They are directly integrated into the development environment, and they are extensible; that is, anybody can extend the existing snippets or provide new ones. Over time Microsoft will continue to supply new code snippets, and members of online communities will contribute their snippets as well. Code snippet extensibility is a really nice feature that helps people share useful features in online communities.

- **Data-enabled applications**   With these applications you can connect to Microsoft SQL Server 2005 Express Edition and add databases and code to access the data in your applications. In addition, a new editor has been added to help you develop applications that use data. As mentioned earlier, LINQ is one of the big new features of .NET 3.5 included with Visual Studio 2008, and you will see how to use it in Chapter 8, "Managing the Data."

- **Windows Forms Designer and WPF Designer**   With these new tools, you can easily design your Windows application using either Windows Forms or WPF, including features such as snap lines, which make sure your controls are aligned in your form.

- **XAML editor**   The XAML editor lets you edit Extensible Application Markup Language (XAML), which was introduced with .NET 3.0. This new markup language is used extensively in WPF and Windows Workflow (WF) to describe user interface elements in WPF and process logic in WF. (WF is beyond the scope of this book.)

- **XML Web services**   Visual C# 2008 provides easy-to-use tools and wizards that help you connect to published XML-based Web services and utilize their functionalities.

- **New Windows Forms controls**   These comprise an impressive list of controls—a greater selection than in any previous version of Visual C#. They will help you create user interfaces that have a professional look and feel.

- **Smart Tags**   Most Windows Forms controls that come with the product include Smart Tags. As in many applications of the 2007 Microsoft Office system, a Smart Tag is represented by a little black triangle or an icon and a little black triangle attached to a control. A Smart Tag gives you access to the most common actions you can perform on a control.

MORE INFO
XAML is also used in Silverlight for Web applications, but this is beyond the scope of this book.

- **Refactoring** The Visual C# 2008 IDE includes robust and powerful refactoring support. By *refactoring*, developers can automate many common tasks related to restructuring code. *Restructuring* code is when you want to change some of your source code elements and apply that change to all files and occurrences of that element. For instance, you'll be able to rename variables throughout a project, promote local variables to parameters, extract methods, and do much more. The Visual C# 2008 IDE gives you a nice preview feature so that you can see the changes before you make them. You'll be able to access the refactoring features either by opening a context-sensitive menu while editing your source code or by using a Smart Tag. For more information on refactoring, please visit *http://www.refactoring.com/*, and for more examples on how to implement these features in the Visual C# 2008 IDE, visit *http://msdn2.microsoft.com/en-us/ library/719exd8s(VS.90).aspx*.

- **Organizing Using feature** Related to the refactoring feature, the Organizing Using feature lets you clean your source code by removing unused *using* statements or sorting them without changing the behavior of the source code. Over time you might add features requiring the addition of new assemblies, which usually means new *using* statements. Over the course of your application's development, you might change your mind, and then your code might be bloated with unwanted artifacts such as *using* statements. With the Organizing Using feature, you can delete the ones you are not using in your code. You can also remove and sort them in one pass.

- **ClickOnce deployment** With this feature, you can easily publish your applications to the Internet, on a local area network (LAN), on a network share, or on a CD or DVD. It also simplifies publishing updates. With this edition of Visual Studio, you can now handle with the ClickOnce wizard the Windows Vista User Account Control (UAC) so that your application runs in the lowest user security context it needs. Usually you want to aim your software development on Windows Vista for regular users. This has the effect of reassuring the user that your application won't perform unsafe operations without their knowledge.

- **Edit and Continue** While you are debugging your application, the Edit and Continue feature lets you modify the code, move back and forth in the debugger, re-execute code, add functionality, or fix bugs on the fly without stopping program execution.

- **Debugger visualizers**   While you are debugging your application, visualizers give you an easy way to get readable representations of your application data. They give you a human-readable representation of the stored data, even for more complex types found in ADO.NET or XML.

- **Community Access and Start pages**   With these features, you can access additional information from online communities and from different sources of online help, including diverse RSS feeds. (RSS can stand for Rich Site Summary or Really Simple Syndication and is a family of XML file formats; it is widely used by the blog community and news Web sites.)

- **Simplified development environment**   Everything in the development environment was created so that you can easily access key functionalities, tools, and objects.

As you can see, Visual C# 2008 Express Edition includes many nice features to help new programmers develop applications in a fast and fun way. These features will provide guidance even when you're not necessarily sure what syntax or components to use and will greatly expedite learning the product.

In Summary...

You now know that .NET is a framework composed of compilers, tools, languages, debuggers, and an execution engine. The CLR is that execution engine, and it is responsible for loading and executing managed applications. In essence, .NET is like a house with the CLR as the foundation and all other services built on top of it. You also learned that the CLR didn't change with Windows Vista and Visual Studio 2008, but a lot of new building blocks have been added so you can take advantage of features provided by Windows Vista and make developing applications easier.

In addition, you learned that C# is an object-oriented programming language. You also started to learn what object-oriented programming is and the basics of OOP in Visual C# 2008.

This chapter gave you the opportunity to hear about the most important features of Visual C# 2008 Express Edition. In the next chapter, you'll learn how to install Visual C# 2008 Express Edition.

Chapter 2

Installing Visual C# 2008 Express Edition

Preparing to Install Visual C# 2008 Express Edition, 18

Installing Visual C# 2008 Express Edition, 19

In this chapter, you'll install Microsoft Visual C# 2008 Express Edition and start getting to know what components are included with it. I'll guide you through all the steps of this installation so that you will be ready to start building applications using Visual C# 2008 Express Edition right away. In addition, I will talk about some common installation scenarios, give you some tips for installing the product, and also cover what to do if the unexpected happens.

The installation process is easy and straightforward, following in the spirit of the Visual Studio Express editions.

You have a couple of options for installing Visual C# 2008, particularly if you've had previous versions installed or if you installed an early (prerelease) version of the product. Before you start the installation, make sure your computer meets the software and hardware recommendations. Review the introduction to this book for all the necessary information. You will also want to be sure that your computer has the latest updates from Windows Updates (*http://windowsupdate.microsoft.com*) and Microsoft Updates (*http://update.microsoft.com*). Installing the latest updates will ensure that your computer has all the latest security updates along with some installation prerequisites before starting the product installation.

If you have an antivirus or antispyware application installed and running, it might prompt you to allow certain setup tasks to proceed. For instance, with the latest Microsoft Windows Defender (*http://www.microsoft.com/athome/security/spyware/software/default.mspx*), I was asked two times to allow certain tasks to proceed, and a few other times the antispyware product recognized the source and simply mentioned it and continued. If you are using a different antispyware application, your experience might vary slightly, but it will bear some similarities to this process. These antivirus and antispyware products are giving you an opportunity to confirm the origin of the product you're about to install. When you're sure it's from Microsoft, let the setup application continue its job by choosing to allow the action.

During the installation, if something goes wrong, you're probably not the only person to encounter the problem, so your first step is to look at the latest Readme information maintained by the setup team on MSDN and follow the steps provided to solve installation problems. Here is a link to the MSDN resources: *http://www.microsoft.com/express/support/*.

Side-by-Side Installation

CAUTION

Please make sure you carefully read the MSDN article at *http://msdn2.microsoft.com/en-us/vs2008/bb964521.aspx* before starting the uninstall process!

If you have a previous version of Microsoft Visual Studio on your computer, say Visual Studio 2003 or Visual Studio 2005, installing Visual C# 2008 Express Edition (or any Visual Studio 2008 product) will be straightforward. This is considered a *side-by-side* execution, and you can go straight to the "Installing Visual C# 2008 Express Edition" section about installing the software.

Prerelease Versions of Visual C# 2008 Express Edition

When you uninstall a prerelease version of any software, you might encounter problems. At some point, you might have no choice but to reformat your hard disk and reinstall your operating system. This situation is not uncommon when you work with prerelease software, but this problem has a solution. Before beginning the uninstall procedure, and as a precautionary measure, be sure to back up all your data. If possible, it's good practice to avoid installing any prerelease versions of any products on your main computer. Using a test machine (or virtual software) will help you avoid losing any important data and won't slow your productivity in the event that something goes wrong. You can learn more about the virtual solution that Microsoft offers, called Microsoft Virtual PC 2007, at *http://www.microsoft.com/windows/virtualpc/default.mspx*.

Luckily, with Visual Studio 2008, all Community Technology Preview (CTP) and pre–Beta 2 versions were "time-bombed" virtual images provided by Microsoft; therefore, the chance of ruining your main computer has been almost eliminated. You simply have to delete the Virtual PC image provided by Microsoft, and you should be good to go with the released version of the product. But if you installed Visual C# 2008 Express Edition Beta 2 and you didn't use a Virtual PC image, you will have to uninstall the beta version before you proceed with installing the released version.

MORE INFO
Because of a new feature called *multitargeting*, you can compile any project to .NET 2.0, .NET 3.0, or .NET 3.5. After successfully installing Visual C# 2008 Express Edition, you can safely uninstall Visual C# 2005 Express Edition because with Visual C# 2008 Express Edition, you can target .NET 2.0 and also get all the benefits and new features of Visual C# 2008 Express.

NOTE
Even though Microsoft doesn't officially support prerelease versions of the software, you will find resources on Microsoft's Web site to help you with installation. In particular, you will find information on how to uninstall (and in what order to uninstall) the products. Look at the forums at the following address for help on uninstalling any Beta 2 installations (you'll need to sign-in using a Windows Live ID to get to this article): *http://forums.microsoft.com/msdn/showforum.aspx?forumid=1346&siteid=1.*

Installing Visual C# 2008 Express Edition

Now that we've addressed a lot of potential issues and your computer is ready, you can proceed with the installation. You will find a companion DVD with this book that contains a full working edition of the product. Simply insert it into any available CD/DVD drive in your system, and follow the steps listed next.

TO INSTALL VISUAL C# 2008 EXPRESS EDITION

If autorun is enabled, the installation process should start automatically. If it doesn't start automatically after a few seconds, follow these steps:

1. Click the Start button, and then click Computer.
2. Right-click the CD/DVD drive that has the product media, and select Explore.
3. In the list of files, locate and double-click Setup.hta to start the Installation Wizard.
4. On the Welcome to Visual Studio 2008 Express Editions Setup page, click Microsoft Visual C# 2008 Express Edition.

Within a few seconds, you should see that the setup program is copying all necessary installation files to a temporary folder, as shown in Figure 2-1.

Figure 2-1
Copying setup files locally to a temporary folder

When the setup program is done copying the files, the setup application loads into memory. While the application is loading, you'll see an initialization progress bar, as shown in Figure 2-2.

Next, you'll be greeted by the Welcome to Setup page (Figure 2-3), which provides some information about the product and the possibilities you'll have working with it. You can select the check box if you want to send anonymous data about your experience installing the product to Microsoft. This program is collecting only anonymous data,

Figure 2-2
Initializing the setup process

and you can read the policy to see exactly what type of information will be sent. Click Next to continue or Cancel to exit the installation program.

To continue the installation process, you must read and accept the license terms (Figure 2-4). Please read the terms carefully to see what you can and can't do with this product. When you have finished and you're ready to accept the license agreement, select the option button that says you have read and accepted the license, and then click Next to continue.

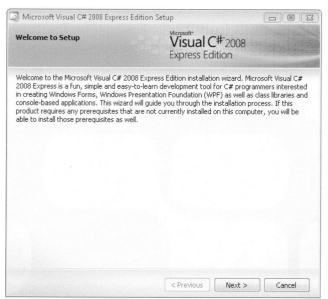

Figure 2-3
Welcome to Setup page

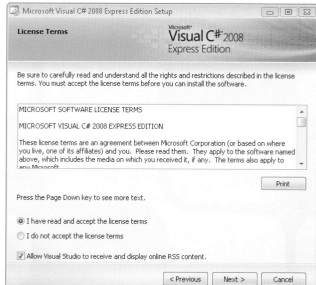

Figure 2-4
License agreement page

The Installation Options page appears, as shown in Figure 2-5. On this page, be sure to specify that you want access to the Help system (MSDN Express Library) and Microsoft SQL Server 2005 Express Edition.

SQL Server 2005 Express Edition is a relational database management system (RDBMS) with which you can easily manipulate data in your application. This is an important step. For example, if you're creating the DVD collection management application that exists as one of the Starter Kits, all the data related to your DVD collection will need to be stored in a database using SQL Server 2005 Express Edition.

> **NOTE**
> The only reason not to install the local MSDN Help or SQL Server 2005 Express Edition is limited hard disk space. Be sure you understand the consequences of your selections. If you don't install MSDN Express Library, you'll need access to the Internet to get help from MSDN Online. If you don't install SQL Server 2005 Express Edition, you won't be able to create applications that need to access other sources of data, such as Microsoft Access database information, XML files, or other types of RDBMS information. In addition, some sample files from this book won't work automatically, and you'll have to perform some manipulations or re-installations to get them to work.

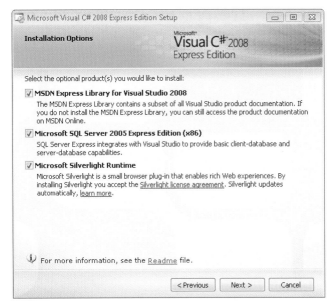

Figure 2-5
Setting your installation options

The last product to install is Silverlight, and although we won't use Silverlight directly in this book, I strongly recommend you install it, because you will have a smoother and richer experience on many Web sites. Silverlight 1.0 will not take a lot of space, because it is only a few megabytes.

When you're done with your selections, click Next to continue.

The Destination Folder page appears, as shown in Figure 2-6. This page will ask you where to install the software on your computer. I recommend you use the default location.

Click Install to start the installation. The installation progress bar appears, which means the installation is underway! (See Figure 2-7.) This might be a good time to get something to drink because the installation could take some time.

Figure 2-6
Destination Folder page

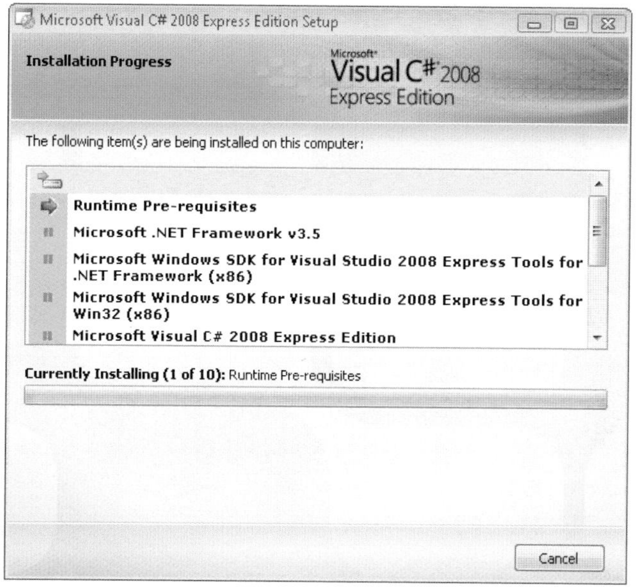

Figure 2-7
Installation Progress page

Here is the list of components that will be installed:

■ **The .NET Framework 3.5**   This is the outer circle of the image in Figure 1-1.

■ **Visual C# 2008 Express Edition**   This is the tool itself.

■ **Microsoft SQL Server Compact 3.5**   This is a version of SQL Server that lets you, as the developer, embed a compact database on smaller devices, such as Windows Mobile–based phones or even on your Windows–based desktop or laptop.

■ **MSDN Express Library**   This was described earlier.

■ **SQL Server 2005 Express Edition**   This was described earlier.

When the Setup Complete page appears (see Figure 2-8), you are now finished with the installation. That wasn't too painful, was it? Before you click the Exit button, please read the following notes.

Whenever you install a new application, it's always a good habit to go to Microsoft Update (*http://update.microsoft.com*) or Windows Update (*http://windowsupdate.microsoft.com*) to get all the high-priority updates. Or you can click the Microsoft Update hyperlink on the Setup Complete page of the setup application, as shown in Figure 2-8. I prefer Microsoft Update because you get all the updates you need for all the Microsoft software already installed on your hard disk. You'll get updates for Windows, the Microsoft Office system, SQL Server, Windows Defender, and the .NET Framework along with your hardware drivers updates, all in one stop!

It's also important to verify that your antivirus application and its signatures are up-to-date and that you have updated antispyware installed. Finally, in Control Panel, open the Security Center, and make sure all lights for the firewall, virus protection, automatic updates, and all other security settings are green. If not, address those issues to prevent any security hazards.

Click the Exit button when you are done. If you elected to send the feedback of your installation to Microsoft on exit, the setup application will send it to Microsoft's servers, as shown in Figure 2-9.

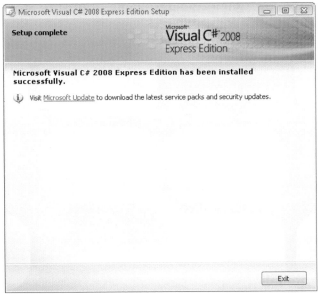

Figure 2-8
Setup Complete page

Figure 2-9
Sending installation feedback to the Microsoft servers

In Summary...

This chapter focused on installing Visual C# 2008 Express Edition. It addressed most issues that you might encounter during the installation, it covered different setup scenarios, and it provided links to MSDN for more help.

After working through this chapter, you should now have the .NET Framework 3.5, Visual C# 2008 Express Edition, MSDN Express Library for Visual Studio 2008, SQL Server Compact 3.5, Silverlight 1.0, and SQL Server 2005 Express Edition installed and ready to go. Your computer should also be up-to-date with all updates installed and all security settings on green.

Whenever you're ready to explore the integrated development environment (IDE) and write your first two applications, just jump to the next chapter.

Chapter 3
Creating Your First Applications

Three Types of Applications: What's the Difference?, 28

Getting Started with the IDE, 30

Building the Projects, 33

You've installed Microsoft Visual C# 2008 Express Edition, so now it's time to create your first application. You'll start this chapter by learning about the differences between console applications, Windows applications, and Windows Presentation Foundation (WPF) applications. You'll then look at the integrated development environment (IDE). As its name implies, the IDE is the application that provides all the tools you need to design, plan, develop, and distribute your applications. You could use any text editor, such as Notepad, for example, to create your applications, but in this chapter and for the reminder of the book, you'll be using the IDE.

Most programming books usually start with a fairly simple application called "Hello, World." Your first application will be a simple application as well, but you'll be creating an application that does a little bit more than just say "Hello" to the world. Specifically, you'll learn to create an application that adds two numbers together and outputs a result. With this application, you'll also learn about Solution Explorer as well as the documentation and Help system built into Visual C# 2008 Express Edition.

Three Types of Applications: What's the Difference?

MORE INFO

Simple text (also called *ASCII characters*) is the usual output of a console application, but some console applications use ASCII graphic characters. (ASCII stands for American Standard Code for Information Interchange.) An ASCII code is the numerical representation of a character (such as 0 or #) or an action of some sort. Pressing Enter in a word processor to move a line of text is an action represented by an ASCII character, for instance. The ASCII graphic character set, also called *extended ASCII characters*, includes vertical lines, vertical double lines, corners, and much more. ASCII characters are sometimes used to create boxes around text in console applications. Unicode characters are similar to ASCII but are not encoded in the same way. They are more extensive and can represent different locales.

NOTE

Please note that console applications are still executed in Windows but in the console.

NOTE

Console applications can be written in many different programming languages (C, C++, C#, Visual Basic, and so on) and scripting languages (Perl, Python, or JScript).

In this chapter, you'll create two versions of the same application: a console application and a Microsoft Windows application. You might wonder why you even have to worry about the type of application when you're creating a program. Often the type of application you create depends on the purpose of the application and how users will interact with it.

Sometimes your application doesn't need to have a graphical interface. For instance, some applications need to be executed in a script or a batch file, or they don't need a graphical interface because no user usually interacts with the application except for launching it. This type of application is called a *console application* because everything is displayed in a system console window. You might have heard these types of windows referred to by many different names: a *DOS window*, a *command prompt window*, or simply the *command window*. The most common output in a console application is simple text.

Figure 3-1 shows the result of the famous "Hello, World" application as a console application.

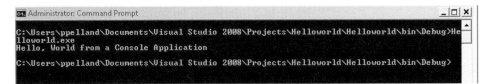

Figure 3-1
Console application

Console applications can be much more complex than the "Hello, World" example shown here. In fact, they can have as rich a set of features as Windows applications. The only difference is that they don't have a graphical interface. For example, in corporate data centers, many applications execute all day and night, producing a large amount of data. It would be time-consuming and problematic to rely on people to verify the data. So, data centers are usually highly automated to facilitate this job; they use console applications that produce, manipulate, and verify the data in scripts or batch files.

In contrast to a console application, a *Windows application* has a graphical interface, as shown in Figure 3-2. (This type of application is also called a *Windows Forms application* in .NET.)

These applications are usually accessible from the Windows Start menu, and by default they share some common characteristics, such as a Close button, a Maximize button, and a Minimize button, as shown here.

Another type of application—a *WPF application*—also has a graphical interface and looks similar to a Windows application; however, it uses a completely different set of libraries to generate the executable. For our work in this chapter, it is enough to say that WPF applications can provide a richer experience and are using a different approach for their design.

Figure 3-3 shows a WPF application in action, and I will explain them much more fully in Chapter 6, "Modifying Your Web Browser." The overall effect with this application is not that different from a normal Windows application even though it is much more powerful. In Chapter 6, you'll be able to see applications that have been designed by professionals, and you'll be able to see for yourself what *richer* means.

Figure 3-2
Windows application

NOTE

A *Windows service* is a type of Windows application that runs on Windows in the background—it doesn't have a user interface, doesn't produce any visual output, starts when Windows starts, and doesn't even require a user to be logged in to start executing. Windows XP Service Pack 2 (SP2) and the Windows Vista operating system come with roughly four dozen Windows services. For example, one built-in Windows service validates your user name and password at start-up.

Figure 3-3
WPF application

To get started writing the code for the first version of the application, you'll need to start Microsoft Visual C# 2008 Express Edition. To do this, follow these three easy steps: click Start, click All Programs, and click Microsoft Visual C# 2008 Express Edition.

Before we go further, let's pause and admire the IDE in all its glory. Look at Figure 3-4, and feel the excitement.

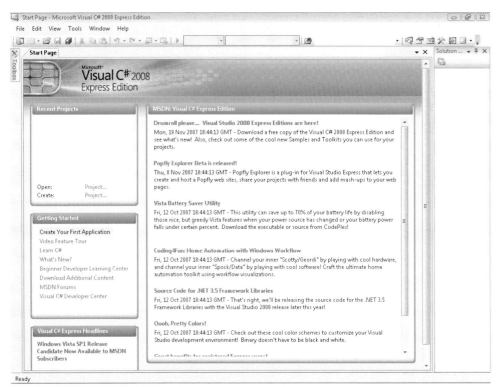

Figure 3-4
The IDE in all its glory

If you're not feeling the excitement yet, you soon will be. The development environment has been designed to make a lot more information available up front and to make you more productive more quickly. From this screen, everything you need to build an application is available in a couple of clicks. This is where you type your code, compile your code, launch the application, find your mistakes and fix them, get help on the syntax, and perform many other tasks. Furthermore, the Visual C# 2008 Express Edition IDE is designed to generate a lot of code for you so that you have less to type. If you didn't have the IDE and you wanted to write a Windows Forms application, you would have to type a lot more code, and this is prone to errors. With the IDE, most of the actions you'll perform will automatically generate the code for you behind the scenes.

NOTE
I will show you how and where to look for this generated code in Chapter 5, "Using Rapid Application Development Tools with Visual C# 2008."

As you spend more time with the IDE, you'll find that there are many ways to perform the same actions. For instance, to complete a specific action, you can use a series of menu choices, you can use a keystroke shortcut, you can click an icon on a toolbar, you can click a hyperlink in a page, or you can right-click and choose an option from a context-sensitive menu. Before diving into our first application and before writing some code, we'll go through each big component of the IDE.

The first page you see when you start the IDE is a really useful one: the Start Page. It contains a lot of useful information:

TIP
The first and only rule of this book is to not be afraid to experiment. Click, look, read, and try whenever possible. This is really the best way to learn. I'll show you some important material, tips, and tricks throughout this book, but my advice to you is to go beyond these examples and just try and try and try.

- **Recent Projects pane**   Here you'll get the list of projects or solutions that were recently opened. You can also create a new project or open an existing project that is not in the list.

- **Getting Started pane**   I call this useful pane "Help Central" because if you need quick help, this is one of the best places to get answers. Whether you need help with some Visual C# constructs, you want to see a list of how-to articles, or you simply want hyperlinks to communities of programmers, you can often find these items in the Getting Started pane of the IDE.

- **Visual C# Express Headlines pane**   This is where you find specific news about Visual C# Express Edition coming from Microsoft. These product headlines deliver special messages specific to Visual C# 2008 Express Edition and announce new updates, new releases, new code snippets, or anything that needs attention on your part.

NOTE
Some hyperlinks on the Start Page require a live connection to the Internet. So if you are unable to read the hyperlinks, please verify your Internet connection status.

NOTE

The Microsoft Developer Network (MSDN) is a set of online and offline services designed to help developers write applications using Microsoft products and technologies.

MSDN feeds   This pane of the Start Page includes hyperlinks to articles from one of the Microsoft Developer Network Really Simple Syndication (MSDN RSS) feeds. You can configure these articles to any valid RSS feed from the Web. The default is set to the MSDN Visual C# 2008 Express RSS feed. These articles are usually different from the ones under Visual C# Express Headlines; occasionally they might be the same, but the articles from MSDN cover not only Visual C# Express Edition but topics including Visual Studio Team Systems, Microsoft SQL Server, Web services, and so forth. You can modify the feed by clicking Tools and then Options, expanding Environment, selecting Startup, and updating the Start Page News Channel field with a valid RSS feed of your choice.

Some important components of the IDE are not part of the Start Page:

Menu bar   This is where you can select and perform almost all possible actions related to your projects, files, and Help. The options available change based on the current context. For example, when you don't have a project open, you have fewer menu choices: File, Edit, View, Tools, Window, and Help. When a project is open, the menu choices will also include Refactor, Project, Build, Debug, and Data.

TIP

If you don't see Startup and other settings in the Options dialog box, ensure that you selected the Show All Settings check box in the lower-left corner of the Options dialog box.

Main toolbar   This toolbar contains icons that are essentially shortcuts to popular actions that you can also perform by going through the menus.

Toolbox   The Toolbox contains controls that are used in your applications. If you move your mouse pointer over the Toolbox on the left side of the Start Page, the Toolbox will expand. If you don't have a project open, the Toolbox will be empty. At this point you can think of controls as visual elements in Windows applications that possess a graphical interface. For instance, once a project is opened, the Toolbox will include buttons, labels, text boxes, menus, toolbars, and so on. I'll explain these controls in greater detail in Chapter 5.

TIP

If you accidentally close the Start Page and you want to display it, you can always display it again by clicking View, Other Windows, Start Page.

Solution Explorer   This feature lists the files and components in your project. If no project is open, it will be empty. You'll learn more about Solution Explorer later in this chapter.

- **Status bar** The status bar displays a wide variety of information corresponding to the state of certain active operations. For instance, when you load a project, you'll see a message on your screen such as "Loading project c:\blabla\blabla.csproj from your hard drive." When you're building an application, you'll see something like "Build started," and when the application has finished, you'll see "Build succeeded" or "Build failed" depending on the success of the process.

Building the Projects

From this point on, you'll focus on what you really came here to do: build some projects. Let's start with your first application—the console version of the application that adds two numbers together.

Building a Console Application

We've been talking about what a console application can do and what it will look like, so why don't we build one? In this section, you'll create a simple mathematic application.

TO BUILD A CONSOLE APPLICATION

1. If Visual C# 2008 Express Edition is not running, start it by clicking Start, All Programs, Microsoft Visual C# 2008 Express Edition.

    You can choose to start building your application either by clicking the New Project icon on the toolbar, by selecting Create: Project from the Start Page, or by clicking File, New Project on the menu bar.

2. In the New Project dialog box, select Console Application in the Templates section, and type **MyFirstConsoleApplication** in the Name box. The New Project dialog box should be similar to the one in Figure 3-5. Click OK to create the project.

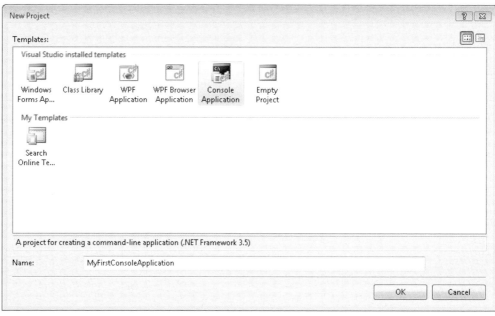

Figure 3-5
Creating a console application using the New Project dialog box

NOTE

By default in Visual C# 2008 Express Edition, when you click OK, projects are created in a temporary location. When you save or close the project, files are saved in Documents\Visual Studio 2008\Projects. (On Windows XP and Windows Server 2003, you'll find them in My Documents\ Visual Studio 2008\Projects.) You can change the default project location by clicking Tools, Options, Projects and Solutions and finding the first text box named Visual Studio Projects Location. We'll look into what files are created and what their content is in Chapter 5.

You should now see the IDE in an idle state waiting for you to write the application's code. Your screen should look like the one shown in Figure 3-6. (If you do not see the Properties window at the bottom right, click View, Properties Window.)

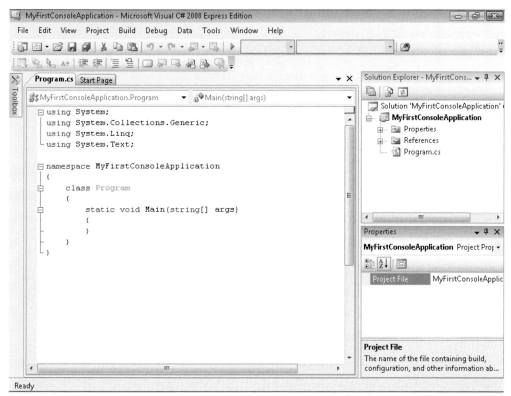

Figure 3-6
MyFirstConsoleApplication without the code

Getting to Know Solution Explorer

Before you write the code, you need to learn about Solution Explorer. Shown on the right side of the screen in Figure 3-6, Solution Explorer provides an organized view of your projects and all the files associated with them, as well as some useful commands in the form of a toolbar. You'll find all the source code files, the project settings, the resource files (such as the application icon), the configuration files, and so on, in Solution Explorer.

TIP
If you accidentally close Solution Explorer, you can get it back by clicking View, Solution Explorer.

If you want more information about Solution Explorer, you can always do a search in the Help system and product documentation. Before trying to perform a search, please read the next section; you'll learn a lot about all the information that is at your disposal.

Getting Help: Microsoft Visual Studio 2008 Express Edition Documentation

If you want to read more about Solution Explorer, you need to be introduced to Help and the documentation system. You access the documentation by pressing F1 from within Visual C# 2008 Express Edition or by using the Help menu. The first time you press F1 or use the Help menu, you'll be greeted with the Online Help Settings dialog box, as shown in Figure 3-7.

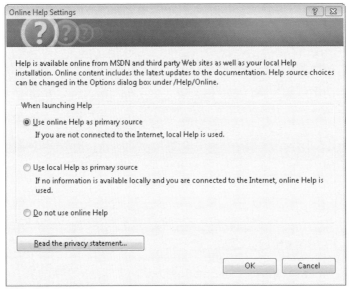

Figure 3-7
Online Help Settings dialog box

This dialog box prompts you to choose a primary Help source; you can choose online Help as a primary source, local Help as a primary source, or no online Help at all. Think about your options carefully. If you don't have a broadband (cable, DSL, or satellite) Internet connection, I suggest you choose local Help as the primary source; otherwise, choose online Help as your primary source since it is the best source for the latest information.

Once you've made your selection, you'll see the documentation's graphical interface, as shown in Figure 3-8.

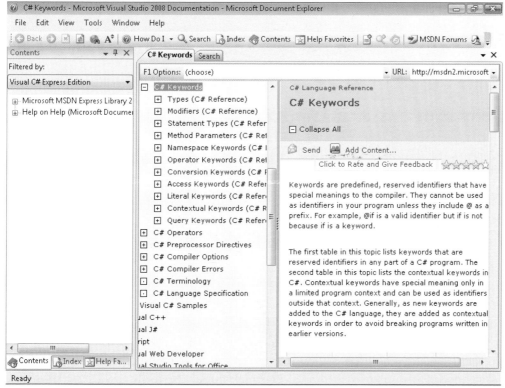

Figure 3-8
Microsoft Visual Studio 2008 Express Edition documentation

The toolbar at the top of the window includes several interesting elements that will help you find exactly what you need. Figure 3-9 shows the most important buttons on the toolbar.

Figure 3-9
Important buttons on the toolbar

For example, let's say you want to learn more about Solution Explorer. Click the Search button on the toolbar, and the search page opens. Enter your search query (in this example, type **Solution Explorer**), and either press Enter or click the Search button. The Help results come from four sources:

- **Local Help**   This source is fed by the MSDN Library (part of the product installation) and is installed on your hard disk (if you selected it during installation).

- **MSDN Online**   This source contains the most up-to-date information from MSDN Online.

- **Codezone Community**   The Codezone Community is a set of Web sites based on Microsoft developer products. To see a list of all Web sites that are researched, click Tools, Options, and then select Online under Help in the list of items at the left. Figure 3-10 shows the dialog box you will see. Notice the list of Web sites on the right that are part of the Codezone Community. In the future, this list might expand to show more sites to provide even better coverage of the community.

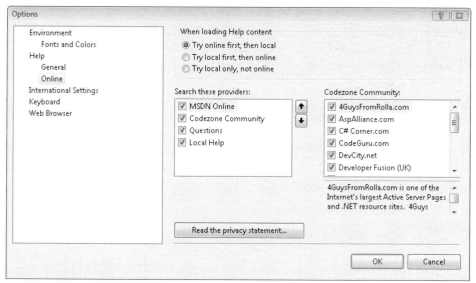

Figure 3-10
Options dialog box with the online settings, including the Codezone Community Web sites

In the same dialog box, you can customize settings related to the Help system. On the General tab, you can set up how the Help system retrieves and presents information. You can set up the international setting to get local Help in the language of your operating system, if available, and get online Help in a predefined list of languages supported by MSDN. You can also view the keyboard shortcuts for menu commands used throughout the product (for example, notice that the shortcut for Copy is Ctrl+C) or assign new shortcuts to commands that might not have one already.

■ **Questions**   This type of query searches the MSDN Online forums (*http://forums. microsoft.com/msdn/*). These forums are hosted by Microsoft and are an excellent source of information because they have questions and answers on topics asked by other programmers of all levels and experience. There's a good chance that somebody has already had the same problem or the same question as you, so your chances of finding

NOTE

MVPs stands for Most Valuable Professionals. MVPs are professionals who are not Microsoft employees but are recognized by Microsoft as experts in their fields.

an answer to your problem in the MSDN Online forums are good. Furthermore, you can have confidence in the answers you get because answers on the MSDN forums are often validated by Microsoft employees or MVPs. A check mark in a green circle tells you which answer has been validated as correct.

Coding Your Console Application

Now that you know how to get help if needed, you are ready to code your first console application.

TO CODE A CONSOLE APPLICATION

1. To begin, type the following code in your code window (minus the line numbers):

```
1   using System;
2   using System.Collections.Generic;
3   using System.Text;
4
5   namespace MyFirstConsoleApplication
6   {
7       class Program
8       {
9           static void Main(string[] args)
10          {
11              //  Declaring two integer variables that will hold
                //  the 2 parts of the sum and one integer variable to
                //  hold the sum
12
13              int number1;
14              int number2;
15              int sum;
16
17              //  Assigning two values to the integer variables
18              number1 = 10;
19              number2 = 5;
20
21              //  Adding the two integers and storing the result in the
                //  sum variable
```

Microsoft Visual C# 2008 Express Edition: Build a Program Now!

```
22              sum = (number1 + number2);
23
24              // Displaying a string with the 2 numbers and the result.
25              Console.WriteLine("The sum of " + number1.ToString() +
                    " and " + number2.ToString() + " is " + sum.ToString());
26          }
27      }
28  }
```

2. Now that the code is in the window, you can save your work by clicking the Save button. This will save the current file. Or you can click the Save All button to save all modified files in the project.

TIP

You can also save your project by pressing Ctrl+S to save the current file or by pressing Ctrl+Shift+S to save all the files.

3. Now it is time to build (or *compile*) the application. Click the Build menu, and then click Build Solution.

If you typed the code exactly as it appears, you should see the message "Build succeeded" in the status bar at the bottom of the window (see Figure 3-11). If something went wrong, you'll see errors in the Error List (as shown in Figure 3-12). If you typed the code and have errors, try copying and pasting the code from the completed code samples (*http://www.microsoft.com/mspress/companion/9780735625426/*) instead of typing it. Then build the code again.

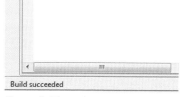
Build succeeded

Figure 3-11
Status bar with "Build succeeded" message

IMPORTANT

Comments in the source code start with either // or /*. Developers use comments so that their code is easy to maintain and understand. It's not rare to see developers staring blankly at their own source code a few months after it was written. Use comments to comment pieces of code that are more complex or that you think are more important. Do not comment pieces of code that are obvious.

Error List					
⊗ 1 Error	⚠ 0 Warnings	ⓘ 0 Messages			
	Description	File	Line	Column	Project
⊗ 1	The name 'Consle' does not exist in the current context	Program.cs	26	10	MyFirstConsoleApplication

Figure 3-12
Error List with errors

In Chapter 7, "Fixing the Broken Blocks," you'll learn about all the debugging techniques you can use when you get an error.

4. To see the execution results of your application, click the Start Debugging button in the main toolbar (or hit F5).

Wow! That was fast, wasn't it? You probably saw a command window for a few seconds, and then it disappeared. It didn't leave you a lot of time to see whether your application displayed the expected output. In the next section, you'll look at a new way of running your application to solve this problem. To do this, you'll need to customize the IDE.

Customizing the IDE

You can easily customize the IDE to fit your needs. Here, you want to execute your application and then have the application pause automatically at the end of the last instruction to give you as much time as you need to view the output. You'll do this by adding an icon and its attached command to the toolbar. The name of the command you'll add to the IDE is Start Without Debugging.

TO CUSTOMIZE THE IDE

1. Click the View menu, click Toolbars, and then click Debug.

2. Click the Tools menu, and then click Customize.

3. In the Customize dialog box, select the Commands tab.

4. In the Categories area on the left side of the window, select Debug.

5. Scroll down in the Commands area, and select Start Without Debugging.

Your screen should now look like the one in Figure 3-13.

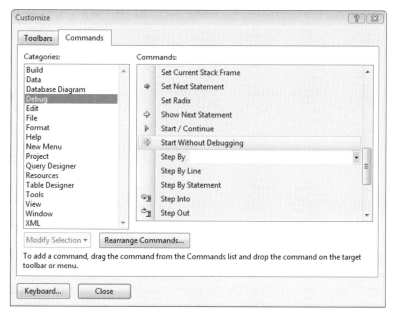

Figure 3-13
Customize dialog box with Start Without Debugging selected

Now you must add the command to the toolbar to the right of the Start Debugging button. To do that, drag Start Without Debugging from the Commands area, and drop it on the Debug toolbar to the right of the Start Debugging button. (Figure 3-14 shows a "before" and "after" look at the toolbar.) When finished, click Close in the Customize dialog box.

Figure 3-14
Before and after customizing the toolbar with the Start Without Debugging command

NOTE
Figure 3-14 shows the "before" version toward the left and the "after" version toward the right, overlapping the "before" version.

To make sure the customization worked, click the new icon on the toolbar. (Or, press the keyboard shortcut Ctrl+F5.) You should see a command prompt window with the expected output, which is the string "The sum of 10 and 5 is 15." You should also see the message "Press any key to continue...," as shown in Figure 3-15.

Figure 3-15
Command prompt window with the expected result and a message indicating a paused execution

As you probably realize by now, the effect of the new command is to display the "Press any key to continue..." message and pause the execution after the last instruction executes. Press any key to close the command prompt window and return to the IDE. When you're done, you can close the project by clicking File, Close Solution. You'll be prompted to save or discard your changes. Click Save, and then if the name and location are fine, click Save again in the Save Project dialog box.

Creating a Windows Application

You just built a console application. The next step is to develop the same application but as a Windows application. What you will develop is a real and fully functional Window application, but it won't do much; you'll create a fully functional Windows application in Chapter 5.

TO BUILD A WINDOWS APPLICATION

1. When creating the console application, you saw the New Project dialog box. Open it again by clicking File, New Project.

2. This time, select Windows Forms Application from the Templates section, and type **MyFirstWindowsApplication**. Make sure your screen looks like the one in Figure 3-16, and then click OK.

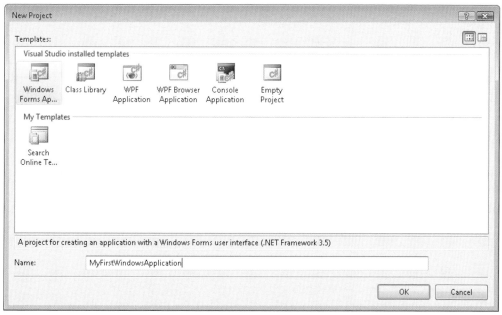

Figure 3-16
Creating a Windows application by using the New Project dialog box

You'll immediately see that the result of this operation is quite different for the Windows application process than it was for the console application process. You should see the Windows Forms Designer, as displayed in Figure 3-17.

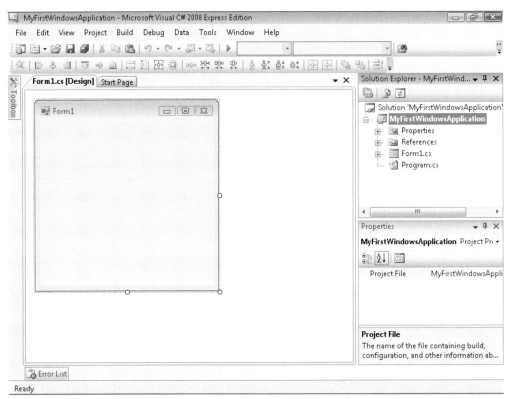

Figure 3-17
IDE with the Windows Forms Designer and an empty form

3. On the left side of the IDE, move your mouse pointer over the Toolbox to open it. Click the plus (+) sign next to Common Controls. You'll see a list of form controls that are common in a Windows application.

4. Drag the button control to the designer surface. Your form should look like the one in Figure 3-18.

   You now have a full and valid Windows application without having written a single line of code. The application doesn't do anything very useful at this point, but it works! You can easily verify this by running the application. Just hit F5 to see for yourself. This is part of the magic of using the Visual Studio IDE environment for programming instead of using a text editor such as Notepad. Visual Studio writes a lot of code for you, and in Chapter 5, we'll look at some of the activity that's taking place behind the scenes to make it appear like magic. When you have finished, click the Close button on the form to return to the IDE.

Double-click the button on the designer surface. You'll get the familiar source code window but with different content this time. For now, type or copy the code under *static void Main(string [ ] args)* from the console application you created previously to the *button1_Click* method, as shown in Figure 3-19. (You'll learn more about this method and the whole process behind the double-click in Chapter 4, "Creating Your Own Web Browser in Less Than Five Minutes.")

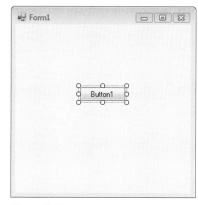

Figure 3-18
Windows Forms Designer surface with a button control

```
MyFirstWindowsApplication.Form1                    button1_Click(object sender, EventArgs e)
    {
        public Form1()
        {
            InitializeComponent();
        }

        private void button1_Click(object sender, EventArgs e)
        {
            //  Declaring two integer numbers variables that will hold the 2 parts
            //  of the sum and one integer variable to hold the sum
            int number1;
            int number2;
            int sum;

            //  Assigning two values to the integer variables
            number1 = 10;
            number2 = 5;

            //  Adding the two integers and storing the result in the sum variable
            sum = (number1 + number2);

            // Displaying a string with the 2 numbers and the result.
            Console.WriteLine("The sum of " + number1.ToString() + " and " + number2.To
        }
```

Figure 3-19
Button-click method with the code from our previous example

5. In the source code, find the words *Console.WriteLine*, and replace them with the words *MessageBox.Show*. Then build and execute the application by hitting F5.

6. When the form opens, click the button, and you'll see the result of your application: a message box with the same string you saw in the console application. It should look like Figure 3-20. Click OK in the message box, and then quit the program by clicking the Close button on the main form.

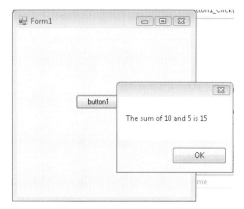

Figure 3-20
Output of MyFirstWindowsApplication

Congratulations! You just created your first two applications: a console application and a Windows application.

In Summary...

In this chapter, you learned some key information that will help you build on the skills you started developing in the previous chapters. You learned the differences between console applications, Windows applications, and WPF applications. You started Visual C# 2008 Express Edition, explored the IDE, and learned its major components. You created two versions of the same application: a console application and a Windows application. While learning about console applications, you also learned what Solution Explorer is as well as how to search and use the product documentation and the Help system. In the next chapter, you'll build on this knowledge and write a simple Web browser.

Chapter 4

Creating Your Own Web Browser in Less Than Five Minutes

What Is a Project?, 44

What Is the Design Layout?, 45

Putting It All Together, 52

Now that you've gotten a little experience creating simple applications in Microsoft Visual C# 2008 Express Edition, you'll build a more complicated application in this chapter and finish it in Chapter 6, "Modifying Your Web Browser." In this chapter, you'll start with the basic framework of the application; in the next two chapters, you'll continue to learn new features and then use them to enhance your project.

Specifically, in this chapter you'll learn how to build your own basic Web browser, and you'll be able to do it in five minutes or less!

In the previous chapter, you created a project to hold your source code. I'll now take a moment to explain what a project is and what information it contains. A *project* is a container for all the items in your application, such as forms, source code, and resources. It also stores important configuration data that belongs to the application as a whole: the location of the executable (that is, binaries) on your hard disk, the version information, and many more settings that affect the characteristics of your application. For instance, a project stores programmer-defined application settings that are important for the user experience. Users love to customize their software environment to reflect their comfort level and personal styles, for example. You've probably set up specific user preferences in Windows Internet Explorer, such as your home page address, your home page settings, which toolbars are displayed, whether your toolbars are locked in size, and so forth. A typical use of application settings in a project is to make sure the application can preserve user customizations from one execution to another.

In the next chapter, you'll learn about some of the most important settings stored in the project configuration file and how to use them in your application. In the final chapter of this book, you will use programmatic techniques to preserve the user's settings and customizations.

The name you choose when you create your application becomes your project's name. It also becomes the default folder name on your hard disk where your application is stored when you save it, and this name becomes the default namespace of your application. A *namespace* is used to organize the classes in a program in a single, logical hierarchical structure. It does the same for any other types you might define. The creation of a namespace also helps prevent naming collisions. What is a naming collision? Let's look at an example to illustrate this concept.

Suppose a company called AdventureWorks wrote a new Windows Forms class named *ANewForm*. The company would create a namespace called *AdventureWorks* and put its *ANewForm* class in it to uniquely name the class. The fully qualified name of a class is always composed of the namespace followed by a dot and then the name of the class or classes. Therefore, AdventureWorks's unique class would be *AdventureWorks.ANewForm*.

Now let's suppose you are creating a new project using Visual Studio and decide to name your project MyLibrary. Visual Studio would then create for you a namespace called *MyLibrary*. Suppose you then define a new class and name it *ANewForm*. You might not be aware that a company called AdventureWorks also called its new class using the same name. Even though AdventureWorks might be performing completely different tasks with its class, a problem could arise because the two classes are named the same.

Now suppose you're trying to use both classes called *ANewForm* in your new application. If you simply use *ANewForm*, the compiler will not be able to determine which *ANew-Form* class you want to use—the one from your library or the one from the AdventureWorks library; this is a *naming collision*. By prefixing the class name with the namespace name, you are then telling the compiler exactly which class you want to use (*AdventureWorks.ANew-Form* or *MyLibrary.ANewForm*).

What Is the Design Layout?

You will soon create a new design layout in the form designer. In doing so, you'll be creating what the application contains and how its content is presented when the user executes the application.

To accomplish this phase of a project, you typically do not need to type a great deal of code; as explained later in this chapter, Visual Studio takes care of this code for you. You have to worry mostly about how your application looks. When you're done designing all the visual aspects to your liking, your next task usually involves attaching the source code to your visual layout so that your application reacts to and acts upon the user's input.

In this chapter, you will complete the basic layout. You will learn more advanced layout techniques in following chapters. Let's start the Web browser project now.

TO CREATE A SIMPLE WEB BROWSER

1. Start Visual C# 2008 Express Edition by clicking Start, All Programs, Microsoft Visual C# 2008 Express Edition.

2. Create a new Windows Forms application by using any of the techniques shown in the previous chapters; for instance, you can use either the File menu or the New Project icon in the toolbar. Name the new application MyOwnBrowser.

3. On the design surface, you'll see the empty form with a title bar named Form1. Click the title bar once. By default, you don't see the Properties window. To view it, select the View menu, and then select Properties Window (or press F4). Look at the Properties window on the bottom right of the IDE, as shown in Figure 4-1.

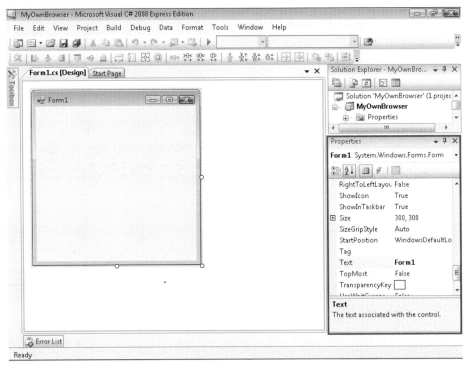

Figure 4-1
Properties window for MyOwnBrowser application Form control

We'll be using most of the properties you see listed here. Right now what is important for you to understand is that most of these properties influence how the control you have selected behaves or what it looks like when you execute your application.

For all the samples in this book, I suggest you sort the Properties window in ascending alphabetical order; it will be much easier to find properties that I reference in the examples. To sort the properties in ascending alphabetical order, click the Alphabetical button (with the AZ icon) in the Properties window toolbar. The other option is to arrange the controls by category, but this might slow you down as you progress through this book.

Whenever you select a property, you'll see a brief description of its usage at the bottom of the Properties window. Refer to Figure 4-1 as an example. In this case, the *Text* property is selected, and at the bottom of the Properties window, you can see a succinct message describing the function of the *Text* property.

As mentioned in Chapter 3, "Creating Your First Applications," my best advice for learning this software is to try, try, and try again. Visual C# 2008 Express Edition comes with a variety of tools and therefore many possibilities. You will learn to use most of these tools by performing the exercises in this book, but it's impossible to learn all the variations and possibilities if you don't do some exploring on your own. With that in mind, to understand the effect of changing a particular property, try all the possible values. Each time you modify a property, build and verify the execution. However, don't make more than one change at a time. If you do, it will be difficult for you to know which one of your changes actually triggered a visual modification. By exploring possibilities one at a time, you'll be able to see the effect of your changes immediately.

4. Make sure you have selected the Form control named *Form1* as directed in step 3, and then modify the properties using the values in Table 4-1. The property name to modify is located in the left column, and the value to which to set the property is located in the right column. You may have already completed this step, but to facilitate your data entry, verify that you have sorted the properties in ascending alphabetical order.

IMPORTANT

Some properties have a plus (+) sign beside them, which means they're tree view properties. Whenever you click the +, you'll expand this property to display the property's attributes, which you will then be able to set. Whenever you are asked to enter values for properties that are in a tree view, I will use the notation structure *Size:Width*, which refers to the *Size* property and the *Width* attribute.

Property	Value
Text	My Own Browser
Size:Width	640
Size:Height	480

Table 4-1
Form Properties to Change

You'll now add three Windows Forms controls to your browser application: a text box control in which to enter the destination URL, a button to navigate to the Web page, and a WebBrowser control in which the Web page content will be displayed.

5. Drag a WebBrowser control to the designer surface. The WebBrowser control is located in the Toolbox on the left side of the IDE; it's the last control in the Common Controls section. By default, this control will fill the designer surface entirely. Because you don't want that behavior for this particular application, you'll click the black triangle shown here, which will produce the content of a Smart Tag.

In this particular example, the Smart Tag helps you undock the control from its parent container (the form). Click the Smart Tag, and select Undock in the Parent Container.

6. Expand the control so that it occupies almost the entire designer space. To do this, click any of the control handles to change its size.

7. Select the WebBrowser control by clicking anywhere on the control. Then go to the Properties window, and modify the values for the properties listed in Table 4-2. Modify the values in the same way you modified the form controls in step 4.

Property	Value
(Name)	myBrowser
Size:Width	607
Size:Height	385
Location:X	12
Location:Y	12

Table 4-2
WebBrowser Control Properties to Change

8. Drag a text box control and a button control from the Toolbox's Common Controls section to the form so that it looks like Figure 4-2. Change the properties of the controls as you did with the WebBrowser control in step 7. Select one control at a time, and modify its properties with the data in Table 4-3.

9. At this point, you have a complete Web browser—congratulations! You can compile and execute your application by pressing F5.

If you followed the previous steps exactly, your application should now be running. Because we didn't code any functionality, entering a URL and clicking the GO button will not do anything.

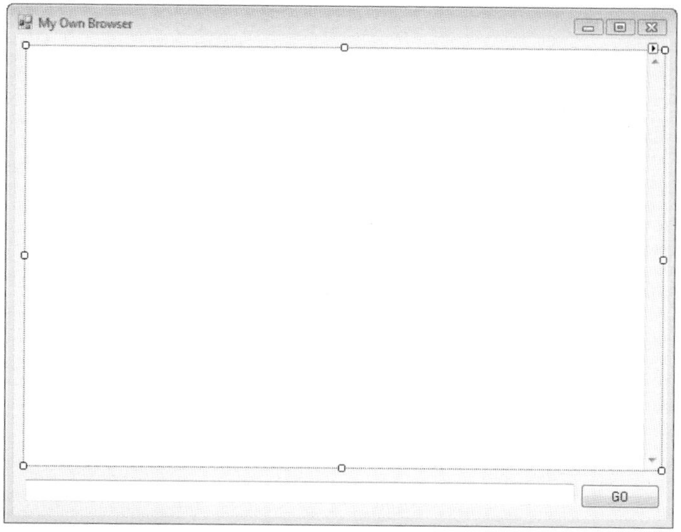

Figure 4-2
MyOwnBrowser application

Control	Property	Value
Textbox	(Name)	tbURL
Textbox	Location:X	12
Textbox	Location:Y	411
Textbox	Size:Width	526
Textbox	Size:Height	20
Button	(Name)	btnGo
Button	Location:X	544
Button	Location:Y	409
Button	Text	GO

Table 4-3
Controls, Properties, and Values

You first have to "wire up" the controls to the functionality that they will perform. I will use an analogy to explain this fundamental concept. A light bulb by itself is not a useful piece of hardware. To obtain light from it, you need to connect two wires carrying electricity. Similar to what an electrician would do to create this electrical circuit, you need to attach, or *wire*, the control and the action together by writing code to handle the event of clicking the GO button. Keep this analogy in mind when you see references to the term *wire* or *wiring* used in this book.

Before we wire up the click action to the button, I'll explain the line of code you'll add in the following instructions, and I'll explain how it relates to the OOP concepts previously introduced in Chapter 1, "Introducing Microsoft Visual C# 2008 Express Edition."

When you dropped the controls onto the designer surface, you created instances of the class represented by those controls. For example, when you dropped the WebBrowser control, you created an instance of the class *System.Windows.Forms.WebBrowser* that you then named *myBrowser*. The *WebBrowser* class has many methods, and the *Navigate* method is the one you'll use. As its name implies, this method allows the *WebBrowser* class to navigate to a URL. The URL is passed as an argument to the *Navigate* method. An argument, also called a *parameter*, is used to pass data to a method.

The argument in this case is the text the user will enter in the instance of the *System.Windows.Forms.TextBox* class that you appropriately named *tbURL*. To retrieve the content of the text box control named *tbURL*, you use the *Text* property of that control. A property enables you to set or retrieve the content of a data member in a class without accessing the data member directly. That way, the provider of the class (for example, Microsoft) can modify the implementation of the *Text* property without concerning the user with the implementation details. In OOP, this is called *encapsulation*. You can compare this process to a person driving a car: you don't need to know how the engine and transmission work to drive the car. Another good example is the *Navigate* method. You don't need to know how it's implemented; you simply want it to do its job. As mentioned earlier, many things are happening when you design a form with Visual Studio. You have seen that you don't need to create any of the classes or instances representing your controls because Visual Studio is doing all of that for you!

TO WIRE THE CLICK ACTION TO A BUTTON

1. Close the running application, and return to the IDE. Double-click the button control. You'll see the code window shown in Figure 4-3.

```
MyOwnBrowser.Form1                              btnGo_Click(object sender, EventArgs e)
    namespace MyOwnBrowser
    {
        public partial class Form1 : Form
        {
            public Form1()
            {
                InitializeComponent();
            }

            private void btnGo_Click(object sender, EventArgs e)
            {

            }
        }
    }
```

Figure 4-3
Code window for the btnGo_Click *event*

NOTE

If you try to type some code and it doesn't work, your application is probably still running. If you don't close the application and you return to Visual C#, you won't be able to modify the source code. A good way to verify that you have closed and terminated the application is to look in the Visual C# Express Edition title bar. If you see the name of your application followed by the word *(running)*, this means your application is still active and you won't be able to add code. If you try to add code, the status bar will report that you are in read-only mode with the following message: "Cannot currently modify this text in the editor. It is in read-only."

If you terminated the execution of your application properly, you should see the source code window with the *btnGo_Click* event template. When you double-clicked the button control, you signaled to Visual Studio that you wanted to wire the click action to the button control. Typically, each control can trigger multiple events depending on which behavior you want to intercept with your code. Each control has a default event that becomes available to the programmer for coding by double-clicking the control on the designer surface. In this case, Visual Studio created the *Click* event template so that you could enter the following code.

2. Type the following code at the cursor:

```
myBrowser.Navigate(tbURL.Text);
```

NOTE

Everything in C# is case-sensitive, so *tbURL* and *tbUrl* are two different values.

3. Press F5 to compile and execute the application. If you named your controls correctly in step 8 in the previous exercise and entered the line of code as shown in step 2 of this exercise, you should now have your own Web browser application that takes you to a Web page when you enter a URL. Of course, you won't have all the bells and whistles of Internet Explorer, but be patient—we're getting there. Try going to your favorite URLs to see whether your browser is working as expected. For instance, I went to *www.microsoft. com*, and it worked just fine! You can see the result in Figure 4-4.

Figure 4-4
MyOwnBrowser showing the Microsoft.com Web site

Putting It All Together

MORE INFO

Philosophies differ when it comes to naming the variable that represents controls on the design surface. In this book, I'll use up to three letters to describe and identify the control type by looking at its name, such as *btn* for a button control. The variable name then becomes *btnGo*. I will introduce the list when I talk about common controls in Chapter 5, "Using Rapid Application Development Tools with Visual C# 2008."

You've just seen that when you drag a control to the design surface, you're actually creating an object of that control class. When you're naming the control in the Properties window, you're actually assigning a name to the variable you've just created—which is exactly what you did for the three controls used in your browser. In fact, this is why you want to give your controls meaningful names so that you can use them later programmatically.

As you now know, a great deal of activity was taking place when you dropped controls on the designer surface. To help you understand what took place in the background, we talked about important OOP concepts behind the line of code you added to respond to the *Click* event.

Now that you've run the application, here is a list of questions you may have:

- What happens if I put nothing in the text box and hit Enter?
- What happens if I enter an invalid URL?
- What happens if I enter anything I want?

My answer to you is simply, "Try it. Try it now." The real deal is that your Web browser will actually behave like any other Web browser and will navigate to whatever URL is typed into the text box. If you don't type anything, clicking the GO button will have no effect. If you type something that isn't a URL, the browser control will come back with a Page Not Found or Code 404 page.

Now is your time to experiment. Remember this book's rule: try, try, try. Play with it. Change some of the properties, and see the results at run time. Although we haven't used many features yet, you'll add more in Chapter 6. This project is far from over! By adding new features, you'll arrive at a point where your application will start to look much more familiar.

IMPORTANT

Before moving on, I invite you to look at a video on the MSDN Web site that talks about object-oriented programming. You've read a good introduction to OOP both in this chapter and in Chapter 1. To understand the concept from another angle, navigate to *http://msdn2.microsoft.com/en-us/beginner/bb308750.aspx* and view Lesson 6.

Links to More Information

Other good sources of information are the videos from MSDN that were created to cover Visual C# 2005 Express Edition but are still applicable. The videos for Lessons 2 and 7 cover some of the topics you have just learned and will provide you with another point of view. You can find the videos for Lessons 2 and 7 by visiting the following hyperlinks:

For Lesson 2: http://msdn2.microsoft.com/en-us/beginner/bb308738.aspx

For Lesson 7: http://msdn2.microsoft.com/en-us/beginner/bb308753.aspx

In Summary...

In this chapter, you learned how to build a Web browser; in the process, you did the following:

- You added more than one control to the designer surface.
- You set properties in the Properties window.
- You wired an event to a control and learned how to add code that will execute when the event is triggered.

In this example, you saw many OOP concepts in action by using only one line of code. You added the code to respond to the button click event by calling the *Navigate* method of your Web browser object. Your Web browser navigated to a URL passed in as an argument to the *Navigate* method. The argument for the *Navigate* method was passed in using the text box control's *Text* property. Everything was completed and fully working just by tweaking some properties and adding only one line of code! That's what I call productivity.

In the next chapter, you'll continue this process by learning more about the major features of Visual C# 2008 Express Edition. You'll become more productive at developing applications by learning about features such as IntelliSense, snap lines, code snippets, Smart Tags, refactoring, and much more.

Chapter 5

Using Rapid Application Development Tools with Visual C# 2008

Snapping and Aligning Controls Using Snap Lines, 64

Using IntelliSense—Your New Best Friend!, 66

Renaming and Refactoring, 74

Exploring Common Windows Controls, 80

What Happens When an Event Is Triggered?, 83

In Chapter 4, "Creating Your Own Web Browser in Less Than Five Minutes," you started building your own Web browser, and in Chapter 6, "Modifying Your Web Browser," you'll add to its capabilities. But before you do that, I'll introduce some Microsoft Visual C# 2008 features that will help you develop your Microsoft Windows programming knowledge and skills. In this chapter, we'll look into some of the more useful rapid application development (RAD) features of Visual C# 2008 Express Edition.

NOTE

You can find all the RAD features described in this chapter in every edition of Visual Studio 2008. If you already know how to use these features in Express Edition and decide to explore any of the other editions of Visual Studio 2008, you'll find it much easier to switch and be productive.

Snapping and Aligning Controls Using Snap Lines

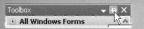
Not being a very skilled user interface designer myself, I've always had problems working on a program with many controls to align. Even more difficult was trying to get the alignment right the first time I dropped the controls onto the form. I've always had to go to the Properties window and align the controls manually by entering their *x* and *y* coordinates, which slows down the development process quite a bit! One of the philosophies the Visual C# 2008 team had in mind when creating this awesome new product was to make sure you didn't have to perform multiple steps at several different places to accomplish a simple task. And they succeeded with a lot of important features built into the designer; one of these is the snap lines feature with which you can easily align objects on the designer surface. Let's do an exercise so you can see the snap lines feature in action.

TO CREATE A NEW WINDOWS FORM USING SNAP LINES

1. Start Visual C# 2008 Express Edition by clicking Start, All Programs, Microsoft Visual C# 2008 Express Edition. Create a new Windows Forms Application project using any of the techniques shown in the previous chapters (using either the File menu or the New Project icon in the toolbar). Name the new application TestProject.

2. You should see the designer surface. If you don't, right-click the filename Form1.cs in Solution Explorer, and select View Designer. Then, using the Toolbox, drag three label controls and three text box controls to the design surface.

3. Stack the label controls vertically. A thin blue line (a *snap line*) appears on either the right side or the left side of the labels to help guide the alignment. When the labels are aligned correctly, release the label control.

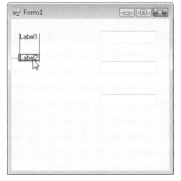

Figure 5-1
Snap lines in action with two label controls

As shown in Figure 5-1, a small blue horizontal line also appears to the left of the label control. This line represents the minimum space between a control and another control or between a control and its container.

4. After aligning the labels vertically, do the same with the text boxes immediately to the right of each label. The designer surface should look like the one shown in Figure 5-2.

5. Notice that the labels are aligned with the bottom of the text box controls. For a cleaner appearance, the labels should align with any text that will be entered in the text box. To align the labels correctly, move each label until you see a horizontal fuchsia line instead of a blue line, as shown in Figure 5-3. In Figure 5-4, Label1 and Label2 have been properly aligned with the baseline of the corresponding text box contents, but Label3 is still aligned with the bottom of the text box.

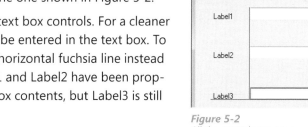

Figure 5-2
All the controls are now aligned.

Figure 5-3
Example of alignment with the common text baseline

Figure 5-4
Runtime execution of an alignment problem. The bottom label is aligned with the bottom of the text box but not its content.

IMPORTANT
Do not close the test project; you'll need it for the sections that follow. If you close the test project and Visual C# 2008 Express Edition and then re-open them later, you might lose the current view and your form, and any code you enter might not show up automatically. If you do happen to close the test form, click the View Code button on the Solution Explorer toolbar to view the code for the selected form, or click the View Designer button to open the designer for the selected form. Alternatively, you can right-click the form filename, in this case *Form1.cs*, and then select View Code to view the source code or View Designer to open the design surface.

Using IntelliSense—Your New Best Friend!

NOTE

As a beginner, one of the toughest aspects of programming to learn is the syntax, including knowing when you can use a particular keyword, and so on. Well, IntelliSense in Visual Studio 2008 really gives you a hand. It's smart enough to bring you only those suggestions that you can use in the context you are in and therefore removes a lot of potential errors for using a construct in the wrong place.

IntelliSense is one of the greatest tools developed for both beginner and experienced programmers. This feature provides contextual language references within the code editor and can even complete typing for you. This means you can get immediate code syntax help specific to the code you're writing without leaving the code editor. For example, if you're working with a form and you ask IntelliSense for help (you'll see how in a minute), you'll get access to code constructs that make sense for that particular form. You've already experienced IntelliSense while doing the previous examples without really knowing that's what you were using.

Opening IntelliSense: Pressing Ctrl+Spacebar

One of the easiest ways to open the IntelliSense window is to press Ctrl+Spacebar. Figure 5-5 shows an example from the project currently open in my code editor. You can see in this figure a list of possible choices based on the context of a form element named *Form1*.

MORE INFO

A neat feature in Visual Studio tracks the changes you make to the source code, similar to the Track Changes feature in Microsoft Office Word. In Visual Studio, however, whenever you modify your code, a colored line is added to the beginning of that line. A yellow line indicates that a change was made but has not been saved yet. If the line is green, it means the change was saved and is now part of the code even if you exit Visual Studio. It's a really useful feature, and if you want to turn it on, just click Tools, Options, and then select the Show All Settings check box at the bottom left of the window. In the tree view, expand Text Editor, select General, and then select Track Changes. In Visual C# this feature is enabled by default, but if you change this setting, you can always change it back.

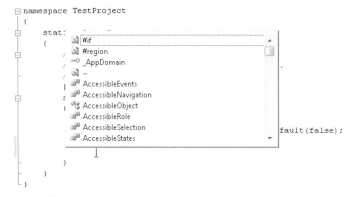

Figure 5-5
 You can invoke IntelliSense by pressing the Ctrl+Spacebar keystroke combination.

Opening IntelliSense: Typing a Period or Left Parenthesis

Another way you can get help using IntelliSense is by typing a period (.) after an element. The IntelliSense window will show up whether you are using .NET objects or your own objects. For example, I requested the list of possible constructs involving the variable *Form1*. In this example, I was looking for the variable *textBox1*, which represented the first text box on our form. By typing **this** and then a period (.)—as in **this.**—I received the list of all relevant objects in this context. Then by typing the letter **t**, I received the list of all relevant components that have names beginning with that letter. I just had to scroll down to the item I wanted: *textBox1*. Figure 5-6 illustrates these steps in the code editor (after you insert the button control in the following section). Finally, I pressed the Tab key to insert my selection, *textBox1*, in the code.

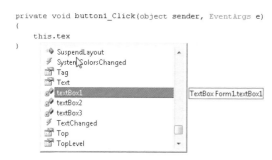

Figure 5-6
Getting help from IntelliSense by typing a period (.) after a valid object

TO USE INTELLISENSE

1. From the Toolbox, drag a button control to the form.

2. Double-click the button to open the button click event handler in the code editor. Then, where the cursor is blinking, press Ctrl+Spacebar. The IntelliSense window opens.

3. Type the letter **t** and then the letter **h**. In most cases, *this* should now be selected in IntelliSense. Press Tab, and then type a period (**.**).

4. Start typing **textbox**. Before you finish the word, IntelliSense should open textBox1. Press the Tab key to insert the component.

5. Type a period (.) again, type **text**, and then press the Tab key or the Spacebar. The code line should look like this one:

```
this.textBox1.Text
```

6. Now add the equal sign (**=**) and the string literal "**Hello, World**"; in the end, the line should look like this:

```
this.textBox1.Text = "Hello, World";
```

> **TIP**
> At any time you're using IntelliSense, you can press the Tab key to move quickly through the selections IntelliSense presents if the item you're looking for is already selected.

You can now build and execute the application by pressing F5 and verify that it works. When you click the button you created, you should get the string "Hello, World" in *textBox1*, which ordinarily should be the first one of the three text boxes because it was the first one dropped on the design surface. If you drop a bunch of controls onto the form in the designer, just increment the number at the end of the control type, as in *textBox1*, *textBox2*, *textBox3*, and so on.

You can get additional help from IntelliSense if more than one choice is available for your situation. Typing a left parenthesis displays a list of all the possible choices. For instance, when we created the console application in Chapter 3, "Creating Your First Applications," we wrote to the console using the *Console.WriteLine* method. We used this method with a string argument, but you can do more with *Console.WriteLine* than just use a string as an argument. IntelliSense will indicate whether there is more than one option. For *Console.WriteLine*, IntelliSense indicates there are 19 possible variations, as you can see in Figure 5-7. I was looking for the second variation, which is a Boolean argument. Now it's your turn to try it.

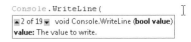

Figure 5-7
IntelliSense lists all the possible variations of using the WriteLine *method.*

TO SELECT FROM A LIST OF OPTIONS IN INTELLISENSE

1. If the source code is not visible, just click the tab at the top of the code editor where you see the filename Form1.cs. Add a new line in the *Button1_Click* event, type **MessageBox.Show**, and then type **(**. The IntelliSense window opens and shows there are 21 possible variations for *MessageBox.Show*.

2. Scroll through the list of options using the up or down arrow on your keyboard. Once you find the one you want to use, simply use the code constructs as IntelliSense indicates to you. In this case, that means using the option identified as "1 of 21" in the yellow rectangle, which is called a *tooltip*.

3. Complete the following line of code so that it looks like this:

```
MessageBox.Show("Hello Again");
```

4. Build and execute the application. When you click the button, you should see the "Hello, World" string in *textBox1*, and then a dialog box should show up with the "Hello Again" message.

IntelliSense Filtering: Preselecting the "Most Recently Used"

You might have noticed that when the IntelliSense window appears (except for the first time you invoke it), you immediately jump to an element in the list. IntelliSense has preselected this element because it's the most recently used construct. Therefore, to be more productive, IntelliSense picks it up automatically to save you some typing. Another type of filtering is selection based purely on the context you're in at the moment of the IntelliSense invocation. For instance, if you're in the code for handling an exception, say in a *catch* statement in a *try-catch* block, then IntelliSense presents you with the exception types. That's IntelliSense filtering at its best.

Using IntelliSense Code Snippets: The Time-Saver

Code snippets were invented for only one reason—developer productivity. The code snippets in C# are related to language constructs but can be extended to include other code snippets. In Visual C# you can add code snippets in two ways: You can insert them, or by using an existing block of code, you can surround that block of code with a code snippet. The first option is simple. At any point in your source code you can right-click, select Insert Snippet..., and then select the code snippet that best fits the context.

The second option needs a bit more explanation. Let's say you have an existing block of code that reads a line of text in a file and then parses some data. In the process of developing your application, you realize you need the code to read the whole file, not only one line. This means you need to add a looping construct. With the Surround With... option it's quite easy to add the block of code to do the looping. You just have to select the block of code you want to have in a loop, right-click, and select Surround With.... Then you need to select the instruction you want to surround your block of code with. In this example, you would surround the code with a *while* statement. Then you just have to double-click the *while* statement, and your code will be automatically embedded in the *while* block.

MORE INFO
See the "Finding Additional Information" section later in this chapter for more information about code snippets.

Figure 5-8 gives you a glimpse of the Visual C# code snippets. All code snippets are made with customizable fields, which means they contain fields that are replaceable with code elements from your own applications. Going forward, you will be able to download additional code snippets from various sources such as the MSDN Web site, online communities, and other .NET vendors. You will also be able to add your own code snippets to the code snippets library to fulfill your needs in other projects.

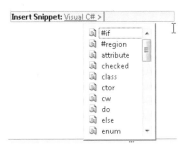

Figure 5-8
IntelliSense code snippets menus

Invoking Code Snippets

You can invoke the code snippets in the code editor in two ways: by right-clicking and choosing Insert Snippet or Surround With and also by selecting Edit, then IntelliSense, and then Insert Snippet... or Surround With... Each way has its own keyboard shortcut: press Ctrl+K, X for Insert Snippet, or press Ctrl+K, S for Surround With.

TO USE CODE SNIPPETS

1. Using the previous test project, return to the code editor in the *Button1_Click* event, and then open the IntelliSense Snippet menu by using either method described earlier.

2. Click the Visual C# menu choice, and then scroll down to the *for* statement. Look at Figure 5-9 to get a feel for which menu choices you should have on your screen. Double-click the *for* statement to insert the code into the code editor.

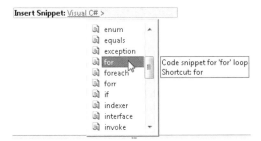

Figure 5-9
Code snippets within the Visual C# language menus

3. Once you select the *for* statement, a generic template for the C# *for* language construct appears. As shown in Figure 5-10, the green fields in the "before" version (on the left) are replacement fields prepopulated with some default values that you can modify. Before you go to the next step, edit the code to match the "after" version (on the right).

```
for (int i = 0; i < length; i++)        for (int i = 0; i < 10; i++)
{                                        {
                                             this.textBox2.Text += i.ToString() + ",";
}                                        }
```

Figure 5-10
"Before" (left) and "after" (right) look at the for statement code snippets

4. Build and execute your application by pressing F5, and then click the button on the form to execute the code snippet you've just inserted. In the second text box, you should see the numbers 0 through 9 separated by commas. This output is the result of the *for* statement looping 10 times, adding the index value string representation and a comma to the text box with each loop. In this sample, the index is *i*.

5. Just below the right curly brace (}) of the *for* statement, type again the following line of code:

```
this.textBox2.Text += i.ToString() + ",";
```

6. Select the line of code you just typed, right-click, and select Surround With.... You should see a list of items similar to the Insert Snippet... choices. Double-click the *for* statement in that list. You should see the same code snippet you saw in step 3 with your line of code embedded in it.

7. Now start your index *i* at 10 instead of 0, and instead of increasing the index, decrease it by typing **i--**. Look at Figure 5-11 to see the "before" and "after" Surround With... versions.

Figure 5-11
Before (left) adding the code snippet using Surround With and after (right)

8. Now build and execute by pressing F5, and when you click the button, you should see the suite of 0 to 9 and then 10 to 1 in *textBox2*. You might need to resize *textBox2* to be large enough to hold the suite of numbers.

Using IntelliSense Automatic *Using* Statements

Let's say you want to work with an XML file and you want to load it in memory. The *XmlDocument* class is in the *System.Xml* namespace, and for IntelliSense to recognize it, you need a *using* directive at the top of your file. Automatic *using* statements in IntelliSense help you continue to type your code without leaving the place where you need the new class. For instance, below the right curly brace (}) of the second *for* loop statement, type the following code:

```
XmlDocument
```

A red Smart Tag will appear. If you click it and then click the drop-down list, you'll see that the first choice you'll have suggests inserting the *using System.Xml* directive at the top of the file. This will be done automatically without you having to type a single line of code. Great productivity! After the *using* directive is added, *XmlDocument* changes from black to cyan indicating that IntelliSense picked up the *using* directive and that it is now a recognized class. Look at Figure 5-12 for the "before" (left) and "after" (right) versions. Note the yellow line on the left margin in the editor indicating that the *using* statement was added since the last save, hence proving it was added automatically for you.

Figure 5-12
Using the automatic using *statement feature, and the* using *directive added at the top of the file*

Organizing *Using* Statements

The next IntelliSense feature I'll discuss is the Organize Usings command. This is a new feature for Visual C# 2008, and it helps you keep your code clean. It helps you do that by eliminating *using* statements you are not using anywhere in your code. It could be a tedious job to do this manually and check that every statement has its place in your code. In fact, to show how it works, delete the *XmlDocument* line you entered in the previous section. Then right-click, select Organize Usings, and then select Remove Unused Usings or Remove and Sort. Either of these actions deletes the *using System.Xml* line. Look at Figure 5-13 for the "before" (left) and "after" (right) versions. Note that you can also simply sort the *using* statements for the clarity and readability of your code.

Figure 5-13
Using the Organize Usings command to clean your code of unused using *statements*

Automatically Generating a Method Stub

IntelliSense can also automatically generate a method stub for you. This feature is an IntelliSense automatic code generation feature that provides you with an easy way to create a new method declaration as you write the code to call it. You just have to let Visual Studio infer the declaration from the call. For instance, in this example, after the second *for* loop, type the following line of code:

```
DisplayNumbersInDescendingOrder(10, 1);
```

When you type the terminating semicolon, Visual C# puts a blue underline symbol under the letter *D*. Resting your mouse pointer on that blue underline gives you the option to

OOP Terminology

Although this book is not an OOP book, we'll certainly use many OOP constructs in the applications we'll build. I talked about OOP in Chapter 1, "Introducing Microsoft Visual C# 2008 Express Edition," and in Chapter 4, but if you want to learn more about this paradigm, you can go to the Start Page. If it's not visible, just click View, Other Windows, and then select Start Page. On the Start Page, click the Learn C# hyperlink in the Getting Started section. Locate C# Language Primer, and then find Classes. Click and read whenever you want to learn more about OOP and the Visual C# language. The online information is not a complete OOP book, but it's more than enough for what you'll be doing in this book.

generate a method stub for *DisplayNumbersInDescendingOrder*. Select this option, and you should see a method stub with the correct signature and parameters. By default it adds a line of code in the method's body that throws an exception to make sure you have a visual indication at run time if you forget to implement it. Look at Figure 5-14 for the "before" (top) and "after" (bottom) versions.

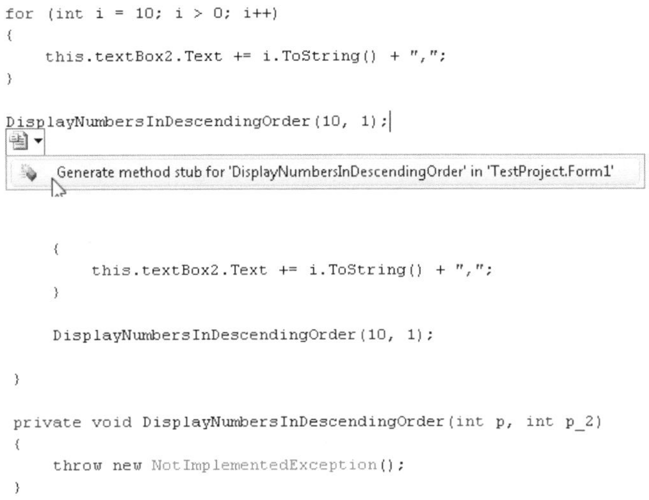

for (int i = 10; i > 0; i++)
{
this.textBox2.Text += i.ToString() + ",";
}
DisplayNumbersInDescendingOrder(10, 1);
Generate method stub for 'DisplayNumbersInDescendingOrder' in 'TestProject.Form1'
{
this.textBox2.Text += i.ToString() + ",";
}
DisplayNumbersInDescendingOrder(10, 1);
}
private void DisplayNumbersInDescendingOrder(int p, int p_2)
{
throw new NotImplementedException();
}

Figure 5-14
Using IntelliSense to automatically generate a method stub to create a method out of a method call.

Renaming and Refactoring

Visual C# 2008 Express Edition has added great support for refactoring. Refactoring helps developers automate many common tasks when they restructure their code. In Visual C# 2008 Express Edition, you can use this feature to do two of those restructuring tasks: rename symbols and extract methods. Let's look at them.

The rename feature in Visual C# 2008 is quite useful. It provides you, the programmer, with an easy, automatic, and effective way of changing source elements in a selective way where the symbol is referenced in the code. You can update variables, controls, comments, strings, and any other items in your applications to meaningful names using the renaming symbol functionality.

Why Should You Rename?

So far in the test project we've worked in, we haven't paid attention to the controls' names because we didn't have to write much code and because the project was a quick prototype to test new features. At this point, our controls are all named something like *textBox1*, *textBox2*, *label1*, and so on. That's OK for what we've been doing, but when you develop your own applications, you'll always want to give meaningful names to your controls and variables so that your code becomes self-documenting and easier to read and maintain.

Using the Rename Feature

As mentioned, we have defined some text boxes, labels, and other controls in our test project, but they all have their autogenerated names (for example, *textBox1* or *label1*). We can use the rename feature to give meaningful names to these controls, starting from three different places within the IDE: the Properties window, in the code, and Solution Explorer.

The first place we can use the renaming feature is in the Properties window at design time. So far in our test project, we've used the form name *Form1*. In the next exercise, we'll rename *Form1* to *TestProjectForm*. The expectation is that this change gets propagated throughout the code in the project. But just to see how the functionality works, we'll look into all files where the *Form1* symbol is used.

Behind the Scenes

This is a good point to introduce a new button in the Solution Explorer toolbar. The Show All Files button looks like this in the toolbar:

By clicking the Show All Files button, you can see files that are part of the project but that you do not need to work with in most circumstances. For instance, you'll see the output files of your application. They are important but not in the context of Visual Studio.

TO USE THE RENAME FEATURE

1. In Solution Explorer, expand the Form1.cs file by clicking the plus sign (+) beside Form1.cs.

2. Right-click the filename Form1.Designer.cs, and then select View Code. Figure 5-15 shows what you should see in Solution Explorer just before you select View Code.

3. Now I'll introduce you to a useful feature: search. With the Form1.Designer.cs source code in the code editor, press Ctrl+F, and then type **Form1** in the Find What text box. Before you click the Find Next button, make sure to select Current Project from the Look In list box.

   Figure 5-16 shows how the search should be configured.

Figure 5-15
View Code option on a source code file

4. Search for all occurrences of *Form1* in the code by clicking the Find Next button. You should see that the search goes through three files: Form1.cs, Program.cs, and Form1.Designer.cs.

5. Once all instances of *Form1* have been found, a dialog box will display a message saying that the search is complete and that there are no more occurrences of your search criteria.

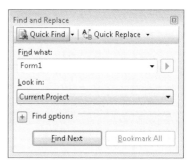

6. You can now rename the form. To do that, select the Form1.cs [Design] tab to return to the designer surface. Then click the title bar to select the form.

Figure 5-16
Find and Replace dialog box

7. In the Properties window, be sure the form control named *Form1* is selected. Modify the (*Name*) property by changing *Form1* to *TestProjectForm*. Press Enter to begin renaming. A small blue circle (the wait cursor in the Windows Vista operating system) appears while the renaming is in process.

8. Now repeat the search from steps 3 and 4, and you'll see that the only occurrence left is a string that corresponds to the form control's *Text* property (that is, the title bar name).

9. You can also rename a symbol directly in the code. In Form1.cs, place the cursor anywhere in the word *textBox1* in the following line of code:

```
this.textBox1.Text = "HelloWorld";
```

10. Right-click, select Refactor, and then select Rename; a dialog box like the one on the left of Figure 5-17 appears. Delete the text *textBox1*, and type **tbMessage** in its place; the dialog box should now look like the one on the right of Figure 5-17. You have three check boxes that can control how deep your rename will go; select all of them.

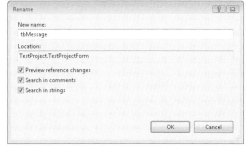

Figure 5-17
Rename dialog boxes: before (left) and after (right) a rename

11. Click OK to start replacing all occurrences of *textBox1* with *tbMessage*. You should see a dialog box that will give you a preview of all the changes that will be made by refactoring. The upper section shows you where the string was found, and the bottom portion shows you what the change will look like if applied to the selected item. The check boxes allow you to select only the changes you really want to perform. One neat feature is that they are organized by type of change: one for the code elements, one for the comments, and finally one for the strings. Look at the top of Figure 5-18 to see the Preview Changes dialog box's upper window completely scrolled, and look at the bottom of Figure 5-18 for the first selected change preview.

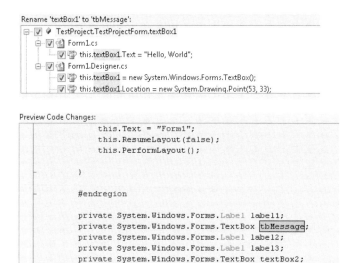

Rename 'textBox1' to 'tbMessage':

```
☐ ✓ ● TestProject.TestProjectForm.textBox1
  ☐ ✓ 🔲 Form1.cs
        ✓ 🔲 this.textBox1.Text = "Hello, World";
  ☐ ✓ 🔲 Form1.Designer.cs
        ✓ 🔲 this.textBox1 = new System.Windows.Forms.TextBox();
        ✓ 🔲 this.textBox1.Location = new System.Drawing.Point(53, 33);
```

Preview Code Changes:

```
            this.Text = "Form1";
            this.ResumeLayout(false);
            this.PerformLayout();


        }


        #endregion

        private System.Windows.Forms.Label label1;
        private System.Windows.Forms.TextBox tbMessage;
        private System.Windows.Forms.Label label2;
        private System.Windows.Forms.Label label3;
        private System.Windows.Forms.TextBox textBox2;
        private System.Windows.Forms.TextBox textBox3;
        private System.Windows.Forms.Button button1;
    }
}
```

Figure 5-18
Rename dialog box: previewing changes

12. Click Apply to perform the renaming. It's that easy. Imagine how much time you would save using the rename feature if you had 10 files with hundreds of lines of code. Not only would you be sure to find every occurrence, but the code would be a lot easier to read.

13. The third way to rename a symbol, and in this case only for project elements, is to do it directly in Solution Explorer. Even though earlier we changed the *Form1* variable into something more meaningful, the filename Form1 hasn't changed because it's not in the source code; it's in Solution Explorer and contained in the project, so it's still Form1.cs. For consistency, right-click the filename Form1.cs in Solution Explorer, select Rename, and change the filename to TestProjectFormOtherName.cs. Two things will happen: first, you'll see that the filename and all dependent filenames are automatically changed to the new name; second, you'll see that all project references to *TestProjectForm* are now changed to *TestProjectFormOtherName*. You can verify this renaming change by pressing Ctrl+F and performing a search on the old name (Form1.cs).

Refactoring: Using the Extract Method Command

It's common when you develop an application that a block of code turns into a mega-method that does a lot more than the original functionality it was supposed to provide. Therefore, you need to reorganize your code and perhaps break the problem into smaller pieces. That's where the refactoring feature's Extract Method command will become your friend. With this refactoring functionality you just have to select a block of code within a method, right-click, select Refactor, and then select Extract Method.... Visual C# 2008 Express will then create a private method with the selected block of code and call that method where the code was. If the block of code uses local variables from the original method, they will be automatically passed as arguments to the new method. Look at Figure 5-19 to see what it looks like before the refactoring (top), during it (middle), and after (bottom) the refactoring.

```
using (StreamWriter sw = new StreamWriter(this.safeFileDialog1.FileName))
{
    // Add the three text boxes to the file
    sw.WriteLine(this.tbMessage.Text);
    sw.WriteLine(this.textBox2.Text);
    sw.WriteLine(this.textBox3.Text);
}
```

```
    using (StreamWriter sw = new StreamWriter(this.safeFileDialog1.FileName))
    {
        WriteTextBoxContent(sw);
    }
}

private void WriteTextBoxContent(StreamWriter sw)
{
    // Add the three text boxes to the file
    sw.WriteLine(this.tbMessage.Text);
    sw.WriteLine(this.textBox2.Text);
    sw.WriteLine(this.textBox3.Text);
}
```

Figure 5-19
The Extract Method command in action before, during, and after the refactoring

I will not spend a lot of time here explaining all the details and properties of each control in the Toolbox. This book is not a reference about Windows Forms programming. Other books do a great job with that topic. However, Table 5-1 provides a quick introduction to the most common controls you will find in most Windows applications.

Many more controls exist than the ones shown here, but this table should make it clear that you have a plethora of controls available to perform many tasks. To save time and effort, you can usually find a control to provide the results you want with very little effort. It is especially desirable if the control you pick can restrict choices or restrict how the data is selected without having to perform any other validation. In software development, always keep the 80/20 rule in mind: 80 percent of results for 20 percent effort. In other words, do not re-invent the wheel. Keep it simple.

Visual Representation	Name	Description
Button1	Button	The button control lets a user communicate a decision or initiate an action. In your application, a button clicked by the user triggers an event that your code needs to handle.
	TextBox	The text box is used to get user input. On the screen it can be a single or multiline control. It can also provide password character masking if you need this behavior in your application. It's a good choice for the user to input information that is not restrictive in choices, such as a Boolean decision (yes/no or on/off) or a list of specific choices (such as a list of country names). It's good for names, addresses, phone numbers, URLs, and so on.

Table 5-1
Common Windows Applications Controls

Visual Representation	Name	Description
Label1	Label	The label control is usually simple text used to describe other controls. It is generally not an interactive control.
○ Grayscale ○ Color	RadioButton	This control is used when multiple choices are offered but the user can pick only one from the list. Let's say you have an application and you want to provide the option to print in grayscale or color. You could use two radio buttons so that the user can select the desired method.
□ AC □ CD Changer □ Metallic Paint □ ABS	CheckBox	A check box is great for Boolean choices (for example, on/off, yes/no, and so on). It can also be used in a group of check boxes to indicate characteristics of a single entity. For instance, in a car-ordering tool that is part of a dealership application, you could have check boxes for all the car characteristics (that is, AM/FM radio, CD changer, heated seats, metallic paint, and so on).
[▼] [▼] Alabama Arkansas California Connecticut Washington	ComboBox	A combo box is a combination of a text box and a drop-down list with valid choices. It's great for displaying an editable text box with a list of permitted values. You can have auto-complete, and the values can be sorted. The values can come from static entry or from other sources of data such as a database. For instance, a good example is selecting a state. You can either enter the state name or select it from the list of possible values.

Table 5-1 (continued)
Common Windows Applications Controls

Visual Representation	Name	Description
Joe John Brad Mark Jim Joe John Brad Mark Jim	ListBox	A list box is a short list of valid choices for the domain this component represents. This control is great when there is a list of possible choices that is not too big in number. It does not allow the user to enter text but lets the user select one or more than one choice by using Ctrl or Shift.
Name [ ] Customer Name	ToolTip	The tooltip control is helpful for displaying information about a control when a user holds the mouse pointer over the control.
1971 ⬍	NumericUpDown	This control is really useful when you want the user to select a numerical value in a defined set of numbers. It allows the user to select a single numerical value from the list using the up or down button to increment and decrement the number. It's a perfect way to force the user to pick a numerical value for the year component of a date.

Table 5-1 (continued)
Common Windows Applications Controls

What Happens When an Event Is Triggered?

All Windows applications are event-driven. This means that whenever you select a menu item, click a button, or even move from one text box to another, you are generating an event. Blocks of code attached to each of your actions execute as you work. Events are generated not only by your actions but also by the surrounding environment, namely, Windows or external sources. To understand what "external sources" means, think about an Internet messenger application, such as Windows Live Messenger. When you chat with someone and exchange data back and forth, you are actually generating events. In non-technical terms, data coming from your friend over the Internet is an event.

These events exist for a multitude of actions you often take—probably without even realizing they are events. Some events are handled for you by autogenerated code, such as clicking the red X in the right corner of an application, and others need to be handled by your code.

In this section, we'll start to work on wiring source code to events. For practice, we will wire two objects from our test project. Before beginning, use what you've learned so far to make the test project look like Figure 5-20.

When an event is triggered, the code that is wired to handle the event is executed. If there is no code attached to a particular event, nothing happens. Our application is basically in that stage right now (except for the button that was doing some work for us, as shown previously). We will add some functionality to our test project application by wiring the Save menu item and the toolbar Save button to the source code that will save all the content of the text boxes to a simple text file in the current directory. Because the Save and Open file dialogs boxes are standard (and also to get a consistent feel across applications), the Visual C# development team decided to write save and open controls and make them available to you. You'll take advantage of this shortcut in the exercise.

Figure 5-20
Customer Info form

NOTE
To add the menus and toolbar buttons, go to the Toolbox in the Menus & Toolbars category. Add a MenuStrip control and a ToolStrip control to the form. Next, select each control, open the Smart Tag menu, and select Insert Standard Items.

Using Comments in Your Code

One good habit you should start embracing when writing code is to comment your code. Right now, the code for the problems we are solving isn't too complicated. But keep in mind that adding comments serves the following purpose: your code becomes much more maintainable because you can return six months later and, if the comments are good, be able to understand what you developed. It also makes your code more readable and facilitates getting help from somebody. Write your comments in plain language without too much jargon. The comments are never compiled in the application you execute, so they will never slow down the performance of your application.

As you can see in the code in step 7 of the following section (code for the FileOK event), you can comment your code by inserting two forward slashes (//) for a one-line comment or by using /* and */ on the same line or on a separate line for a multiline comment. Your comment should appear in green; if not, then the compiler does not consider your line to be a comment. Another good way to comment your code is to use two buttons from one of the toolbars. Let's say you decide that the code in the FileOk event is not the code you want to execute because you want to test something else. You do not want to delete all the text, but you can comment out the code by selecting it and then clicking the Comment Out the Selected Lines button. And if you want to uncomment a block of code, you just have to select the code you want to uncomment and then click the Uncomment the Selected Lines button.

TIP

If you want to look at all the possible events that can be fired for a particular control, you can click the yellow lightning icon at the top of the Properties window. To return to the properties, you just have to click the little sheet symbol to the left of the yellow lightning icon.

Figure 5-21
Design-time representation of the SaveFileDialog control

TO WIRE SOURCE CODE TO EVENTS

1. Drag a SaveFileDialog control located in the Toolbox's Dialogs category to the form. This control has no design-time representation; it will appear only in the component tray, which is the gray section below the designer surface along with the MenuStrip and ToolStrip controls. See Figure 5-21 for the location of the SaveFileDialog control.

   We'll use the SaveFileDialog control to wire the click event to both the Save button on the toolbar and the Save item in the File menu. To have the same operation performed when either event occurs, we'll write a block of code called a *method*, and we will call this method in all the places we need it. The block of code will perform the same operation whether it is triggered by the button on the toolbar or by the menu selection.

2. Click the blue disk icon on the ToolStrip control to select it. Refer to the Properties window to be sure you have the correct control, which should be called SaveToolStrip-Button, as shown in Figure 5-22.

3. Double-click the blue disk on the designer surface, and you will be presented with the default event template for this control, which is the *Click* event.

4. Add the following line of code to the *saveToolStrip-Button_Click* event procedure. (I will explain what it does in a moment.)

Figure 5-22
Verify that the name and type of control is the one you intend to work with.

```
this.saveFileDialog1.ShowDialog();
```

This block of code displays the SaveFileDialog1 dialog box by calling the *ShowDialog()* method on it. At this point, if you want to see the effect of the change, just build and execute the application by pressing F5, and then click the Save button icon to see that the Save dialog box does appear.

5. In every SaveFileDialog dialog box, there is a Save button and a Cancel button. The Cancel button is automatically taken care of for us. But we need to wire what is going to happen when the user clicks the Save button of that new dialog box.

6. Make sure you have stopped the execution of the application. Now, to wire the Save button, select the saveFileDialog1 icon in the component tray, and double-click it to get to the most common event, which is the *FileOk* event in this case.

7. Whenever the user clicks the Save button, your application will take the content of the three text boxes and write them into a file on the hard disk. When you have finished, your code should look like the following code. Examine the comments to understand what we are trying to accomplish. You can use the Insert Snippet feature and use a *using* snippet.

SaveFileDialog1_FileOk Method

```
private void saveFileDialog1_FileOk(object sender, CancelEventArgs e)
{
    // By using the using statement, not to be confused with the using
    // directive on top of the file, we are making sure that if an
```

Finding Additional Information

Some good information on how to create new code snippets and how to modify existing code snippets is available at http://msdn2.microsoft.com/en-us/library/ms165393(VS.90).aspx.

The MSDN videos are another good source of information. I suggest you watch the following two lessons (even though they were made for Visual C# 2005, they still apply); they will reinforce a lot of topics covered in this chapter:

Lesson 2 video: http://msdn2.microsoft.com/en-us/beginner/bb308738.aspx

Lesson 3 video: http://msdn2.microsoft.com/en-us/beginner/bb308741.aspx

These two lessons are a pretty good visual complement to this chapter.

```
    /* exception is happening that a finally is executed to close the
     * file.  The using is in fact a try - finally block. */
    using (StreamWriter sw = new  StreamWriter(this.saveFileDialog1.FileName))
    {
        // Add the three text boxes to the file
        sw.WriteLine(this.txtMessage.Text);
        sw.WriteLine(this.textBox2.Text);
        sw.WriteLine(this.textBox3.Text);
    }
}
```

8. Using the IntelliSense automatic *using* statement feature, click the red and yellow underline on *StreamWriter*, and add the following *using* directive to the top of the code file:

```
using System.IO;
```

9. Now we just need to attach the same event code to the File, Save menu selection. Double-click the Save choice in the File menu, and add the same code as in step 4. Build the application, and execute it by pressing F5. Type some text in the text boxes, and then save the content to a file by using the Save menu or the Save toolbar button. You should verify that the content of the file your application saved is really what was on the form. So to verify it worked properly, open the file with Visual Studio by clicking File, Open File and then browsing to the location of the saved file. Open it to view its contents.

You just handled two events, but I want to point out that you already handled events previously by coding *Button1_Click* and modifying properties of other controls. For instance, you modified the *Text* property of the text box controls when you handled the button click. And you were able to do that by using the control's *Name* property.

In Summary...

Wow, this was a big chapter that covered a lot of features. These features will definitely help you write applications on your own. Specifically, the chapter covered IDE features such as snap lines to help you align the controls on the form. It also covered the rich features of IntelliSense, which help type your code by either suggesting appropriate choices, completing code sentences for you, or providing you with code snippets. In the end, IntelliSense reduces the amount of typing you do, helps you learn the language, and helps your productivity. On top of that, it is a great feature for beginners.

You then saw the benefits of the new refactoring feature to rename elements in your source code, elements such as code elements, comments, and even string literals. Then you saw that the refactoring feature's Extract Method command lets you restructure your code by extracting blocks of code and automatically creating new methods with all the supporting code. It is especially useful for replacing autogenerated variable names with more meaningful variable names. You examined the most common controls you will find in every Windows application with some graphical examples and learned when to use them. Finally, the chapter ended with an explanation of how event-based programming is performed.

In the next chapter, you'll put into practice everything you just learned in this chapter. You'll also take a look at some new features, controls, and concepts that you'll use as we continue with the Web browser project.

Chapter 6
Modifying Your Web Browser

*Opening Your
Application, 90*

*Interacting Through
Dialog Boxes, 100*

*Having a Professional
Look and Feel at Your
Fingertips, 106*

Redoing the Browser, 118

After learning about the avalanche of new concepts presented in the first few chapters, you're now ready to apply your skills and take your Web browser to the next level. In this chapter, you'll add rich features to your browser such as a splash screen, an About dialog box, tool strips, menu strips, a tool strip container that will give you a rich user experience "à la Internet Explorer," a status strip control, a progress bar, and professional-looking toolbars with "déjà vu" icons. You'll also learn about features such as the Document Outline window and how to respond to events coming from the WebBrowser control. Finally, you will learn about Windows Presentation Foundation, because you will modify your Web browser project using this new technology.

When you load an application, you often see something called a *splash screen*. Some good examples of splash screens are the opening information boxes you see for Microsoft Office and Microsoft Visual Studio 2008. Although the splash screens are often very nice looking, they aren't there just to display the software version and some appealing artwork or to make sure you're not bored. These screens serve a function. Once you've started an application, a lot of processing is happening; for instance, the application is connecting to databases, populating controls with data from the database, getting saved configurations for user interface (UI) preferences, and so on. Displaying the splash screen while all of this processing is happening helps inform the user that the application is indeed working.

Technically speaking, a splash screen is a Windows form that does not allow any input from the user. It usually has a nice presentation form with some artwork, the application name, its version, and often some legal text. One of the first features you'll add to your Web browser application is a splash screen.

TO CREATE A SPLASH SCREEN

1. To start, you'll give Form1 a more meaningful name. (Keep in mind that every name in your application needs to be meaningful for readability and maintainability.) In Solution Explorer, rename Form1.cs to Browser.cs. When asked whether you want to rename all references to Form1 in the project, click Yes.

2. To add a regular form to your project, you can either go to the Project menu and select Add Windows Form... or go to Solution Explorer, right-click the project name (in this case, MyOwnBrowser), select Add, and then select Windows Form. The Add New Item dialog box appears and asks which type of form you want to add.

3. Select Windows Form, and name the file Splash.cs. Look at Figure 6-1 to see what the Add New Item dialog box should look like.

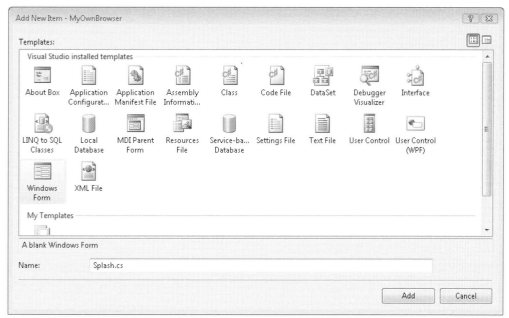

Figure 6-1
Add New Item dialog box for the creation of the splash screen

4. A splash screen has particular properties because it is not designed for user interaction. It is purely informational and should not appear in the task bar, should not be resizable, and more. Now make sure you select your new form in the Properties window and set those particular form properties using Table 6-1.

   The image for the background is located in the Images folder under Chapter6 where you installed your companion content. (If you installed the companion content at the default location, then it should be at the following location on your hard disk: Documents\ Microsoft Press\VCS 2008 Express\.)

5. Add three label controls to the form, and name them *lblApplicationTitle*, *lblVersion*, and *lblCopyright*. Use the Properties window to set the properties specified in Table 6-1.

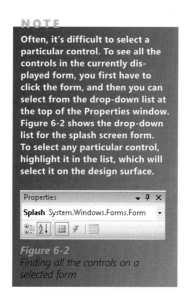

NOTE
Often, it's difficult to select a particular control. To see all the controls in the currently displayed form, you first have to click the form, and then you can select from the drop-down list at the top of the Properties window. Figure 6-2 shows the drop-down list for the splash screen form. To select any particular control, highlight it in the list, which will select it on the design surface.

Figure 6-2
Finding all the controls on a selected form

NOTE

When one of the steps says to add a control and then name it XYZ, it means you need to add the control onto the design surface, and then go to the Properties window and change the (Name) property of the control to XYZ.

Control Name	Control Type	Property	Value
Splash	Form	FormBorderStyle	None
Splash	Form	ShownInTaskbar	False
Splash	Form	StartPosition	CenterScreen
Splash	Form	Size:Width	450
		Size:Height	375
Splash	Form	BackgroundImage	www.jpg
Splash	Form	BackgroundImageLayout	Stretch
lblApplicationTitle	Label	Text	Application Title
lblApplicationTitle	Label	BackColor	Web:Transparent
lblApplicationTitle	Label	Font	Microsoft Sans Serif, 20pt
lblApplicationTitle	Label	ForeColor	Web:White
lblVersion	Label	Text	Version
lblVersion	Label	BackColor	Web:Transparent
lblVersion	Label	Font	Microsoft Sans Serif, 12pt
lblVersion	Label	ForeColor	Web:White
lblCopyright	Label	Text	Copyright
lblCopyright	Label	BackColor	Web:Transparent
lblCopyright	Label	Font	Microsoft Sans Serif, 8.25pt
lblCopyright	Label	ForeColor	Web:White

Table 6-1
Splash Screen Controls and Properties

6. Look at Figure 6-3 to see where the three labels are located and place them there in the designer. The text in the image is for reference only; the application title, version, and copyright information are all obtained dynamically. This means the form will get the values from a variable or a setting somewhere in your project. In fact, at run time those three pieces of information are obtained when the splash screen is loaded by looking up application settings stored in the Project Designer Application pane.

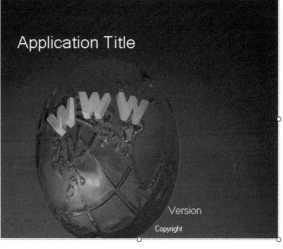

Figure 6-3
Splash screen with the background image and the labels' location

7. Now you have to hook up the splash screen to the application; to do this, you have to modify the Browser form constructor. Open the code for the Browser form (not the splash screen form), and modify the constructor so that it looks like the following:

```
public partial class Browser : Form
{
    Splash splashScreen = new Splash();

    public Browser()
    {
        InitializeComponent();
        splashScreen.Show();
        Application.DoEvents();
    }
}
```

8. The previous step displays the splash screen, but you need to close it and make it disappear whenever the other form is ready to be displayed. The last event before the form is displayed is the *Activated* event. So, you need to select the Browser form in Design view and then go to the Properties window. Then click the Events button (yellow lightning) at the top of the Properties window, and double-click the *Activated* event. The *Browser_Activated* event handler is displayed in Code view. Add the following code:

```
private void Browser_Activated(object sender, EventArgs e)
{
    Thread.Sleep(3000);
    splashScreen.Close();
}
```

9. Place your cursor in the *Thread* text. You should see the familiar yellow and red Smart Tag. This Smart Tag lets you know that the *Thread* class is in the *System.Threading* namespace and that you don't have a reference to this namespace in your *using* directives at the top of the file. Rest your mouse pointer over the Smart Tag, click the down arrow, and then select *using System.Threading* to add it to your list of *using* directives.

TO VIEW THE APPLICATION TITLE, VERSION, AND COPYRIGHT PROPERTIES

1. Select the MyOwnBrowser project in Solution Explorer, right-click, and choose Properties.

   The Project Designer page opens. The Project Designer page has a series of information tabs (as shown in Figure 6-4). You'll work mainly on the first tab for now, which is the Application pane. You'll configure several elements on this pane. All the elements you'll modify will affect how the application looks.

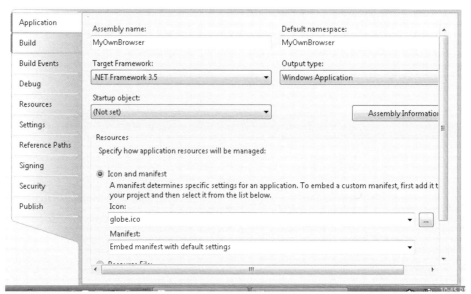

Figure 6-4
Project Designer page

Microsoft Visual C# 2008 Express Edition: Build a Program Now!

2. To change the application icon, click the Icon drop-down list, and select <Browse...>. Find the Chapter6 directory where you installed the book's sample files, and look for the globe.ico file in the Images folder. (If you installed the companion content at the default location, then the file should be at the following location on your hard disk: Documents\Microsoft Press\VCS 2008 Express\Chapter6\Complete\Images.)

You've changed the icon of your application assembly; in other words, you've changed the icon of the executable binary (.exe) file itself. If you build the application and look on your hard disk where the application is compiled (as you learned in a previous chapter, all your projects are by default located at a path such as Documents\Visual Studio 2008\Projects\MyOwnBrowser\MyOwnBrowser\bin\Debug or \bin\release), you'll find that your application, MyOwnBrowser.exe, has the globe icon that you just selected instead of a default icon.

NOTE
You're not changing the icon of the main form when doing this application icon change. To do that, you need to change the form icon's property by assigning a bitmap image. You'll change the main form icon later in this chapter.

3. Click the Assembly Information... button. You should see a dialog box that looks like Figure 6-5.

4. Change the Copyright text box by replacing the word *Microsoft* with your name, and keep the rest of the information as it is. (If the Copyright text box is not already filled with your information, change it to match your name or company information.)

5. Insert spaces in the word *MyOwnBrowser* in the Title text box. (This string is used to display the application title on the splash screen.) Specifically, insert two spaces to get the following title: My Own Browser.

6. Click OK to close the Assembly Information dialog box.

Figure 6-5
Assembly Information dialog box

NOTE
The assembly version information you see here is also what the application will display on the splash screen you're creating. You'll see the source code that will display the information on the splash screen later in the chapter.

Now that you have all your assembly data entered in the Project Designer Application pane, you need to get it onto your splash screen form and in the correct labels. You need to do this in the splash screen constructor to obtain the information from where it was entered. The idea here is to make the splash screen generic enough that you could reuse it in another project. I've used the same methods that are found in the About dialog box template, as you'll see in a minute. Open Splash.cs in Code view, and modify the code so that it looks like the following. (If you don't want to type all this code, you can copy it from the completed application in the Chapter6 folder.)

```csharp
1 using System;
2 using System.Collections.Generic;
3 using System.ComponentModel;
4 using System.Data;
5 using System.Drawing;
6 using System.Text;
7 using System.Windows.Forms;
8 using System.Reflection;
9
10 namespace MyOwnBrowser
11 {
12     public partial class Splash : Form
13     {
14         public Splash()
15         {
16             InitializeComponent();
17             this.lblApplicationTitle.Text = AssemblyTitle;
18             this.lblCopyright.Text = AssemblyCopyright;
19             this.lblVersion.Text = "Version: " + AssemblyVersion;
20         }
21
22         #region Assembly Attribute Accessors
23
24         public string AssemblyTitle
25         {
26             get
27             {
28                 // Get all Title attributes on this assembly
29                 object[] attributes =
                       Assembly.GetExecutingAssembly().GetCustomAttributes(
30                       typeof(AssemblyTitleAttribute), false);
31                 // If there is at least one Title attribute
32                 if (attributes.Length > 0)
33                 {
34                     // Select the first one
```

```
35                        AssemblyTitleAttribute titleAttribute =
                              (AssemblyTitleAttribute)attributes[0];
36                      // If it is not an empty string, return it
37                      if (titleAttribute.Title != "")
38                          return titleAttribute.Title;
39                  }
40                  // If there was no Title attribute, or if the Title
                    // attribute was the empty string, return the .exe name
41                  return System.IO.Path.GetFileNameWithoutExtension(
                        Assembly.GetExecutingAssembly().CodeBase);
42              }
43          }
44
45          public string AssemblyVersion
46          {
47              get
48              {
49                  return Assembly.GetExecutingAssembly()
                        .GetName().Version.ToString();
50              }
51          }
52
53          public string AssemblyDescription
54          {
55              get
56              {
57                  // Get all Description attributes on this assembly
58                  object[] attributes =
                        Assembly.GetExecutingAssembly().GetCustomAttributes(
59                      typeof(AssemblyDescriptionAttribute), false);
60                  // If there aren't any Description attributes, return an
                    // empty string
61                  if (attributes.Length == 0)
62                      return "";
63                  // If there is a Description attribute, return its value
64                  return
                        ((AssemblyDescriptionAttribute)attributes[0])
                        .Description;
65              }
66          }
67
68          public string AssemblyProduct
```

```
69              {
70                  get
71                  {
72                      // Get all Product attributes on this assembly
73                      object[] attributes =
                            Assembly.GetExecutingAssembly().GetCustomAttributes(
74                          typeof(AssemblyProductAttribute), false);
75                      // If there aren't any Product attributes, return an
                        // empty string
76                      if (attributes.Length == 0)
77                          return "";
78                      // If there is a Product attribute, return its value
79                      return
                            ((AssemblyProductAttribute)attributes[0]).Product;
80                  }
81              }
82
83              public string AssemblyCopyright
84              {
85                  get
86                  {
87                      // Get all Copyright attributes on this assembly
88                      object[] attributes =
                            Assembly.GetExecutingAssembly().GetCustomAttributes(
89                          typeof(AssemblyCopyrightAttribute), false);
90                      // If there aren't any Copyright attributes, return an
                        // empty string
91                      if (attributes.Length == 0)
92                          return "";
93                      // If there is a Copyright attribute, return its value
94                      return ((AssemblyCopyrightAttribute)attributes[0])
                            .Copyright;
95                  }
96              }
97
98              public string AssemblyCompany
99              {
100                 get
101                 {
102                     // Get all Company attributes on this assembly
```

```
103            object[] attributes =
                    Assembly.GetExecutingAssembly().GetCustomAttributes(
104                 typeof(AssemblyCompanyAttribute), false);
105             // If there aren't any Company attributes, return an
                // empty string
106             if (attributes.Length == 0)
107                 return "";
108             // If there is a Company attribute, return its value
109             return ((AssemblyCompanyAttribute)attributes[0]).
110                 Company;
111         }
112     }
113     #endregion
114   }
115 }
```

7. Save the application (pressing Ctrl+Shift+S saves all the files, and pressing Ctrl+S saves the current file), and then press F5 to run it. Look at Figure 6-6 to see the splash screen in action with the dynamic information collected from the Project Designer Application pane.

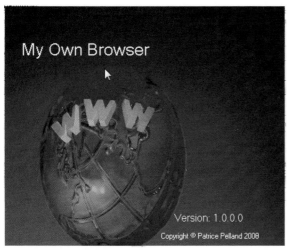

Figure 6-6
The splash screen in action

The dialog boxes you create help the user interact with the software. They are additional forms you add to your application. In the following sections, you'll add two dialog boxes to your Web browser: an About dialog box and a Navigate dialog box.

Adding an About Dialog Box

The first dialog box you'll add is an About dialog box, which exists in most Windows applications. This dialog box contains essentially the same information as the splash screen but sometimes contains more legal, system, and version information.

TO ADD AN ABOUT BOX DIALOG BOX

1. On the Browser form, delete the *txtURL* and *btnGo* controls. Delete the *btnGo_Click* event handler by removing its signature and content from the Browser.cs file.

2. On the Browser form, select the WebBrowser control, and using the Smart Tag, select Dock in Parent Container.

3. As you did for the splash screen, add a new item to your project, but this time when presented with the templates, choose the About Box template. Then name it AboutBox.cs.

Similar to the splash screen, the About dialog box will be populated with information from the project settings in the Project Designer window. At this point, if you run the application, there is no link between your About dialog box and the rest of your browser, so it won't show up anywhere. Usually, the About dialog box shows up when you request it from the Help menu, so you'll add this missing link now.

TO LINK THE ABOUT BOX TO THE HELP MENU

1. Select the Browser.cs [Design] tab to return to the Browser form's Design view. Drag a MenuStrip control from the Toolbox to the design surface to add it to the Browser form.

An empty menu appears on the form, and a component appears in the component tray. Name it msBrowser.

2. To add the Help menu, select the menu strip on the form, click the Smart Tag, and then select Insert Standard Items. You'll get a familiar Windows application menu strip and its menu choices with their submenus, icons, and keyboard shortcuts.

3. Delete all menu choices except the Help menu and the About... menu choice in the Help menu. To perform this cleanup, select any menu choice, right-click to open the contextual menu, and select Delete to remove it. Also remove the menu separators (that is, the lines separating menu choices).

4. To wire the new About form to the About... menu choice, double-click the About... menu choice to get to the *aboutToolStripMenuItem_Click* event handler.

5. Add the following line of code to the Browser.cs file just above the browser constructor, that is, *public Browser()*. Adding this line of code means you can exchange data with this form when needed:

```
AboutBox myAboutBox = new AboutBox();
```

Then add the following code to the *AboutToolStripMenuItem_Click* event handler:

```
myAboutBox.ShowDialog();
```

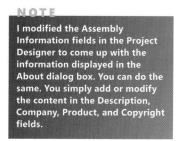

NOTE
I modified the Assembly Information fields in the Project Designer to come up with the information displayed in the About dialog box. You can do the same. You simply add or modify the content in the Description, Company, Product, and Copyright fields.

6. Save the application, and then run it. Select Help, About.... The screen should resemble Figure 6-7. The *ShowDialog()* method opens the form in the middle of the executing application, and nothing else can happen until you click one of its buttons or the red X to close the dialog box. In this case, it has only the OK button.

You're probably wondering why the application worked when you clicked the OK button even though you didn't write any code to handle this event. This is an example of the productivity gains you'll get when using templates. The template includes the code to handle the button click event. Review the source code for the dialog box by right-clicking the AboutBox.cs filename in Solution Explorer and selecting View Code.

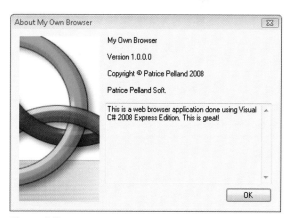

Figure 6-7
About My Own Browser dialog box in your newly refined browser application

Now that you've added the About dialog box, it should be easy to add another that will let your users navigate to Web pages.

Adding a Navigate Dialog Box

You saw earlier that deleting the button and the address controls removed the ability to navigate to a Web page. This, of course, is not useful for a Web browser. Now you'll add a dialog box that will give your user another way to navigate to Web pages.

TO ADD A NAVIGATE DIALOG BOX

1. As you did for the About dialog box and the splash screen, add another new item to your project. Using the templates, select a Windows Form template, and name it Navigate.cs.

2. You'll now add the components for the Navigate form. These are pretty generic to any dialog box form you would want to create.

3. First add a table layout panel control with one row and two columns. Use the Smart Tag to adjust the rows and columns.

4. Add one button in each column of that table layout panel control. Name your buttons *btnOk* and *btnCancel*, respectively.

5. Using Table 6-2, set the various properties on the form, table layout panel, and buttons.

Control Name	Control Type	Property	Value
Navigate	Form	AcceptButton	btnOk
Navigate	Form	CancelButton	btnCancel
Navigate	Form	FormBorderStyle	FixedDialog
Navigate	Form	MaximizeBox	False
Navigate	Form	MinimizeBox	False

Table 6-2
Navigate Dialog Box Controls and Properties

Control Name	Control Type	Property	Value
Navigate	Form	ShowIcon	False
Navigate	Form	ShowInTaskbar	False
Navigate	Form	Size:Width	450
		Size:Height	150
Navigate	Form	StartPosition	CenterParent
tableLayoutPanel1	TableLayoutPanel	Anchor	Bottom,Right
btnOk	Button	Text	Ok
btnOk	Button	DialogResult	Ok
btnCancel	Button	Text	Cancel
btnCancel	Button	DialogResult	Cancel

Table 6-2 (continued)
Navigate Dialog Box Controls and Properties

That's it; those are the properties you will find in any dialog box.

6. Add a label and a text box:

   a. Name the label *lblInfoUrl*, and set the *Text* property to *Type an Internet address and My Own Browser will open it for you.*

   b. Name the text box *txtUrl*, set the *AutoCompleteMode* property to *SuggestAppend*, and set the *AutoCompleteSource* property to *AllUrl*. Next set the *Modifiers* property to *Public*.

7. Size and position the controls so that the Navigate form looks like the one in Figure 6-8.

You've set some of the autocomplete properties of the text box to behave the same way they do in Windows Internet Explorer. This means

Figure 6-8
Navigate form

the text box will suggest and append URLs based on the letters the user types. You'll now wire this form to the application using a new menu called Navigate.

TO WIRE THE FORM TO THE APPLICATION USING THE NAVIGATE MENU

1. Return to the Browser form in Design view, and look at the top of the Browser form. You already have a menu strip with the Help menu; now add a new menu to your menu strip by clicking beside the Help menu and typing **&Navigate**. The & in front of the *N* will create an underscored *N* so that the user can press the keystroke combination Alt+N to fire the click event on the Navigate menu.

2. You'll see that the Navigate menu shows up to the right of the Help menu. To move a menu choice, simply select it, and drag it where you want. In this case, select it and drop it to the left of the Help menu.

3. Before adding the code for the event, you need to add an important line of code. Remember that in C# everything is an object, and if you want to manipulate another form and exchange data between the two forms, you first need to create an object of that type that is visible to your main form (the Browser form)—in this case, an object of type *Navigate*. Create an instance of the Navigate form outside the source code of any event handler by writing the following line of code in Browser.cs:

```
Navigate navigateWindow = new Navigate();
```

Refer to Figure 6-9 to see where to insert it.

```
public partial class Browser : Form
{
    // The about box and navigate form
    AboutBox myAboutBox = new AboutBox();
    Navigate navigateWindow = new Navigate();
    Splash splashScreen = new Splash();

    public Browser()
    {
        InitializeComponent();
        splashScreen.Show();
        Application.DoEvents();
    }
```

NOTE
If you don't get IntelliSense when typing *navigateWindow. txtUrl.Text*, be sure you set the *Modifiers* property on *txtUrl* to *Public* as described earlier.

Figure 6-9
Creating a new instance of the form Navigate

Microsoft Visual C# 2008 Express Edition: Build a Program Now!

Now that you have an instance of the *Navigate* form class, you can write code to exchange data back and forth between the two forms. And that's exactly what will happen. When the Navigate form displays and the user clicks the OK button with a URL in the text box, the WebBrowser control will navigate to the specified URL. Also note that the URL text box will clear after navigating to the URL to make sure it's empty the next time the user accesses it.

4. On the Browser form, double-click the Navigate menu to add the *navigateToolStripMenuItem_Click* event handler.

5. Add the following code to the *navigateToolStripMenuItem_Click* event handler:

```
if (navigateWindow.ShowDialog() == DialogResult.OK)
{
    this.myBrowser.Navigate(navigateWindow.txtUrl.Text);
}
navigateWindow.txtUrl.Text="";
```

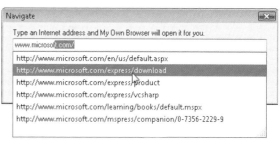

6. Build and execute the application by pressing F5. The form should resemble Figure 6-10 when the user selects the Navigate menu.

Figure 6-10
Execution of My Own Browser using the Navigate form with autocomplete

7. Now, test the application with all the modifications you've made. Verify every new aspect:

    ◾ Does pressing Alt+N take you to the Navigate form?

    ◾ Can you click Cancel with or without content?

    ◾ Can you navigate to a good URL or a bad URL?

    ◾ Is the text box empty when you return to the Navigate form (that is, after you've performed all the other steps and pressed Alt+N)?

MORE INFO

It's important for you to start learning how to test your own code by doing what's known as *black box* testing. At a high level, this consists of testing what the user can do and what is presented to the user. This means you need to test every little detail in the UI as well as the situations the UI offers to the user. When you perform a task such as this, I suggest you create a spreadsheet that contains a matrix of all the test cases. Then fill it in as you test. This gives you a visual representation of all tests and features. You're now doing this manually because your application is small in scope, but you'll quickly realize that with a bigger application or an application you might sell, you'll need some sort of automated mechanism to make sure the tests are all executed and that you're not forgetting any. You'll then require a UI testing tool, and in most situations you'll need to build your own tools. But that's out of context for this book; I just wanted to emphasize the importance of testing your application.

In the following sections, you'll continue to add functionality to your browser using components that you might have seen in other Microsoft applications. You'll add appealing and professional touches to your application quickly and easily.

Adding a Tool Strip Container and Some Tools

A tool strip container is a new control that ships with Visual C# 2008, and with it your users can customize your application like they customize the toolbars in Microsoft Office Outlook or Microsoft Office Word. The tool strip container has five panels, one on each side of the screen, and a content panel in the middle. You can have all of them on the screen turned on at one time or choose them selectively at design time. You can also control them with source code. You can put a tool strip and a menu strip in a tool strip container at design time, and at run time your users have the opportunity to arrange their workspace the way they like. The tool strip container gives your application the same look and feel as Outlook (see Figure 6-11). For instance, I was able to put two tool strips on the left of my screen. This means those tool strips are embedded in the tool strip container's left panel. But I could easily move any visible toolbar back to the top, the right, or the bottom. With a tool strip container, you give your users control over the layout of their tool strips and menu strips, which is a great feature to have.

Figure 6-11
Tool strip container example in Outlook

TO ADD A TOOL STRIP CONTAINER

1. Drag a tool strip container to the Browser form's design surface.

2. Rename *toolstripcontainer1* to *mainFormToolStripContainer*.

3. Use the Smart Tag on the tool strip container to select Dock Fill in Form.

Wait a minute…where is the WebBrowser control? Don't worry, it didn't disappear. The control's z-order has changed. The WebBrowser control is visually under the tool strip container, and its parent is not the tool strip container but the Browser form.

NOTE
The *z-order* is a control's position relative to the other windows or controls on the screen; think of it as the third dimension or as being on top of or beneath other controls.

The Document Outline window is a valuable tool that can help you solve this problem and save you a lot of time. For those of you familiar with previous versions of Visual Studio, this window existed before but only for HTML and ASPX documents. With Visual Studio 2008, it has been extended to Windows Forms applications. To have the Document Outline window in your IDE, simply click View, Other Windows, Document Outline, or press Ctrl+Alt+T. This view lets you manage all the controls on your form. It shows how the controls are arranged on the screen and which controls belong to another control. For instance, right now you cannot see the WebBrowser control, but if you open the Document Outline window, you'll see that the WebBrowser control is at the same level as the newly added tool strip container (see Figure 6-12). To rearrange the order and change how the controls are displayed, follow the next two steps.

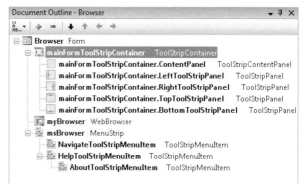

Figure 6-12
The Document Outline window for the My Own Browser project

TO REARRANGE THE ORDER OF CONTROLS

1. In the Document Outline window, select the WebBrowser control called *myBrowser*, and drag it just below the tool strip container content panel called *mainFormToolStripContainer.ContentPanel*. (When you drag the WebBrowser control, a black line indicates where the control will be dropped if you release the mouse button.)

2. Now display the form again. The WebBrowser control is in the middle of the form. But as you can see, the MenuStrip control is not in the tool strip container. Repeat step 1 for the MenuStrip control, but instead of dropping it in the content panel, drop it in the top panel of the tool strip container (*mainFormToolStripContainer.TopToolStripPanel*).

Now the only thing missing from the new menu strip is a dotted grip like the one shown earlier in Figure 6-11. Without this grip, a user is unable to select the menu strip at all; it is fixed in the top panel.

MORE INFO
If your application design demands it and if you want to constrain the user in any way, you can also hide panels and prevent users from docking any tool strip or menu strip in a panel. Let's use the current application as an example. If you want to do this, select the tool strip container control named *mainFormTool-StripContainer*. You can select it from either the Properties window or the Document Outline window. Then modify the visible property of the panel you want to hide. For instance, if you want to hide the bottom panel, set the *BottomToolStripPanelVisible* property to *false*.

TO ADD A DOTTED GRIP TO THE MENU STRIP

1. From the Document Outline window, select the menu strip called *msBrowser*, go to the Properties window, and set the *GripStyle* property to *Visible*.

2. Run the application by pressing F5. Move the menu strip from one panel to the other. You now have an application as cool as Outlook.

Adding a Status Bar to Your Browser

Your application is becoming rich in features, but to get it closer to most Windows applications, you need a status bar to report information about what's going on at any moment during the execution. To accomplish this in your browser, you'll add a StatusStrip control, and within this status strip, you'll add a progress bar.

TO ADD A STATUSSTRIP CONTROL AND A PROGRESS BAR

1. In the Design view for Browser.cs, click the bottom panel handle to expand it. (Note that the glyph arrow direction reverses when you click it.) The tool strip container's bottom panel appears as a blue strip.

2. Drag a StatusStrip control to the tool strip container's bottom panel. After you drop it onto the bottom panel, it should expand to cover the whole panel surface.

3. Rename the StatusStrip control from *StatusStrip1* to *sscBrowser*.

4. Change the *RenderMode* property of the StatusStrip control to *Professional*. This allows the application to present a status bar to the user using the operating system colors. For instance, if the themes in Windows XP are blue, then the status bar will be blue as well.

5. Add a label control to the status strip by clicking the down arrow of the StatusStrip Add Control button and then selecting StatusLabel.

6. Rename the control from *ToolStripStatusLabel1* to *lblApplicationStatus*.

7. Add a progress bar to your status strip just as you did for the label control.

8. Rename the control from *ToolStripProgressBar1* to *pbStatus*.

When the status strip and the progress bar are displayed to the user, they usually display important information about the events that are occurring during the execution. Think of it like a letter arriving at your house. You hear the mail truck and realize the mail has arrived. This is the event that is raised. You open your mailbox and the envelope to learn that it's your credit card bill. The bill is one of the pieces of information that comes along with the event. To analogously populate the controls in the status strip, you'll have to configure your application to extract this information from all controls (that is, the envelope) when events are happening (that is, the mail truck arriving). And you'll do that programmatically by writing code in event handlers.

TO POPULATE CONTROLS WITH INFORMATION

1. On the design surface, select the My Own Browser form by clicking its title bar. Look at the Properties window to make sure the Browser form is selected, and click the Events button (yellow lightning) in the Properties window. Find the *Load* event, and double-click it to open the default event handler: *Browser_Load*. (The form *Load* event is raised just before the form displays to the user, so, it's a good place to change properties that affect the visual aspects of a form.)

2. Add the following code to the event (*Browser_Load*) to modify the status message label (*lblApplicationStatus*) in the status strip:

```
this.lblApplicationStatus.Text = "Ready";
```

   You'll now attach some code to the progress bar and modify the label on the status strip to indicate the location where the user is navigating. When the page is fully downloaded to the client PC, you'll reset the label content in the status strip to the word *Ready*. You'll also modify the browser title to include the URL to which the user navigated. Whenever the OK button is clicked in the Navigate form, the WebBrowser control named *myBrowser* raises the *Navigating* event. That's where you'll start writing code.

3. In Design view, select the *myBrowser* control, and then go to the Events list in the Properties window. Double-click the *Navigating* event, and enter the following code:

```
//Modifying the label in the status strip with the URL entered by the user
this.lblApplicationStatus.Text = "Navigating to: " + e.Url.Host.ToString();
```

Once the user enters a URL and the document is being downloaded, the progress bar will need to update. Periodically, the WebBrowser control raises the *ProgressChanged* event. That's where you'll update the progress bar in the status strip.

4. Make sure you have the *myBrowser* control selected in the Properties window, and then go to the Event list. Double-click the *ProgressChanged* event. Enter the following code (look at the comments to understand the source code):

```
/* The CurrentProgress variable from the raised event
 * gives you the current number of bytes already downloaded
 * while the MaximumProgress is the total number of bytes
 * to be downloaded */
if (e.CurrentProgress < e.MaximumProgress)
{
    // Check whether the current progress in the progress bar
    // is >= to the maximum; if yes reset it with the min
    if (pbStatus.Value >= pbStatus.Maximum)
        pbStatus.Value = pbStatus.Minimum;
    else
      // Just increase the progress bar
      pbStatus.PerformStep();
}
else
      // When the document is fully downloaded
      // reset the progress bar to the min (0)
      pbStatus.Value = pbStatus.Minimum;
```

When the user's document is fully downloaded, the browser will raise the *Document-Completed* event. When this event is raised, the application title needs to be updated to the current URL, and the application status label in the status strip will need to change to the Ready state.

5. In the *myBrowser* event list, double-click the *DocumentCompleted* event. Then add the following code to it:

```
// The About box is retrieving this information in a nice clean method, so
// let's reuse it.
// If you don't have an About box, you can just create this method using
// the code from the About box. We don't need to validate if the title is
// empty; the method is doing it.
// If it's empty, it will use the .exe name
```

```
this.Text = myAboutBox.AssemblyTitle + " - "+ e.Url.Host.ToString();

this.lblApplicationStatus.Text = "Ready";
```

As you can see, this source code is similar to what you used for the About dialog box and the splash screen.

6. Save all the files, and run the application now. You should have a working progress bar, and all the new information should be displayed, meaning the modified title window and status strip label.

Personalizing Your Application with Windows Icons

In this section, you'll continue to personalize your browser by adding some icons that come from known Microsoft applications. After this section, you'll have a working Internet browser with most navigational features fully implemented—maybe not with all the functionality of Internet Explorer, but you should be proud of yourself. Look at Figure 6-13 to see what you will have accomplished after this section.

Figure 6-13
Your browser after completing this section

As you can see, you'll implement a nice list of features in this section. Here's what you're going to accomplish:

- You'll link all buttons to browser functionalities.
- You'll manage the Go button and the Enter key on the Address text box in the tool strip.
- You'll change the Browser form icon to the same globe icon you set for the application icon on the hard disk.

First you'll add two new tool strips and all their buttons. You'll also add the code to handle all those new buttons. Each time you add a button, rename it before writing the event-handling code. You should do this to make sure you have the correct variable names, which is just a matter of consistency and good practice.

TO ADD TOOL STRIPS AND BUTTONS TO YOUR BROWSER

1. Start by adding two new tool strips to the Browser form right below the menu strip. Name the first one *tsIcons* and the other one *tsNavigation*. Use the Document Outline window to make sure they are under the top panel of the tool strip container that is *mainFormToolStripContainer.TopToolStripPanel*.

2. Select the *tsIcons* tool strip. Then, using the Add Tool Strip Item drop-down list, add six buttons, and name them *tsbBack*, *tsbForward*, *tsbStop*, *tsbRefresh*, *tsbHome*, and *tsbSearch*.

3. To modify the image for each button, change the *Image* property of the ToolStripButton control by clicking the ellipsis button (...) to browse on your hard disk for the icon. Or you can right-click the icon in the tool strip and select Set Image.... You'll then have the same dialog box to import the image files from your hard disk. The images for these buttons are all located in the Images folder under Chapter6 where you installed your companion content.

4. For the *tsbSearch* button, right-click the button, select Display Style, and set it to ImageAndText.

5. Modify the *Text* property of the *tsbSearch* button to *Search*. Change all your other controls to meaningful names.

6. For each button, add the respective functionality. (You'll see how easy it is to add the desired functionality because the WebBrowser control was well designed to provide methods for the most important functionalities.) Double-click one button after the other, and you'll get to the *Click* event for each one. In each *Click* event, add the code in Table 6-3, which lists the corresponding button name and event source code.

Button Name	Event Code
tsbBack	myBrowser.GoBack()
tsbForward	myBrowser.GoForward()
tsbStop	myBrowser.Stop()
tsbRefresh	myBrowser.Refresh()
tsbHome	myBrowser.GoHome()
tsbSearch	myBrowser.GoSearch()

Table 6-3
Buttons and Their Properties

7. Run the application, and determine whether the buttons are working. Everything should be working except for the navigation buttons.

You'll now modify the behavior of the two navigation buttons in the *tsbIcons* tool strip to make sure they're enabled only when they should be—that is, when there are pages in the browser's history. When you start the application, the buttons should be disabled. The best place to put this code is the *Load* event of the Browser form. It's a good place because the event will happen right before the user actually sees the form. Next, you need to think about where you should put the code that will enable and disable the two navigation buttons. The ideal place for the validation code is where the navigation occurs because you know at that moment the browser will navigate to a new URL.

TO MODIFY THE BEHAVIOR OF NAVIGATION BUTTONS

1. In Browser.cs, add the *ModifyNavigationButtons* method, and modify *Browser_Load* and *myBrowser_DocumentCompleted* to look like the following:

```csharp
private void Browser_Load(object sender, EventArgs e)
{
   this.tsbBack.Enabled = false;
   this.tsbForward.Enabled = false;
   this.lblApplicationStatus.Text = "Ready";
}

private void ModifyNavigationButtons()
{
   // Add the code to enable or disable whenever there are URLs
   // in the browsing session's history
   if (myBrowser.CanGoBack)
     tsbBack.Enabled = true;
   else
     tsbBack.Enabled = false;

   if (myBrowser.CanGoForward)
     tsbForward.Enabled = true;
   else
     tsbForward.Enabled = false;
}

private void myBrowser_DocumentCompleted(object sender,
   WebBrowserDocumentCompletedEventArgs e)
{
   // The about box is retrieving this information in a nice clean method
   // so let's reuse it
   // If you don't have an about box you can just create this method using
   // the code from the about box. We don't need to validate if the title
   // is empty; the method is doing it.
   // If it's empty it will use the .exe name
   this.Text = myAboutBox.AssemblyTitle + " - " + e.Url.Host.ToString();

   ModifyNavigationButtons();
   this.lblApplicationStatus.Text = "Ready";
}
```

2. Run the application to determine whether the buttons behave correctly now.

Next, you'll add the names and controls to the *tsNavigation* tool strip as you did for the previous tool strip. However, this time instead of adding just some tool strip buttons, you'll add different types of controls.

For instance, you'll modify the browser to navigate to the URL specified in the text box when the user presses Enter. You'll also modify the behavior of clicking the Go button to make sure it does the same thing.

TO ADD NEW CONTROLS TO THE TSNAVIGATION TOOL STRIP

1. Use the Add Tool Strip Item drop-down list on the *tsNavigation* tool strip, and add the following controls to the tool strip: a label, a text box, and a button. Name the controls *tslblAddress*, *tstbUrl*, and *tsbGo*.

2. Use Table 6-4 to set the properties of the controls.

Control Name	Type	Properties	Value
tslblAddress	ToolStripLabel	Text	Address:
tstbUrl	ToolStripTextBox	Size:Width	350
tsbGo	ToolStripButton	Text	Go
tsbGo	ToolStripButton	DisplayStyle	ImageAndText
tsbGo	ToolStripButton	Image	Go.bmp

Table 6-4
Navigation Tool Strip Controls and Properties

The *tsNavigation* tool strip is not a dialog box with an OK button or a Cancel button, so you cannot use the *AcceptButton* or *CancelButton* property. Therefore, you need to capture another event that will be triggered whenever the user presses Enter.

The *KeyUp* event is triggered whenever the user releases a key. For instance, whenever the user types a letter, he presses the key of the desired letter. When he releases the key, the *KeyUp* event is triggered. The code you'll add in the next exercise will determine whether the key the user just released was the Enter key. If it was, a new method called *NavigateToUrl* will accept a string representing the URL as a parameter and then navigate to the URL.

You'll use the same method for the Go button. When you develop an application, you never want to duplicate two pieces of code that differ only by a literal. You always want to reuse the source code whenever possible. The way to do that is to create methods that are generic enough to be used by more than one component. Since the *NavigateToUrl* method has only one line of code, you might be tempted to ask, if it's almost the same one line of code, why use a method? The answer is simply that in the future you might have to add some validation. If that one line of code is repeated throughout the source code, you'll have to update it in multiple places. However, if there is only one place where you have to modify the code, your solution is less prone to errors and a lot less tedious.

TO CONFIGURE THE BROWSER TO NAVIGATE TO THE URL

NOTE

By the way, more than one event is being triggered by pressing the Enter key, but the one you'll trap is the *KeyUp* event.

1. Select the *tstbUrl* tool strip text box.

2. In the events list in the Properties window for *tstbUrl*, double-click the *KeyUp* event. The following is the code to determine whether the user pressed and released the Enter key; it also contains the method *NavigateToUrl* that lets you use the same code in more than one place. Add this code to *tstbUrl_KeyUp*, and add the *NavigateToUrl* method.

```csharp
private void tstbUrl_KeyUp(object sender, KeyEventArgs e)
{
    // e is of type KeyEventArgs and contains all the
    // information that triggered the event. The KeyCode
    // is part of that information.
    if (e.KeyCode == Keys.Enter)
        this.NavigateToUrl(tstbUrl.Text);
}

private void NavigateToUrl(string Url)
{
    myBrowser.Navigate(Url);
}
```

3. Double-click the Go button on the *tsNavigation* tool strip, and add the following code to the *tsbGo_Click* event procedure. (Notice that this is the *NavigateToUrl* method.)

```
private void tsbGo_Click(object sender, EventArgs e)
{
    this.NavigateToUrl(tstbUrl.Text);
}
```

You can now modify another piece of code, the Navigate menu click event. You simply have to modify the code so that it calls the *NavigateToUrl* method, as shown here:

```
private void navigateToolStripMenuItem_Click(object sender, EventArgs e)
{
    if (navigateWindow.ShowDialog() == DialogResult.OK)
    {
        this.NavigateToUrl(navigateWindow.txtUrl.Text);
    }
    navigateWindow.txtUrl.Text = "";
}
```

Finally, you'll modify the Browser form's icon so that the user sees a globe when the browser is running or minimized.

TO MODIFY THE BROWSER FORM ICON

1. Select the Browser form, and then look for Icon Property in the Properties window. If you see only events in the Properties window, click the Properties button at the top of the Properties window. Click the ellipsis button (...) to browse for the globe.ico file in the Images folder under the Chapter6 directory.

The result of your hard labor is the finished product—the My Own Browser application, as shown in Figure 6-14.

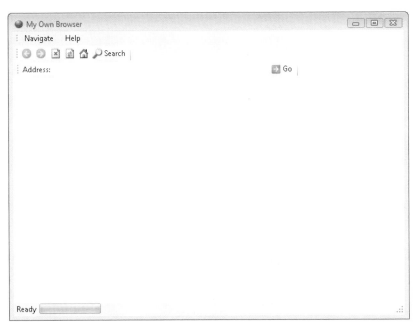

Figure 6-14
Finished product—the My Own Browser application

Redoing the Browser

Now that you have enriched your browser application, it is time to refresh it and make it look like a Windows Vista application. To do that, you'll start learning the new Windows Presentation Foundation (WPF). You'll work on the same browser application so that you can focus only on the new topics at hand.

Microsoft Visual C# 2008 Express Edition: Build a Program Now!

Using Windows Presentation Foundation

What is WPF? First let's look at where it came from—if you refer to Figure 1-1 in Chapter 1, "Introducing Microsoft Visual C# 2008 Express Edition," you'll see that WPF was added with the arrival of .NET 3.0 and shipped with Windows Vista. What is it? WPF is a unified programming model that allows developers and designers to build Windows applications that incorporate rich media (sound, video, and so on) and documents.

WPF uses your graphical processing unit (GPU) via a technology called DirectX, which is a software platform and technology used mostly for games and other graphical-intensive applications. Programming applications directly with DirectX is not easy, and WPF uses the capabilities of DirectX without the need for you to learn them. With WPF, you have the ability to develop richer applications by using the full power of your computer instead of relying only on your central processing unit (CPU).

With WPF, developers and designers are able to work together to come up with high-quality applications; you probably have seen what WPF will let you do in big Hollywood productions such as *The Net*, *Sneakers*, *Disclosure*, *24*, or *Mission Impossible*. For instance, do you remember in *Disclosure* the virtual glove database with its innovative explorer software? Or how advanced the e-mail software was? It's always fascinating to see how Hollywood presents software and how good it looks, but at the same how far it is from the reality. Well, it's now a reality because of WPF.

Before we dig into the technicalities, I invite you to look at the videos on the Mix07 Web site that showcase WPF capabilities. Specifically, look at the nice implementation of a kiosk-based application for a well-known company at *http://sessions.visitmix.com/default.asp?event =1016&session=2017&pid=UNI19&disc=&id=1620&year=2005&search=UNI19*.

> **NOTE**
> There are a few differences between WPF on Windows Vista and WPF on earlier versions of Windows. The following two features are unique to Windows Vista: 3D objects get anti-aliasing only on Windows Vista or newer, and nonrectangular or translucent windows get hardware acceleration (from your graphic card's GPU) only on Windows Vista or newer.

> **MORE INFO**
> Many other videos and presentation and learning tools are available at the same Web site. See *http://sessions.visitmix.com/*.

WPF and XAML

Extensible Application Markup Language (XAML), pronounced "zammel," is a grammar of XML that enables declarative programming in WPF. It is called *declarative programming* because, by using XAML, a developer can define the user interface declaratively, similar to how an XML file describes a document format. It is a programming language because you can create .NET objects by simply using XAML.

A good analogy is the new 2007 Microsoft Office system's document format that uses XML to describe the structure and formatting of your Word 2007 documents, for instance.

XAML enables something that was really difficult previously: designers and developers working together on the same project. With Visual Studio and Microsoft Expression products such as Microsoft Expression Blend, designers can work on the design and user interface and then pass them on to the developers who can write the code. The video referenced previously is a good example of how these separate tasks can come together.

Using XAML simply helps separate the front end, or user interface, from the back end, or business logic. I don't want to get too deep into XAML at this point because that's not the purpose of this book, but we'll start by looking at how XAML defines real .NET objects. Here's how a button is declared in XAML:

```
<Button xmlns="http://schemas.microsoft.com/winfx/2006/xaml/presentation"
 Name="btnGo">Go</Button>
```

If you place this code in a file called Foo.xaml and then fire up Internet Explorer and open this file, you'll see a big button that takes the entire surface, but it's a real WPF button. You don't need to compile the code, and it works. Isn't that great? This means you can write applications that define your interface and then add events such as the *Click* event and have the code in a separate Visual C# file; however, it also means it can't run by itself in a browser. It would look something like this:

```
<Button xmlns="http://schemas.microsoft.com/winfx/2006/xaml/presentation"
Name="btnGo" Click="btnGo_click">Go</Button>
```

So, you now see clearly the separation between the user interface definition and the business logic of your application.

TO CREATE A WPF VERSION OF THE BROWSER

This is an introduction to WPF, so we won't reimplement the whole application here; instead, I'll show parts of the Web browser application but with a reduced set of features. In fact, we will implement almost the same version as in Chapter 4.

You'll first define the interface, and then you'll hook up the browser events so that it actually works:

1. Add a new project to your solution by clicking File, Add, New Project. Select the WPF Application template from the Visual Studio templates, and name it MyOwnWpfBrowser. Your screen should look like the one in Figure 6-15. Then click OK to create the project.

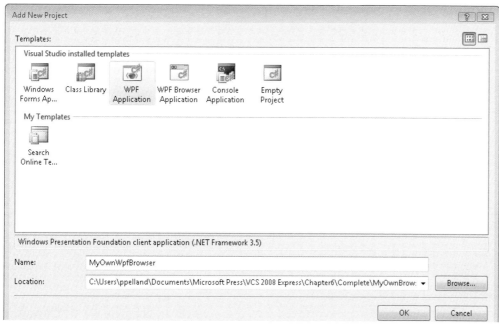

Figure 6-15
Adding the WPF browser project to your solution

You should now have the new designer surface and XAML editor in a split view on your screen. Look at Figure 6-16 for the new WPF design experience. You'll also notice that the Properties window has changed quite a bit.

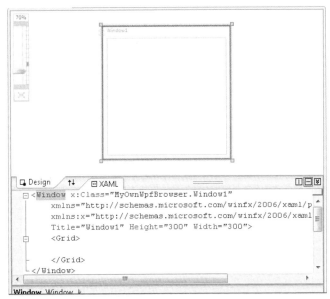

Figure 6-16
The new WPF split view design surface and XAML editor

MORE INFO

You can see that this view is rather different. The view is split between Design view at the top and Code view at the bottom. In the bottom part you see the XAML representation of what you see on the design surface. It's a real-time representation, so if you modify either view, you'll see the change immediately replicated in the other. Figure 6-16 shows the horizontal view, but if you click the vertical glyph on the top-right corner of the XAML window, you'll see the screen split in vertical halves instead of horizontal ones. It's a matter of preference which one you use.

1. In Solution Explorer, rename the file Window1.xaml to Browser.xaml, and in the Browser.xaml.cs file rename the class to *Browser*. Pay attention to the red and yellow underlines indicating that you can use the rename function. Please do, and rename all instances of *Window1* to *Browser*.

2. Next you'll change the title of this new browser window and change the *Window* variable name. To do this, you'll change the XAML directly. Go to the XAML editor, and change the *Title* attribute of the *Window* element to *My Own WPF Browser*. As you do this, look at Design view to see your change being applied in real time. Then change the *Window* variable name by changing the *Class* attribute to *Browser*. The XAML should look like the following at this point:

```
<Window x:Class="MyOwnWpfBrowser.Browser"
    xmlns="http://schemas.microsoft.com/winfx/2006/xaml/presentation"
    xmlns:x="http://schemas.microsoft.com/winfx/2006/xaml"
    Title="My Own WPF Browser" Height="300" Width="300">
```

```
<Grid>

</Grid>
</Window>
```

3. Click the designer surface on the title, and make sure you have the *Window* element in the Properties window. Now delete the values for *Height* and *Width* properties, and change *MinWidth* and *MinHeight* to a 640-by-480 window (which is the width by height). You'll see that Design view will resize in real time and that the XAML code changes in real time as well.

4. This is version 1 of the WPF editor, and the integration and synchronization between Design view/Code view and Solution Explorer are not without bugs. Before you run the project, you need to modify the project settings. Open the App.xaml file by double-clicking it. Locate the Startup URI element, and then change Window1.xaml to Browser.xaml. Save all the files (by pressing Ctrl+Shift+S).

<aside>
NOTE

The fact that most of those changes are in sync everywhere makes it easier to learn XAML and WPF because you can see the changes live. Selecting something on the design surface takes the XAML editor to the corresponding code. So, learning by opening completed samples from the Web helps you learn how to reproduce cool things you see in samples.
</aside>

5. You have two projects in your solution, so in order to have your WPF browser execute when you press F5, you need to make a small modification to your project. In Solution Explorer, right-click the MyOwnWpfBrowser project name, and select Set as StartUp Project. Your project name should now be in bold to indicate it will be the one to start when you press F5.

6. Press F5 to get an empty Windows application "WPF style," as shown in Figure 6-17.

If you remember, I was telling you that WPF uses DirectX and the power of your graphic card. Well, a good way to see that is to use the slider on the design surface to adjust the scale and view a really big close-up or zoom out to see the entire window (even if it's bigger than your monitor). This is a really neat feature that displays the great capabilities of WPF. Look at

Figure 6-17
First view of your WPF browser application

Figure 6-18, for example: on the left side is WPF, and on the right side is the normal Windows form's title bar but magnified. On the left side you can see how great the title bar characters look and how they don't have a jagged contour. This is possible because WPF uses DirectX and because everything is actually drawn to your design surface.

Figure 6-18
WPF (left) vs. Windows form (right)

7. Now you'll copy the globe icon file you used in the Windows Forms project. In Solution Explorer, right-click the globe.ico file in your Windows Forms browser project, and select Copy. Then right-click your MyOwnWpfBrowser project name in Solution Explorer, and select Paste.

8. You will now set some more Window properties. In the XAML editor, press Enter just before > in the *Window* element, and add the following XAML:

```
Icon="globe.ico" SizeToContent="WidthAndHeight"
WindowStartupLocation="CenterScreen"
```

9. Press F5, and you should get the same empty Windows application "WPF style," except this time it should be centered and have the globe icon in the top-left corner of the window.

You'll now add the two menu items on top of your window: the Navigate and Help menus. For the purpose of this example, we will wire only the Navigate menu. To wire the Navigate menu to an event handler, you will add the *Click* event and then the name of the method to call when clicked. If you look in the following XAML code, you might ask what the *DockPanel* element is; well, it enables you to have easy docking within an element, which in this case is the *Grid* element.

1. Select the Browser.xaml file tab at the top of the editor, and then add the following XAML code. Replace all the XAML including the opening and closing *Grid* element. When you're done typing the code, save all the files.

```
<Grid Name="grid1">
    <DockPanel x:Uid="DockPanel_1">
        <! Menu Bar>
        <Menu x:Uid="Menu_1" Background="White" Name="_MainMenu"
          DockPanel.Dock="Top">
            <! Navigate Menu>
            <MenuItem x:Uid="NavigateMenu" Header="_Navigate" />

            <! Help Menu>
            <MenuItem x:Uid="HelpMenu" Header="_Help">
                <MenuItem x:Uid="AboutMenu" Header="_About" />
            </MenuItem>
        </Menu>
    </DockPanel>
</Grid>
```

2. Next build your solution by pressing Ctrl+Shift+B. To see what it looks like, execute your application by pressing F5. You should see your two menus added to the top of the window.

3. Before we can navigate to the Navigate dialog box when we select the Navigate menu, we need to add this window to our project. To add this new window, right-click the project name, MyOwnWpfBrowser, and select Add and then Window…. You'll get the Add New Item dialog box with the Window (WPF) template selected. Change Window1.xaml to Navigate.xaml.

4. In the Navigate.xaml file, delete the current content, and type the following XAML. I'll explain what it means afterward.

```
<Window
    xmlns="http://schemas.microsoft.com/winfx/2006/xaml/presentation"
    xmlns:x="http://schemas.microsoft.com/winfx/2006/xaml"
    x:Class="MyOwnWpfBrowser.Navigate"
```

```xml
        Title="Navigate"
        Height="130"
        Width="500"
        ResizeMode="NoResize"
        ShowInTaskbar="False"
        WindowStartupLocation="CenterOwner"
        FocusManager.FocusedElement="{Binding ElementName=Url}">

    <Grid>
        <Grid.Resources>
            <Style TargetType="{x:Type Grid}">
                <Setter Property="Margin" Value="10" />
            </Style>
            <Style TargetType="{x:Type Label}">
                <Setter Property="Margin" Value="30,0,5,5" />
                <Setter Property="Padding" Value="0,0,0,5" />
            </Style>
            <Style TargetType="{x:Type TextBox}">
                <Setter Property="Margin" Value="30,0,10,10" />
                <Setter Property="AutoWordSelection" Value="True" />
            </Style>
            <Style TargetType="{x:Type StackPanel}">
                <Setter Property="Orientation" Value="Horizontal" />
                <Setter Property="HorizontalAlignment" Value="Right" />
            </Style>
            <Style TargetType="{x:Type Button}">
                <Setter Property="Width" Value="70" />
                <Setter Property="Height" Value="25" />
                <Setter Property="Margin" Value="5,0,0,0" />
            </Style>
        </Grid.Resources>

        <Grid.ColumnDefinitions>
            <ColumnDefinition Width="Auto" />
            <ColumnDefinition />
        </Grid.ColumnDefinitions>

        <Grid.RowDefinitions>
            <RowDefinition Height="Auto" />
            <RowDefinition Height="Auto" />
            <RowDefinition Height="Auto" />
```

```
          </Grid.RowDefinitions>

          <! Label and URL  >
          <Label Grid.Column="0" Grid.ColumnSpan="2" Grid.Row="0">Type
            an Internet address and My Own WPF Browser will open it for
            you</Label>
          <TextBox Name="Url" Grid.ColumnSpan="2" Grid.Column="1"
            Grid.Row="1">
          </TextBox>

          <! Accept or Cancel >
          <StackPanel Grid.Column="0" Grid.ColumnSpan="2" Grid.Row="2">
              <Button Name="okButton" Click="okButton_Click"
               IsDefault="True">OK</Button>
              <Button Name="cancelButton" Click="cancelButton_Click"
              IsCancel="True">Cancel</Button>
          </StackPanel>

      </Grid >
</Window>
```

IMPORTANT

You might see a yellow bar at the top of Design view as you're typing indicating that the document root element has been modified. If you want to see the modification, you need to click the yellow bar to reload the designer. If you do this as you type, you might not be able to see the end result immediately.

You now have a Navigate window in your WPF Designer that should look like the one in Figure 6-19.

Figure 6-19
Navigate dialog box in the WPF Designer

Now let's return to the XAML code. Most of it is self-explanatory because of the nature of XAML. But one feature was new in this part of the sample: the *Grid.Resources* element in which you added styles for all elements found in the grid. This has the advantage of not having to set the styles for each control. Pretend you had 10 text boxes in your grid; it would be tedious to set the styles for each button. Well, because of the style definition of *Grid.Resources*, you have to set the styles just once. What follows in the XAML code is the grid layout in terms of columns and rows and then finally the content of those columns and rows. That's pretty simple, isn't it? You define your user interface, building it piece by piece, and then you attach the functionality in Visual C#. It's a clear separation of UI and logic!

1. Now, we can't navigate to this dialog box because we didn't wire the click event on the Navigate menu item. In the Browser.xaml file, add a *Click* XAML attribute to the Navigate menu item so that it looks like this:

```
<MenuItem x:Uid="NavigateMenu" Header="_Navigate" Click="Navigate_Click" />
```

2. After you add the *Click* XAML attribute, right-click Navigate_Click, and then select Navigate to Event Handler.

Now you'll add the WPF browser control, but wait...it doesn't exist. Not all controls were developed for version 1 of WPF, and you might also have invested some time and code in Windows Forms elements that you want to reuse as-is. For that, the .NET Windows client team has developed a class to integrate Windows Forms elements: *WindowsFormsHost*. You can use this class to use the Windows Forms WebBrowser control that you used previously in this chapter. By using the *WindowsFormsHost* class, you can use a Windows Forms control as if it were a real WPF control.

MORE INFO

For more information, read the MSDN article at *http://msdn2. microsoft.com/en-us/library/ ms751761.aspx.*

3. Add *WindowsFormsIntegration* and *System.Windows.Forms* from the .NET tab as references for your project. (*WindowsFormsIntegration* is the name of the assembly that includes the *WindowsFormsHost* class.) To do this, right-click the MyOwnWpfBrowser project name, select Add References..., and add both references. You can't add them at the same time, so you will have to do the operation twice. Once you're done, save all the files, and build your solution.

4. At the top of your Browser.xaml.cs file, add two *using* statements for those two assemblies:

```
using System.Windows.Forms;
using System.Windows.Forms.Integration;
```

5. Now add the following code to the *Navigate_Click* method:

```
private void Navigate_Click(object sender, RoutedEventArgs e)
{
    // Instantiate the dialog box
    Navigate dlg = new Navigate();

    // Configure the dialog box
    dlg.Owner = this;

    // Open the dialog box modally
    dlg.ShowDialog();

    // Process data entered by user if dialog box is accepted
    if (dlg.DialogResult.GetValueOrDefault() == true)
    {
        NavigateToUrl(dlg.Url.Text);
    }

    dlg.Url.Text = "";
}
```

I'll now explain the previous code a little. The *Click* event handler essentially displays the Navigate dialog box, and if the user clicks OK, it tries to navigate to the URL specified by the user. I am sure you saw that this is a little different from the Windows Forms technique you used previously in this chapter.

6. Add the code for the *NavigateToUrl* method:

```
private void NavigateToUrl(string Url)
{
    WindowsFormsHost host = new WindowsFormsHost();
    WebBrowser browserControl = new WebBrowser();

    host.Child = browserControl;
    this.grid1.Children.Add(host);
    browserControl.ScrollBarsEnabled = true;
    browserControl.Navigate(Url);
}
```

Just to reinforce the concepts, as you can see in the previous method code, we have wrapped the WebBrowser control in an instance of the *WindowsFormsHost* class. Doing this enabled us to use the control and execute it in a WPF application as if it were a real WPF control. Then by adding the *browserControl* element to the *Grid* element as a child, the WebBrowser control becomes embedded in the grid as any regular WPF control. Finally, we turn on the scroll bars for the browser, and we use the WebBrowser control's *Navigate* method to try to get to the URL specified by the user.

7. Save all your files, and then build your application by hitting Ctrl+Shift+B. You will notice that we have two errors left—we don't have a click handler for the *okButton* and the *CancelButton* of the Navigate window. Select the Navigate.xaml tab, right-click okButton_ Click, and select Navigate to Event Handler, which will create the method stub for you. Add the following code to the event handler, and at the same time add the code for the *CancelButton*:

```
private void okButton_Click(object sender, RoutedEventArgs e)
{
        this.DialogResult = true;
}
private void CancelButton_Click(object sender, RoutedEventArgs e)
{
        // Dialog Box Canceled
        this.DialogResult = false;
}
```

NOTE

The sample WPF browser you just created was created this way for learning purposes. If you do real development in WPF, you can follow a set of best practices so that you can have your application translated into different languages. Other design principles apply to the best practices, so if you go on to develop applications commercially in WPF, please visit MSDN for all those best practices.

8. Save all the files, build your solution, and then execute your application.

You should have a functional Web browser developed in WPF. We won't implement more of the Web browser in WPF in this chapter because the goal was to show how different the development approaches are and how a bit more tedious it is for beginner developers to develop in WPF. Nevertheless, I am not discouraging you from using WPF—quite the opposite. I invite you to develop your first applications like we did in this book. When you develop an application for learning purposes, develop both at the same time, one in Windows Forms and one in WPF. That way you'll become more proficient in WPF, and you can then go on to more advanced topics.

In Summary...

In this chapter, you took a simple application and upgraded it to create a professional-looking application with many nice features for your users. You added a splash screen to your application and worked with dialog boxes. You created an About dialog box and a Navigate dialog box to allow your users to navigate to a URL, and you added an autocomplete feature to your text boxes and the autosuggest/append feature using the browser's URL history. You then added tool strips, progress bars, and icons from Windows. You dynamically managed controls, and you learned a lot about new events and how to handle them using event arguments.

After finishing the Windows Forms implementation, you learned how to add a second project and created your WPF Web browser. While doing this, you experimented with XAML and the WPF development technique. You implemented a dialog box that allowed you to enter a URL and navigate to it. You then learned how to use a Windows Forms control and use it in WPF to create a hybrid application.

In the next chapter, you'll learn techniques to use when things don't go well; that is, you'll learn the art of debugging code. You'll also learn about the Edit and Continue feature, data visualizers, tips and tricks, and much more.

Chapter 7

Fixing the Broken Blocks

Debugging an Application, 134

As you'll discover more and more, when you develop an application, you rarely succeed on your first attempt. Most of the time, the process goes like this: brainstorm on paper, look at the users' needs (often yours), perform some analysis, prototype, design, develop, test, fix bugs, test the product again, and finally release it. This is a high-level view of the process; it can be much more complicated or simplified. It all depends on the complexity of the project, the number of people involved, and so on. But this is certain: you always need to debug your applications, and Microsoft Visual C# 2008 provides many tools to help you fix your bugs faster.

To show you how to use the tools and techniques to debug your applications, I've created a sample application that you'll use in this chapter. If you installed the companion content at the default location, the application should be at the following location on your hard disk: Documents\Microsoft Press\VCS 2008 Express\Chapter7\. Look for a folder named Debugger Start in the Chapter7 folder. Double-click the Debugger.sln solution.

This solution has several items you have not learned about yet. First, the solution has more than one project. This is a common practice in developing applications. In this case, the solution (named Debugger) contains two projects: a Microsoft Windows Forms application named Debugger and a managed library named MyLibrary (a managed DLL). The acronym DLL stands for Dynamic Link Library; a DLL is a library of classes and their methods that are called dynamically and as needed by an application. A DLL doesn't contain a main entry point and cannot be executed by itself. Also, multiple applications can use the same DLL at the same time.

Second, the project Debugger has a type of file you haven't seen yet, at least inside Visual Studio: a text file. You can have different kinds of files in your projects, and a text file is not uncommon. In this case, one of the methods called by the Debugger.exe application will use the text file, so to have the file in the output folder, you need to select it in Solution Explorer and then change the *Copy to Output Directory* property to *Copy If Newer.*

> **NOTE**
> The Debugger program is exclusively for the educational purposes of this chapter. It doesn't do anything interesting except teach debugging.

Using a DLL in an Application

When you design an application, you usually have more than one component. In many cases, the components are new classes (types). It is good practice to have those types in a separate source code file instead of keeping them with the user interface code. Often, the classes are grouped in a single library or DLL.

When you want to use a type from a library, you need to make your application aware of all the types and methods contained in that library by adding a reference to the library in the application.

TO ADD A REFERENCE TO YOUR APPLICATION

1. Select the project where you want to add the reference; in this case, select Debugger.

2. Right-click Debugger (look at Figure 7-1 to make sure you're at the right place), and then select Add Reference.

   As you can see from the tabs on the dialog box that appears, the references can come from multiple sources.

3. Select the Projects tab, and then select the MyLibrary project, which contains the managed DLL. Click OK to add the reference to your project.

Because the DLL is in the same solution and you just added a reference to that DLL to your application, Microsoft Visual Studio now knows there is a dependency between the two and will always build the DLL first so that your application builds the executable with the most up-to-date DLL possible.

You can verify that the reference has been inserted by using the following technique: in Solution Explorer, expand the References node, and look for the MyLibrary reference. Click it to see the details in the Properties window. By default, when you create a Windows Forms project, plenty of references are automatically added to the project during its creation. Figure 7-2 shows the references and Properties window for information pertinent to MyLibrary.

When you're done adding the reference, your application can create instances of the new types that are built in the DLL and use them appropriately. The build process (the compiler and linker) will now accept the use of those new types; however, for Visual Studio to have those new types available via IntelliSense and for the compiler to know about those new types, one more step is required. You might already have seen the line of code in the TestApplication.cs file that reads *using MyLibrary;*.

You create a *using* directive to use the types in a namespace without having to specify the fully qualified namespace name.

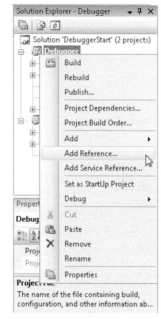

Figure 7-1
Add Reference... menu choice from the Debugger project

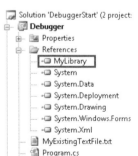

Figure 7-2
All references for this project

> **NOTE**
> A *using* directive does not give you access to any namespaces that are nested in the namespace you specify.

For instance, *Console.WriteLine()* comes from the *System* namespace; by adding it on top, you don't have to type *System.Console.WriteLine()*. This saves time, and it's easier to read. By adding this line of code, you're telling Visual Studio to look into that assembly for the metadata that will enable IntelliSense to be populated with the public/protected elements. After adding this line, you'll have access to those items whenever you have an instance of one of the types built in the library.

Using Breakpoints, Locals, Edit and Continue, and Visualizers

There is no better way to dive into this subject than by going through the code. If the TestApplication.cs source code file is not already open, open it by right-clicking the TestApplication.cs file and selecting View Code. You should see red dots on the left side of the screen; those red dots are *breakpoints*. Figure 7-3 shows the source code and the breakpoints.

TIP

If the breakpoints don't appear, you can add them by clicking in the left margin.

```
public TestApplication()
{
    InitializeComponent();
}

private void button1_Click(object sender, EventArgs e)
{
    Library myObjectLibrary = new Library();
    string myString = "Helloworld";

    MessageBox.Show(myObjectLibrary.Divide(5, 3).ToString());
    MessageBox.Show(myObjectLibrary.Divide(3, 3).ToString());

    MessageBox.Show(myObjectLibrary.ReadFile("MyExistingTextFile.txt"));
    myObjectLibrary.ManipulateStrings(ref myString, 20);
    MessageBox.Show(myString);
    myObjectLibrary.ManipulateStrings(ref myString, 1);
    MessageBox.Show(myString);
    MessageBox.Show(myObjectLibrary.Divide(6, 4).ToString());
    MessageBox.Show(myObjectLibrary.ReadFile("MyNotExistingTextFile.txt"));
}
```

Figure 7-3
Source code and breakpoints from the TestApplication Windows form

When the debugger encounters a breakpoint, it stops executing the application. In this source code, one breakpoint is placed on the call to *MessageBox.Show(myString);*. Another breakpoint appears in Library.cs in the first line of code of the *Divide* method. In the following procedure, you will execute the code and go through a debugging session.

To debug an application, you can do one of the following:

- Press F5, or click the Start Debugging button. The program will start executing normally. If there is a breakpoint in the source code, the execution will stop there. Otherwise, the program will continue to execute unless there is an unhandled exception or error.

- Alternatively, you can debug the application by stepping through the code line by line. To do this, press F11, or click the Step Into button.

For now, you'll jump to the first breakpoint and execute the code in the sample program using the first technique.

TO BEGIN DEBUGGING AN APPLICATION

1. Press F5, or click the Start Debugging button.

2. You will see a Try Me! Button. Click it. The code should stop executing at the first breakpoint in the *Divide* method, and you should see what is shown in Figure 7-4. The yellow highlighted line indicates the next statement to be executed.

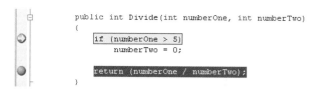

Figure 7-4
Execution stopped at the first breakpoint in the Divide *method*

You're now in debugging mode, so you have access to a plethora of tools and data elements about your application to help you understand what is happening when your application is executed. You can see the content of local variables, parameters, exception messages, the console window, and many more items you'll discover in the next few pages. All that information is useful when an application is not behaving the way it should and you're trying to understand why. With all the information the debugger provides, you can try to uncover where the problem lies and see why you have a bug. You can also use the debugger for learning purposes as you are doing right now. The debugger is an excellent teacher when you're new to a technology, when you're new to a language construct, or when you're simply trying to understand a new element. It is also common to use the debugger to understand someone else's code, and it is especially helpful when you need to modify existing code.

You'll now look at the first series of data elements offered by the debugger while you're stepping through your code. At the bottom of the Visual Studio screen, you can see a series of tabs, which can include Locals, Watch, Immediate Window, Output, and Error List. If you don't see these tabs, you can open these tabs by selecting them in the View and Debug menus. Most of these are not visible when you're working in editing mode. While you're debugging, the Locals tab is usually on top and shows the current variables and object information. Beside it you'll see the Call Stack that displays all methods that have been called, enabling you to follow the execution of your application at any given point during the debugging. Figure 7-5 shows the two windows.

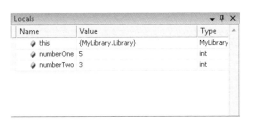

Figure 7-5
Tabs present during debugging in Visual Studio

On the Locals tab, you can see three elements of data from your *Divide* method: *this*, *numberOne*, and *numberTwo*. These are, in order, the instance of the current object and the two parameters. The debugger detects all elements that are in scope in that method and displays them on the Locals tab. The elements in scope are all the elements that are "visible" from where the instruction pointer (that is, the next instruction to be executed) is located. In this case, it could be either local variables or shared variables. This means that throughout the execution of the *Divide* method, you'll be able to follow the values that those items will have. Now it's your turn to see this for yourself.

TO CONTINUE DEBUGGING THE APPLICATION

1. Press F11, or click the Step Into button.

   While debugging, you can always rest the mouse pointer on program elements to get the information you otherwise find on the Locals tab. For instance, if you rest your mouse pointer on the *numberOne* element, you'll see the same value that is shown on the Locals tab, as illustrated in Figure 7-6.

2. Execute the next line of code by pressing F11 or by clicking the Step Into button on the toolbar or in the Debug menu.

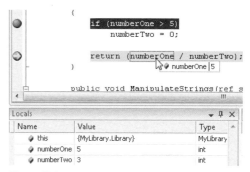

At this point, you can see the results of the division by simply resting the mouse pointer on the division operator. Verify that it's 1. Now let's say it is a more complex operation and you want to see the outcome of a change in the source code or a change in the content of a variable. Previously you would have had to stop the debugging process, change the values, recompile, and see the outcome. But with Visual C# 2008 you can modify your code and verify immediately whether the change you make solves the problem. This feature is called Edit and Continue. As its name implies, the Edit and Continue feature lets you edit an element in the application and continue the execution. In fact, not only can you do this, but you can also modify the next instruction to execute, change the value of a variable, and re-execute the instruction. This can be a huge time-saver because you don't have to stop the execution, make the change, rebuild, and re-execute the new code. You can see the changes right away.

Figure 7-6
Getting the value of the numberOne *local variable in two different ways*

3. Go to the left side of the code window, where the yellow arrow indicates the next instruction to be executed. When you rest your mouse pointer on the yellow arrow, you should see a transparent arrow indicating you can move the yellow arrow. Click and hold the yellow arrow, and slide it up and back over the *if* statement.

4. Change the value of *numberOne* to *-5* by resting your mouse pointer on the variable name, clicking the number 5 in the tooltip that appears, and then modifying it to -5. You can also modify the values on the Locals tab at the bottom of the IDE. Then re-execute the instruction by pressing F11 or clicking the Step Into button.

5. Step into the code until you see a message box with -1 for the first division. If you don't see the message box, you might need to switch to it on the Windows taskbar. Click OK in the message box. Continue stepping into the code until you return to the *Divide* method with a new set of values and you're pointing at the first instruction in the method.

CAUTION

The Edit and Continue feature doesn't work on 64-bit operating systems.

NOTE

There are some limitations to the edits you can make with the Edit and Continue feature. To see a complete list of limitations, simply perform a search in the Help system with the following search criteria: *Edit and Continue [Visual C#]*. Then look for the two sections about unsupported features that explain what you can't do.

When you're back to the *Divide* method, you will not re-execute every instruction because you know that the method should now execute correctly. Instead, you'll step out of the code using the Step Out function. Stepping out doesn't mean you'll skip the execution; stepping out simply means that the debugger will execute all the instructions of the current method and return to the calling point. If you do it on a single instruction, it will simply execute it.

TO STEP OUT OF THE CODE

1. In the Library.cs file, click the red dot at the first breakpoint of the *Divide* method, which is the statement that should be highlighted. Clicking the red dot removes the breakpoint. The red dot should now be gone.

2. In addition to clicking the red dot, you can disable the second breakpoint by using one of three other methods:

   a. Right-click the line of code that has the breakpoint, click the Breakpoint... menu choice, and then click the Delete Breakpoint choice. Look at Figure 7-7 to see this in action.

   b. Click the Debug menu, and then select Toggle Breakpoint or press F9.

   c. Right-click the red dot indicating the breakpoint, and select Delete Breakpoint.

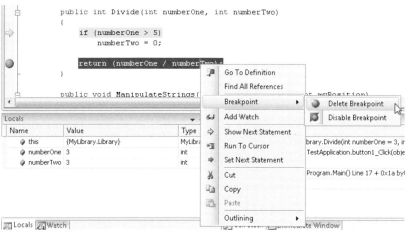

Figure 7-7
Deleting a breakpoint by using a contextual menu in the code editor

3. You should be at the first line of code in the *Divide* method. Press Shift+F11 to step out of the *Divide* method, or click the Step Out button. This executes all the instructions in that method and returns to the caller.

4. Press F5 to execute all the methods up to the next breakpoint.

   You should see another message box with the result 1. Click OK, and then you should be stopped in the source code of the *ReadFile* method.

5. The *ReadToEnd* method reads the content of the open file and puts it into a string variable. Press Shift+F11 and then F11. A message box should display the string variable content. Click OK in the message box. You should now be back at the caller.

6. Step into the code until you get the string "Helloworld" in a message box. Pay attention to the order of execution, and look into the variables and into the content in each of the tab sections.

7. Click OK in the message box, and then step into the code again to get into the *ManipulateStrings* method.

The first instruction in the *ManipulateStrings* method (apart from the *myTempCharArray* variable declaration) is taking the string received in the argument and converting it to an array of characters. The reason for converting the string is because strings are immutable in .NET, and therefore you have to work with them in read-only mode once they're created. Methods modifying a string are actually returning a new string object that contains the modification applied to it.

Therefore, if you want to modify a string character-by-character or if you want to access a single character in a string by using an index, you first need to convert the string into an array of characters.

TO BEGIN STEPPING OUT OF THE MANIPULATESTRINGS METHOD

1. Press Shift+F11 to step out of the *ManipulateStrings* method, or click the Step Out button.

The application stops abruptly. What just happened is an unhandled exception. An unhandled exception happens whenever an error occurs that is not anticipated or handled

MORE INFO

In the *ReadFile* method the *using* block guarantees you're going to dispose of the resources you're using when you exit the block. You can read more about this by searching for *using statement* in the Help system.

MORE INFO

As you can see in the source code, one of the *ManipulateStrings* arguments, *myString*, is passed with the *ref* keyword. When you have an argument that is passed to a method by reference, the called method is receiving a reference to the same memory location used by the caller. Therefore, if the method is modifying the content of that argument, it is modifying the content at this memory location and thus modifying the variable from the caller. In this case, anything that is done to the *myString* argument will modify the value of the variable in the calling code. The other argument is *myPosition*, and it is passed by value. When you have an argument that is passed by value, the method is receiving a copy of the variable from the calling code and thus can't modify the original value from the caller. Therefore, the content will get lost when the method ends and the execution flow returns to the caller.

explicitly by your application. In that case, the execution of your application is halted because there is no way the application can continue in that state without potentially corrupting the memory or opening security holes. One of the .NET runtime (CLR) principles is to make sure that neither ever happens. Therefore, the CLR crashes your application to prevent your application from continuing to execute in an unknown state. Even though the CLR is taking those precautions, which means it is less likely to have insecure code executing in .NET, it is still possible.

To help you find the bug that raised the unhandled exception, Visual Studio includes another useful tool: the Exception Assistant. The assistant is helpful because, based on the context of the exception, it provides information that helps you debug, including error helpers such as the type of exception, troubleshooting tips, and corrective actions that can be applied through the Exception Assistant. Look at Figure 7-8 to see the information provided for the current exception.

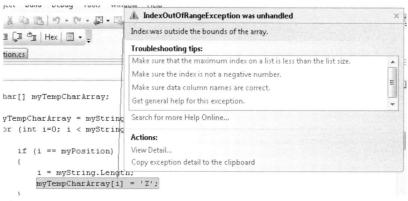

Figure 7-8
Exception Assistant

When you look at the exception name, the troubleshooting tips, and the data visualizers, it should be apparent why an unhandled exception was raised. The exception name alone is self-explanatory: *IndexOutOfRangeException*. The first troubleshooting tip displayed asks you to make sure the maximum index on a list is less than the list size. Arrays in .NET are *zero-based*, which means that the first element starts at index 0. The length of the string received as the argument is 10.

The intent of this method was to modify the last character of the string when the position in the array is equal to a position passed by value to the method. In this particular case, the position passed by value to the method is 1.

Therefore, in the *for* loop, at the second character of that string, the *if* statement will return true, and then the index *i* will get the value of the string *length*. This means *i* is now equal to 10. When the application tries to modify the character at index 10, an exception is generated because index 10 is outside the range of the array. The array has 10 characters with indexes from 0 to 9. Figure 7-9 uses a new visualizer to look at the *myTempCharArray* content.

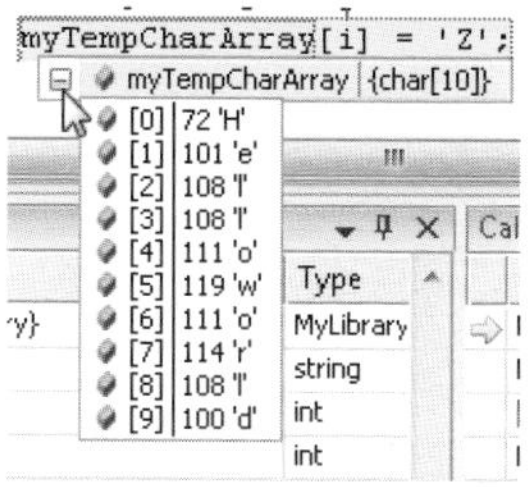

When you move the mouse pointer over program elements, you'll sometimes see a magnifier. If you click the drop-down list, you will see a list of visualizers that display the information in a way that is meaningful to the data type you're seeing. For instance, if you're working with XML or HTML content, the XML or HTML visualizer allows you to see the content as if you were using Windows Internet Explorer or any other XML or HTML tool. You'll use one of the visualizers soon when you debug the *ReadFile* method.

Figure 7-9
Array visualizer

CAUTION

If at any time you use the Edit and Continue feature and you see that your data looks odd or seems corrupted, stop the debugging process and restart the debugging of your application.

TO FIX THE OUT-OF-RANGE PROBLEM

1. Close the Exception Assistant by clicking the X in the upper-right corner.

2. Modify the *ManipulateStrings* method. Subtract 1 from the string *length* when you assign a new value to *i*. The source code should look like this after you modify it:

```
if (i == myPosition)
{
    i = myString.Length - 1;
    myTempCharArray[i] = 'Z';
}
```

3. After modifying this line of code, move your next execution pointer to the *for* statement so that index *i* starts at 0. Step through the code or step out. This time there should be no exception. Continue to step through the code; you should now see another message: "HelloworlZ." The string has been modified because it was passed by reference.

Continue to step through the code, and soon you'll get a second exception, which is a division-by-zero error. Of course, an exception is raised because the *Divide* method assigns

0 to the denominator when the numerator is greater than 5. Using a visualizer, you can see that the numerator is 6, and therefore 0 will be assigned to the denominator.

Again, the first displayed troubleshooting tip helps by suggesting that you make sure the denominator is not 0. To solve the problem, you could add an *if* statement; but before you do that, consider another .NET principle.

It's good practice in .NET to use the exception mechanism to catch those corner cases instead of coding special conditional instructions that bloat the code. The exceptions are an integral part of the .NET Framework, and they're everywhere. I'll now explain the logic behind this decision.

In the real world, your application would not purposely assign 0 to the denominator; therefore, most divisions would result in a correct operation. Adding an *if* statement would result in a conditional instruction executed for every single division. And because most divisions would be valid, you would automatically slow down your application. Using an exception-handling mechanism to catch those corner cases is a much better solution because the exception-handling code will be executed only when necessary, so your application should be faster.

When you insert exception-handling code in your application, it is best practice to always catch exceptions from the most precise to the least precise. In this case, you know that the *DivisionByZeroException* exception is the one most likely to occur; therefore, it's the first one you want to catch.

When you catch an exception, the exception is "handled." You then need to do something about it; either you handle it by mentioning it to the user or you throw the exception back. In this case, you want the user to know that an exception was raised, but you don't want the program to crash. Here's an example that demonstrates this form of handling that I'm sure you already know. If you try to divide by zero in Microsoft Office Excel, Excel won't crash; it simply indicates that your entry results in a division-by-zero error and displays the #DIV/0! message in the cell.

An older way of doing things was to make your method return an integer to indicate success or failure. And that's where people met with trouble, because between two applications, and sometimes between two functions, the same integer code meant two different things. You received an integer that was supposed to tell you why your application failed, but the originating code had two meanings, and it was a nightmare to figure out which one was the valid error code. In addition, when people used error codes, their code was ugly because they either had a switch case or had a series of nested *if* statements.

In .NET, you should never design your methods to return an integer to indicate success or failure, and you shouldn't use a Boolean for the same purpose. This is a poor practice that was used when exceptions did not exist or when people didn't know or want to use them appropriately. *You should never do this.* Instead, use exceptions.

TO ADD CODE TO HANDLE DIFFERENT EXCEPTIONS

1. Click the Stop Debugging button, or press Shift+F5 to stop debugging mode. In TestApplication.cs, modify the *button1_Click* method to look like the following:

```
Library myObjectLibrary = new Library();
string myString = "Helloworld";
string myFile = "";

try
{
  MessageBox.Show(myObjectLibrary.Divide(5, 3).ToString());
  MessageBox.Show(myObjectLibrary.Divide(3, 3).ToString());
  MessageBox.Show(myObjectLibrary.Divide(6, 4).ToString());
}
catch (DivideByZeroException ex)
{
  MessageBox.Show(ex.ToString());
}

try
{
  myFile = "MyExistingTextFile.txt";
  MessageBox.Show(myObjectLibrary.ReadFile(myFile));
  myFile = "MyNotExistingTextFile.txt";
  MessageBox.Show(myObjectLibrary.ReadFile(myFile));
}
catch (FileNotFoundException)
{
  MessageBox.Show(myFile + " doesn't exist!");
}

myObjectLibrary.ManipulateStrings(ref myString, 20);
MessageBox.Show(myString);
myObjectLibrary.ManipulateStrings(ref myString, 1);
MessageBox.Show(myString);
```

2. Remove all the breakpoints in TestApplication.cs and Library.cs, and execute the code. Look at the different message boxes. If a *DivideByZeroException* or *FileNotFoundException* exception occurs, a message box will be displayed.

During this debugging session, you didn't use some other useful tabs. For instance, the Watch tab is important because you can enter variables and expressions that you want to follow and monitor during the execution of the application.

Another useful tool is the Immediate window, where you can type anything and the compiler verifies, compiles, and executes it on the fly! Any effect on the application you are debugging is immediate. Any piece of code that can be evaluated by the compiler and does not require a block of code can be entered on the Immediate window. You could enter a loop, for instance. You also have full access to IntelliSense in this window just as if you were in the code editor. Let's look at a simple example.

TO USE THE IMMEDIATE WINDOW

1. Put a breakpoint at the first instruction in your application (which is *InitializeComponent();*), and run the application by pressing F5.

2. If you don't see the Immediate window, just click the Debug menu, and then click Windows and Immediate. You should have an empty Immediate window at the bottom of your screen.

3. Type **int i = 5;**, and then press Enter.

4. Now type **MessageBox.Show(i.ToString());**, and press Enter.

   The message box that appears should show a 5. You can test code in real time during the execution without executing a single line of code from your application. But beware that if you use variables that are in your application and modify them on the Immediate window, you modify them for the application as well.

5. Click OK in the message box, and then click the Stop Debugging button to stop executing the application.

You're now not only able to build new applications, but you're also aware of the techniques and tools available to debug them.

In Summary...

In this chapter, you learned about breakpoints; about different techniques to step into, step over, and step out of the source code; and about data visualizers to see the data in the most pertinent way based on its content or context. You also learned how to work with a DLL.

You discovered that you can use the Edit and Continue feature to modify variables at run time and continue the execution.

You learned how you can move the next instruction pointer to re-execute some lines of code. You also started to deal with exceptions and learned the dos and don'ts of debugging. You saw how subtle bugs can find their way in—usually because of distractions and some-times simply because you don't possess all of the knowledge and experience yet—but that's OK. Don't worry; you're in a process called *learning*.

In the next chapter, you'll learn about using databases, working with ADO.NET, using LINQ, and manipulating data to and from a Microsoft SQL Server Express Edition data-base. You'll learn how to use this data to populate controls on a Windows form. You'll also learn how to create an application to add, modify, delete, and visualize rows in a car tracker application.

Chapter 8

Managing the Data

What Is a Database?, 150

*Using SQL Server 2005
Express in Visual C#
Express Edition, 158*

*What Are ADO.NET, Data
Binding, and LINQ?, 171*

So far, you've seen how to build a Windows Forms application and examples of the characteristics that type of application contains, but you have not managed a great deal of data. Managing data is always a concern, whether at home, at the office, at school, or even for recreation. For instance, I have many recipes and ideas for great dinners, but when I want to prepare a nice meal, it takes me so much time to find the recipes that usually I change my mind about cooking. If I had this information in my computer, it would be easy to quickly access my recipe for rack of lamb with herb crust and prepare a fabulous meal. I could also add other pertinent information to the recipe file, such as what side dishes were served with the main dish or what wines went well with this recipe. I could even add a picture of the finished meal.

You can manage some data using a word processing program, such as Microsoft Office Word, but it becomes unmanageable as soon as you collect a lot of recipes and need to search for information within that file. Using spreadsheets like those you find in Microsoft Office Excel is also problematic. Trying to find information quickly when using more than one variable is close to impossible. Using the recipe example, suppose you want to retrieve all the recipes that can serve at least six people and that have lamb stew meat but no mint in the ingredients because one of your guests is allergic to mint. Imagine the time it would take to find that information in either a Word file or an Excel spreadsheet. That's where databases come to the rescue.

In this chapter, you'll learn what a database is; how to create a database; how to add, delete, and update data; how to search or query a database; and how to use a database in a Windows Forms application. Accompanying Microsoft Visual C# 2008 Express Edition is Microsoft SQL Server 2005 Express Edition, which is a fully workable version of its big brother, Microsoft SQL Server 2005, but with fewer features. SQL Server 2005 Express Edition is free, easy to use, and geared toward building simple and dynamic applications.

What Is a Database?

A *database* is a collection of data that is stored in files on disks using a systematic structure. Because of this systematic structure, users can query the data using management software called a *database management system* (DBMS). SQL Server 2005 is a *relational database management system* (RDBMS), which means its data is structured using sets (the set theory in mathematics) and logical relations (predicates). Most commercial database products are based on the relational model. In fact, it has been one of the most popular models for the past 20 years. Apart from Microsoft SQL Server, you might have also heard of Oracle or IBM DB2.

NOTE
You'll learn about some of the other elements contained in a relational database later in this chapter.

What's in a Database?

A relational database, such as SQL Server 2005, contains multiple tables that are related. A database can also contain views, stored procedures, functions, indexes, security information, and other elements. In this section, you'll learn about the basic elements of a relational database, which are a table and its components.

A *table* contains columns and rows. A *column* defines the type of data, and a *row* contains the actual data. Because the relational model has strict rules, an RDBMS that uses the relational model must implement them.

MORE INFO
In reality, no popular RDBMS is fully implementing the pure relational model as it was first created in the 1970s.

What Are Data Normalization and Data Integrity?

The rules defining the relational model are called *normalization rules*. Normalization is a process that data architects apply whenever they are at the design phase. Normalization rules exist to reduce the chance of having the same data stored in more than one table; in other words, they reduce the level of redundancy and preserve data integrity in the database. Logically, the normalization process exists to help place data into its own table so that no duplication of information occurs in more than one table. For example, having an application in which a customer's address, city, state or province, ZIP or postal code, and country are duplicated in two different tables is a bad idea. There should be only one link from the customer table to the other table referencing additional customer information. Having duplicate data makes updates and deletions more problematic and also poses the risk of having modified data in one table and not the other. This example demonstrates a data integrity problem.

Let's look at another data integrity problem. Suppose you have both a product table and a table containing customer order details. Now let's say you decide to delete product1, which means removing the row from the product table that corresponds to product1. If the RDBMS would let you do this, it would mean that suddenly all rows in the customer order details table that contained this product would not be able to show which product was ordered because the product would no longer exist. Those rows would be *orphaned*, which could have disastrous results for the company. Although you normalized your data, data integrity does not exist in this example.

As you can see, data integrity is an important concept related to the accuracy, validity, and correctness of the data. To better understand some of these concepts, let's look at another example.

Suppose you are the owner of an online store and want to manage your company using a software application. To use a software application, you must start thinking about using a database. Any company, both small and large, typically has a great deal of data to store. Also, because data is all around us, people want more access to this data so they can create reports and conduct analysis. That is why databases are so useful. Returning to your online store, at a minimum you would like to store information about your customers, products, invoices, purchasing, and inventory. To summarize all these areas, let's take a look at the Product, OrderHeader, and OrderDetail tables, as shown in Table 8-1, Table 8-2, and Table 8-3, respectively.

Column Name	Data Type	Allow Nulls?
ProductID (PK)	integer	Not Null
ProductNumber	nvarchar(10)	Not Null
Name	nvarchar(50)	Not Null
Description	nvarchar(200)	Null
Photo	image	Null
Price	money	Not Null
Taxable	bit	Not Null

Table 8-1
Product Table

Column Name	Data Type	Allow Nulls?
OrderID (PK)	integer	Not Null
OrderDate	datetime	Not Null
DueDate	datetime	Not Null
CustomerID (FK)	integer	Not Null
TaxAmount	money	Not Null
Total	money	Not Null

Table 8-2
OrderHeader Table

Column Name	Data Type	Allow Nulls?
OrderID (PK) (FK)	integer	Not Null
OrderDetailID (PK)	integer	Not Null
ProductID (FK)	integer	Not Null
Quantity	integer	Not Null
LineTotal	numeric(38,6)	Not Null

Table 8-3
OrderDetail Table

You can also represent your Product, OrderHeader, and OrderDetail tables graphically, as shown in Figure 8-1. This is a common way of looking at databases.

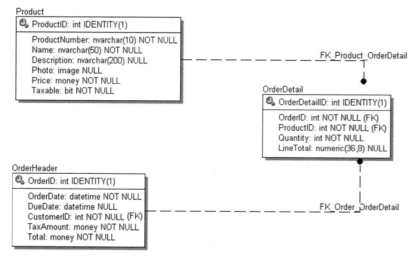

Figure 8-1
Partial database diagram for a small online company

What Is Null?

One of your first observations about the tables is that they each have an Allow Nulls? column, which is also reflected in Figure 8-1. When designing a table, you need to consider what's absolutely necessary (Not Null) and what's not (Null). For instance, when you insert a new row into the Product table, it might not matter whether the product has a photo, but it might be a problem to have a product without a product number. Now let's correlate how allowing null is related to data integrity. Whenever a table is designed with columns that don't allow null, the RDBMS will reject any insertion of a new row that has a column set to null when it is not supposed to be. When you pay attention to those columns that cannot be set to null when designing your tables, you automatically add another data integrity layer by making sure that all the necessary data is present before the record is inserted into the database.

What Are Primary Keys and Foreign Keys?

You can see in the previous tables that some columns have the letters "(PK)," which stands for *primary key*. In Figure 8-1, primary key columns are marked with a yellow key. Some other columns are identified with "(FK)" to indicate that these columns are *foreign keys*. Let's start by talking about the primary key.

Primary Keys

A *primary key* is a value that is used to uniquely identify a specific row in a table. A primary key has the following attributes:

- Can be composed of one or more column names. When it's composed of more than one column, it's called a *composite key*.

- Is often a numeric field.

- Is often generated by the RDBMS, in which case it's called a *surrogate key*. A surrogate key is frequently (but not always) a sequential number. A surrogate key is also called an *identity* in SQL Server 2005. An identity starts at a set number, called the *identity seed*, and increments by another set number, called the *identity increment*. For example, if you create a table named Product, you can have a column named ProductID that is set as an identity, and you can set the identity seed to 1 with an identity increment to 1. When the first row is created in the Product table, the ProductID will be generated by the RDBMS and set to 1. The following row will have a ProductID that is set to 2, and so forth.

- Should be as small as possible but large enough to support the number of rows it will represent.
- Is immutable, meaning its value should never change.
- Is also a natural key when the key has a logical relationship with the rest of the columns in the table. For example, if you had a book table, the ISBN number could be used as a primary key because it uniquely identifies one book. It would be an advantage compared with a generated key because it would take less space and has to exist anyway!
- Is also used to relate two tables together.

In our Product table example, ProductID is the primary key. At design time, it will also be an identity. You can claim that the product number could be a primary key—and you could be right—but in certain scenarios a product number could be used twice. For example, suppose you have product #FG-001 with a revision 1.0. In time, you change the product because of customer complaints and give it a revision 2.0. You want your customers to continue to order the same product number for many business reasons. In your database, you would retire the product revision 1.0 by perhaps changing a column named Active, and you would then add another row in your table with the new product details, including revision 2.0, and set it to Active. Why can't you use the same row? Let's assume that six months after creating the new product revision, you want to create a graph to determine whether your changes to the product mean you had fewer returns from your customers. It would be difficult to come up with good data if you had only one row for the product, but it would be fairly easy to do if you have two rows because they would be unique in the database, with each having a different ProductID.

In the OrderDetail table, you have a composite primary key that is a combination of OrderID and OrderDetailID. This means these two columns would ensure the uniqueness of a row in the OrderDetail table.

In the OrderHeader table, OrderID is the primary key.

Foreign Keys

A *foreign key* is a column in a table that relates to a column in another table. It lets you create relations between tables. A foreign key in a table is always a primary key in another table. Foreign keys are used to enforce data integrity by being part of foreign key constraints. Foreign key constraints are created to make sure referential integrity is preserved and not violated. There are two foreign keys in the OrderDetail table. The first is the ProductID foreign key, and it's related to the primary key named ProductID in the Product table. The second is the OrderID foreign key, and it's related to the primary key named OrderID in the OrderHeader table. Concerning the naming of foreign keys, it's good practice to define them by using the same name as their primary key counterpart; otherwise, it might lead to problems for people looking at your logical data model.

I introduced you to data integrity earlier in this chapter. When doing so, I cited an example that could create similar problems to the one in the Product and OrderDetail example. Adding a foreign key constraint between these two tables would prevent a user from deleting a product in the Product table that could potentially create a large number of orphaned rows in the OrderDetail table. If you look at Figure 8-1, the foreign key constraint between Product and OrderDetail is shown as a line labeled FK_Product_OrderDetail between the two tables. Naming constraints is an easy way to understand their purpose. We have only three tables in our example, but you can imagine that constraints without names that exist between numerous tables would quickly become unclear.

Another foreign key constraint is the one between the OrderHeader and OrderDetail tables; this constraint prevents an order from being deleted before all of its matching order details have been deleted. You can see in Figure 8-1 that the OrderHeader table has a second foreign key called CustomerID. Therefore, another foreign key constraint is between the Customer and OrderHeader tables. Following the same principles found with other foreign key constraints, this prevents a customer in the Customer table from being deleted before all the matching orders in the OrderHeader table and all the detail rows in the OrderDetail table that match the orders have been deleted.

If there were no foreign key constraints in this database, data integrity would be easily violated. The database would be left with a big problem: a time bomb of orphaned rows that take up space and slow down all queries. By adding foreign key constraints, the RDBMS ensures, for example, that all rows in the OrderDetail table that reference a product have been deleted before the product row can be deleted in the Product table.

Interacting with a Relational Database

So far, I've talked about tables in which you can update, add, or delete rows or query the database to get particular results. Perhaps you've been asking yourself, "But how do I talk or interact with the database? How does it return the answers to my queries? And how do you create those tables?" I'm sure you've been asking yourself many other questions as well. The answer to all of these questions is SQL Server 2005 Express Edition.

SQL stands for Structured Query Language and was invented in the 1970s. The acronym is pronounced "sequel" and was also introduced using that same spelling, but because of a trademark dispute in the United Kingdom in the 1970s, the name was shortened to the now well-known SQL acronym. (The other acronym, SEQUEL, means Structured English Query Language.) SQL is an English-based language and is similar to human-language questions. That's why it's easy and fast to learn basic SQL programming. Let's look at two examples:

```
SELECT * FROM CUSTOMER
SELECT COUNT(*) FROM PRODUCT
```

The first line can be translated as "give us all (*) rows in the Customer table" (designated by the asterisk, which is a wildcard character in SQL), or less formally, "give us the list of customers." The second line can be translated as a request to give us the total of all rows contained in the Product table—in other words, a count of how many products this company has.

When you issue a SQL query to a relational database, the database returns a result set that simply contains the rows with the answers to your query. Using SQL, you can also group or aggregate the results of a query. You also use SQL to create tables or delete (drop) tables. You've learned about primary keys, foreign keys, and constraints, but you probably didn't know that they're also created using SQL.

It's also good to know that SQL is an ANSI/ISO standard; therefore, any RDBMS producer needs to obey a set of rules. Basic SQL is a base programming language and as such is usually not sufficient to solve all the possible problems or provide all the analysis needs that an application might demand. It has a rather limited set of keywords. Because the first goal is to query data from a database, the most popular RDBMSs on the market have added extensions to SQL to permit the addition of procedural code. These additions turn SQL into a full-fledged programming language that helps solve more complex problems. The following are popular extensions and their manufacturers: Microsoft Transact-SQL (T-SQL), Oracle PL/SQL, and IBM SQL PL. Recently, in addition to these extensions, RDBMS manufacturers have added support for other programming languages. Microsoft added .NET language support to the database with all SQL Server 2005 editions, while Oracle and IBM have added Java support.

There are more database concepts and theories than those explained here, but I have covered the immediate database needs of this book. You'll now apply those concepts concretely in a Windows Forms application that will use a SQL Server Express 2005 database.

Using SQL Server 2005 Express in Visual C# Express Edition

In this section, you will develop a Windows Forms application. This will be a car-tracking application that lets a user track the prices of cars over time and determine where the listing was observed. You will first use Visual Studio to create the database and the tables, and then you'll add some data and validate some of the concepts you just learned. You will then create a Windows application that will use your data and build a data-centric application that lets users store any amount of data.

Refer to Figure 8-2 for the database diagram pertaining to this section's example.

MORE INFO

SQL Server is well integrated because Visual Studio provides a great software development kit (SDK) for other components to plug into the IDE.

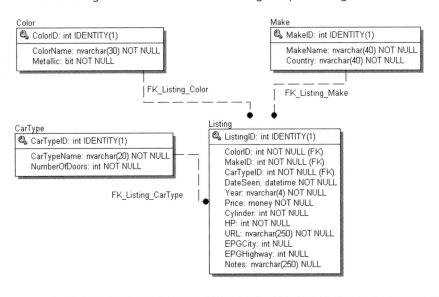

Figure 8-2
Car tracker application database diagram

Creating a Database Using Visual C# 2008 Express Edition

Before using data, you need a place to store the data. In this section, you'll learn how to create a database in Visual C# 2008 Express Edition. You'll also see how easy it is for you to create all the tables you need to satisfy the needs of the car-tracking application because the SQL Server team did a wonderful job of integrating the tools into Visual Studio.

TO CREATE A DATABASE USING VISUAL C# 2008 EXPRESS EDITION

1. Start Visual C# 2008 Express Edition.

2. Create a new Windows Forms application, and name it CarTracker.

3. You will now create the database that will hold the tables for the application. In Solution Explorer, right-click the CarTracker project, select Add, and then select New Item.

4. In the Add New Item dialog box, select Service-Based Database under Visual Studio Installed Templates. Type the filename **CarTracker.mdf**, and click the Add button. By doing so, you'll create a database and attach the database file (CarTracker.mdf) to your CarTracker project.

5. You will then see the Data Source Configuration Wizard. Don't pay attention to this dialog box just yet; you'll learn about it soon. Just click Cancel for now.

   Solution Explorer should now contain a new item within your project: the database file called CarTracker.mdf, as shown in Figure 8-3.

6. You will now start adding tables to your database. To do this, you can either double-click the CarTracker.mdf file or right-click CarTracker.mdf and then select Open. This causes Visual Studio to connect to the SQL Server 2005 Express Edition instance installed on your machine.

   Database Explorer should appear on the left side of the screen where the Toolbox usually opens, as shown in Figure 8-4. If you do not see Database Explorer, click View, Other Windows, Database Explorer.

   Under the database name, you should see a list of database elements represented by folder icons. Although you will not recognize most of them, you will see two elements

MORE INFO

The .mdf file extension is used by the SQL Server family of products. The .mdf file contains the entire database, which means all tables and other elements that exist in the database are located in this file. The only element that is not part of the .mdf file is the log information, which is in an .ldf file that is created whenever you create a database. You can see the .ldf file by clicking the Show All Files icon in Solution Explorer.

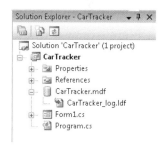

Figure 8-3
Solution Explorer with the newly created CarTracker.mdf database file

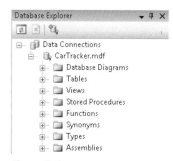

Figure 8-4
Database Explorer with the CarTracker database connected

NOTE

Currently, you have only one database in your project, but it's not unusual to need to connect to and get information from two or more databases. That's why Database Connections in Database Explorer is there as a tree—it's representing each database as a node in that tree. You have only one node in the tree, which is your CarTracker database.

that are already familiar to you: database diagrams and tables. You will use both of these elements shortly.

You'll know that you're connected to the database when you see the database icon with an electric cord icon. When you're disconnected, you will see the database icon with a red X. However, seeing a red X does not necessarily mean you're disconnected. You might have been disconnected earlier but never refreshed Database Explorer. To verify the state of the connection to your database, you should click the Refresh button in the Database Explorer toolbar.

7. Right-click your database named Car-Tracker.mdf in Database Explorer, and select Close Connection. You should now see the red X near your database name.

   You're now disconnected. You can reconnect in three ways. You can double-click your database name (that is, CarTracker.mdf) in the Database Explorer, you can click the Refresh button, or you can right-click the file name in Database Explorer and select Modify Connection.... If you choose the Modify Connection route, you will see a dialog box like the one shown in Figure 8-5.

8. Because it's good practice to test your connection, click the Test Connection button to verify the connection currently specified. This also verifies that SQL Server 2005 Express Edition is ready and able to receive connections from your applications. Click OK to reconnect to your database.

Figure 8-5
The Modify Connection dialog box lets you reconnect to your CarTracker database.

Creating Tables in Your Database

Now you'll create all tables and relationships needed for the CarTracker application. Using the information found in Figure 8-2, you'll create tables, primary keys, identities, and foreign key relationships in the CarTracker database, and you'll do all of this without leaving Visual Studio.

TO CREATE TABLES IN A DATABASE

1. Let's start with the Color table. In Database Explorer, right-click the table's folder icon, and select Add New Table. You should now see an empty grid on the designer surface, which is the Table Designer. You will also see that a new toolbar has appeared, which is the Table Designer toolbar. This toolbar has all the tools necessary to help you create a table without writing a single SQL query.

2. You'll now add a column to the Color table. Type **ColorID** in the Column Name field of the Table Designer. Select int as the data type, and clear the Allow Nulls check box because this column will be the primary key in this table. A primary key cannot be null since it is part of the uniqueness of a row in the table.

3. Before you add the second column in the Color table, you'll set the ColorID column as the primary key. To do so, you need to click the Set Primary Key icon (the yellow key) in the Table Designer toolbar.

4. The database diagram shown in Figure 8-2 illustrates that you also need this column to be an identity; therefore, you need to modify that property in the Column Properties window right below the Table Designer. Scroll down until you see the Identity Specification group. Click the + sign located to the left of the words *Identity Specification* to expand this group. Now click in the (Is Identity) field, and set it to Yes. Leave both Identity Seed and Identity Increment set at 1 for now.

5. To add another column, click in the row under the ColorID column name (or press Tab). Add the two remaining columns based on the diagram shown in Figure 8-2. Set the size of the ColorName nvarchar to 30 by typing **30** in the Data Type field. When done, your table should look like the one shown in Figure 8-6.

> **NOTE**
> From this point onward, for every tree control and every control that is a group (that is, has a + sign), I'll use the word *expand* instead of repeating the words *click the + sign*.

> **NOTE**
> As a reminder, when a column is an identity, SQL Server automatically generates a new number each time a row is created in a table. It starts at the value indicated by the *Identity Seed* property and increases in increments by the value indicated by the *Identity Increment* property.

Figure 8-6
Table Designer with all the columns for the Color table

NOTE

In the Table Designer, the little black triangle indicates the current row.

6. Now that you're done with the design, you need to add the table to the database. To do this, you need to save the table. Click the Save icon, or press Ctrl+S. When the Choose Name dialog box appears, as shown in Figure 8-7, name your table Color, and then click OK.

Figure 8-7
The Choose Name dialog box showing the Color table name

Figure 8-8
Database Explorer with the Tables folder and Color table expanded

7. Expand the Tables folder in Database Explorer to view the list of existing tables in the database; the new Color table should appear. When you expand the Color table to view the list of columns, all three columns you just created should appear, as shown in Figure 8-8.

8. Close the Color table in the Table Designer by clicking the X near Solution Explorer.

9. Click the Save All icon in the toolbar to save your project on disk. Make sure the project name is CarTracker, and click the Save button.

10. Before creating other tables, read this step completely. Now that you have the knowledge to create a table, create all remaining tables (CarType, Make, and Listing) by using the same techniques you've just learned. Make sure all tables and all their columns are

created in the same way as shown in Figure 8-2. Don't worry about establishing the relationships, because you'll create those in the following exercises. Between each table creation, save your new table immediately, and make sure it appears in Database Explorer. Then close the table in the designer surface as shown earlier in step 8 of this section.

Creating Relationships Between the Tables

You have created tables, but they don't have any relationships. You'll now add those relationships and make sure your database has data integrity to avoid any orphaned rows. Like many other elements in Visual C# Express Edition, there's more than one way to create the relationships. One is more visual than the other, and you'll start with this more visual approach so you can stay focused on the main idea of the book, which is being productive.

Before you're able to create the relationships visually, there is a prerequisite to add to your project: a database diagram. It might not look exactly like the one shown in Figure 8-2, but it will be similar.

TO CREATE RELATIONSHIPS BETWEEN TABLES

1. Go to Database Explorer, and right-click the Database Diagrams node located above the Tables node. Select Add New Diagram. A dialog box appears indicating that SQL Server 2005 Express Edition doesn't have all the database objects it needs if you want to create database diagrams.

2. Click Yes to have SQL Server create the components it needs to obtain a database diagram. When it's done creating the components, you'll be asked which tables you want to add to your diagram in the Add Table dialog box.

3. Select all the tables you created, and then click Add. It should take less than a minute for your diagram to appear. Click the Close button to indicate to Visual Studio that you have all the tables you need.

4. Click the Save All button, or press Ctrl+Shift+S. You'll be asked to save your diagram and choose a name. Name your diagram CarTrackerDiagram.

TIP

Whenever you click a column name in Database Explorer, you'll see the properties listed in the Properties window. This is the same Properties window you've been using, with one minor difference: it is a read-only view and therefore does not let you modify information.

TIP

Depending on your resolution, the view might be tight. If you want to view more of the diagram, you might need to unpin or close some windows, such as Solution Explorer or the Properties window; you can return these items to your screen by selecting the View menu and then selecting Solution Explorer or Properties Window. You can also change the zoom value by changing the value in the Zoom drop-down list.

5. If you don't see your database diagram, first go to the Database Diagrams node, expand it, and then open the diagram by double-clicking it. You should see the designer surface with all your tables.

Let's focus on one relationship we need to create. When you look at Figure 8-2, you'll see that the ColorID column is present in the Listing table because there's a relationship to the Color table. The line between both tables is an FK relationship. You need to have this relationship established, or otherwise you'll have orphaned nodes in the Listing table whenever a Color row is deleted. This means you have to establish a relationship between the primary key table and the foreign key table. In this case, you need to create a relationship from the Color table toward the Listing table.

6. In the database diagram, click ColorID in the Color table where you see the small yellow key.

7. Look at Figure 8-9 to see where you should be at the end of this step. Drag ColorID toward the Listing table; you should see a line appear as you drag. Align your mouse pointer so that it's over the column with which you want to create the relationship—in your case, over the ColorID field in the Listing table. When you see a small + appear, drop it.

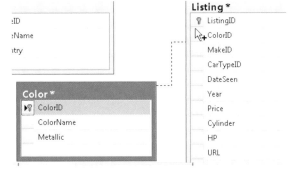

Figure 8-9
Creating the foreign key relationship between the Color and Listing tables

8. If you correctly selected and released the mouse button once you were over ColorID in the Listing table, you should see a Tables and Columns dialog box asking you to confirm the creation of the FK relationship. It's important for each table that ColorID is the column name that appears to link both tables in that dialog box. If the primary key and foreign key tables are correct and the selected column names are correct, click the OK button.

You should then see the Foreign Key Relationship dialog box shown in Figure 8-10.

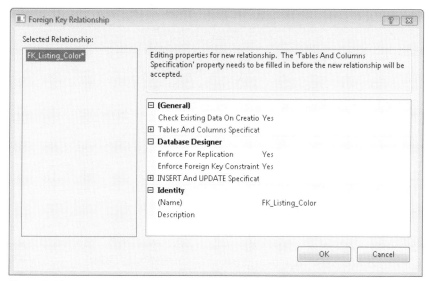

Figure 8-10
Foreign Key Relationship dialog box for the relationship between the Listing and Color tables

9. Although you can change some properties within this dialog box, just click OK for now. See Figure 8-11 to view the diagram with the new relationship created.

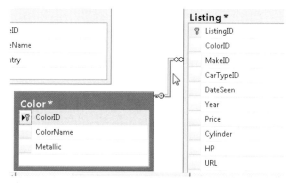

Figure 8-11
Modified diagram showing the new FK relationship between the Listing and Color tables

MORE INFO

To reinforce the concept of establishing relationships between tables, I'll now give you another way of looking at the relationship in this exercise. There are two reasons why the ColorID column is in the Listing table as an FK. First, it is used for a normalization and design principle because you don't want to have duplicate data. Second, it is used for data integrity reasons and, more specifically, for the orphaned rows problem. Let's look at it with some sample data. Suppose there is a Color row called Dark Blue, and the Listing table contains six different ad definitions that are Dark Blue. If you remove the Dark Blue color from the Color table, it would mean that those six ads would have orphaned data. That is why you created a foreign key relationship: to make sure that if an application or a user tries to remove data in the Color table, a process within SQL Server 2005 will prevent this by validating that no "kids" are left behind in the Listing table before allowing the deletion to occur in the Color table.

In Figure 8-11, note the infinity symbol located close to the Listing table and the yellow key located close to the Color table. The infinity symbol on the Listing table indicates the table's cardinality. It indicates that, in this relationship, the Listing table can contain any number of rows with information coming from the matching primary key table. The yellow key indicates from which table the primary key is being taken.

I rearranged the diagram so that the two tables are close together. You can rearrange your tables any way you want by dragging them by the title bar (that is, where the table name is displayed). This is sometimes necessary when you create relationships so that you do not end up with an unusual-looking diagram. I suggest you put your Listing table in the middle of your other tables because it will be easier to create relationships this way. You can also rearrange the tables on your diagram at any time by right-clicking anywhere except on a table on the diagram's designer surface and selecting Arrange Tables. You can also have the labels for every relationship appear on the diagram by right-clicking the diagram's designer surface and selecting Show Relationship Labels.

10. Now create the other FK relationships by using either Figure 8-2 or Table 8-4.

Column	Primary Key Table	Foreign Key Table
MakeID	Make	Listing
CarTypeID	CarType	Listing

Table 8-4
Foreign Key Relationships to Create

MORE INFO
You can review the properties of any relationship by double-clicking the line or by right-clicking and selecting Properties.

When finished, the content of your diagram should resemble the content shown in Figure 8-12. Make sure your relationships are arranged properly by looking at where the infinity symbols and yellow keys are located and by looking at Table 8-4 for verification.

11. Click the Save All button or press Ctrl+Shift+S to commit the changes to the database. Click Yes when asked whether you want to save.

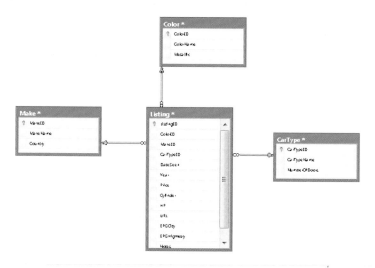

Figure 8-12
Completed CarTracker database diagram

Entering Data in SQL Server Tables Using Visual Studio

Now that you have created all your tables and relationships, you'll start inserting data in your tables and verifying that your constraints ensure the data integrity of your database.

Let's start by adding data in all the tables. You'll first add rows to the Color table.

TO ENTER DATA IN SQL SERVER TABLES USING VISUAL STUDIO

1. To start entering rows in the Color table, right-click the Color table in Database Explorer, and select Show Table Data. Your designer surface should have a grid like the one shown in Figure 8-13.

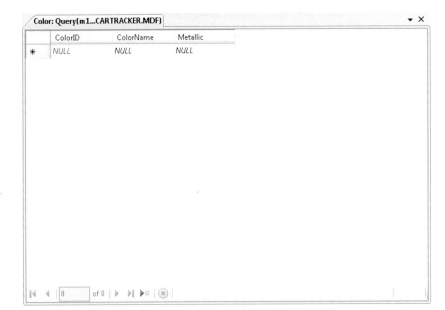
Figure 8-13
Empty Color table in the table data grid

2. Let's add the first color. Click the Color Name field, type **Dark Blue**, and then press the Tab key to go to the next column. Type **true** in the Metallic field. Because that column type is a bit, its values can be either true or false only because a bit type is a binary type. When you're done, press the Tab key to go to the next row.

3. Add three more car colors—Red, Silver, and Black—and set Red as Metallic and the other two colors as nonmetallic (that is, false). When done, the table should look like the one shown in Figure 8-14.

Color: Query(m1...CARTRACKER.MDF)

	ColorID	ColorName	Metallic
	1	Dark Blue	True
	2	Red	True
	3	Silver	False
	4	Black	False
▶*	NULL	NULL	NULL

Figure 8-14
Color table with four new rows of data

4. Add the data in Table 8-5 and Table 8-6 to the Make and CarType tables, respectively.

MakeName	Country
GoodRoadster	Germany
SmallCar	France
BigSUV	USA
ReliableCar	Japan

Table 8-5
Data for the Make Table

CarTypeName	NumberOfDoors
Roadster	2
SUV	5
Hatchback	5
Sedan	4
Coupe	2

Table 8-6
Data for the CarType Table

Don't Add Data to Identity Columns

For all columns you created as identity columns, don't type the data because the field's value will automatically be generated by SQL Server 2005 Express Edition whenever the row is created in the table. If you try to type data in an identity column, you will not be allowed to do so. When the cursor is in an identity column, you'll see near the navigation bar at the bottom of the Table Designer that the cell is read-only.

You might not have realized that by giving a type to your data, you actually added data integrity verification to your database. Try modifying one of the Color rows by changing the Metallic column to read *Helloworld* instead of *true* or *false*. You'll get an error message telling you that the Metallic field is of type Boolean.

To show how data integrity is preserved using the foreign key constraints, you'll add two Listing rows. You will enter more rows when using your Windows Forms application.

5. Right-click the Listing table, select Show Table Data, and add the two rows shown in Table 8-7.

ColorID	MakeID	CarTypeID	DateSeen	Year	Price	Cylinder	HP	URL	EPGCity	EPGHighway	Notes
1	1	1	08/11/2008	2005	42500	6	240	http://www.litwareinc.com/	20	28	This is my dream car, follow regularly.
4	3	2	07/30/2008	2003	39775	8	340	http://www.cpandl.com/	10	15	Too much gas

Table 8-7
Data for the Listing Table

MORE INFO

You can navigate through the table by using the navigation controls at the bottom of the grid. You can use these controls to perform tasks such as moving to the first and last rows, moving to the previous and next entries, moving to a new record, or moving directly to a specific row by entering the row number.

6. You'll now verify that one of your foreign key constraints is working correctly. Open the Make table by right-clicking the Make table and selecting Show Table Data.

7. Let's try to delete the first row by clicking the leftmost field where the pencil usually appears. The row should be selected, and all the fields should be blue. Right-click, and select Delete.

8. A dialog box should appear inquiring whether you really want to delete the row. Click Yes.

9. You should receive the following dialog box error message stating that the row was not deleted because of the foreign key constraint: "Error Message: The DELETE statement conflicted with the REFERENCE constraint 'FK_Listing_Make.'" This statement affirms why the foreign key constraint was created, which was to avoid orphaned rows. Figure 8-15 depicts what the error dialog box looks like and what kind of information is provided to help you debug the problem, if necessary. In this case, it's not a problem but a feature of your creation!

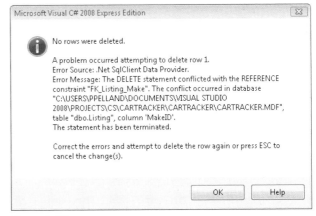

Figure 8-15
Error dialog box showing the foreign key relationship preventing the deletion of a row from the Make table

10. Click OK to exit this dialog box.

11. Test your other constraints related to the Listing table by trying to delete the first row of the CarType table. You should receive the same error message.

Now that you have all your domain tables loaded with some data, you'll learn to use the database in a Windows Forms application. You'll learn about ADO.NET and about data bindings with Windows Forms controls.

What Are ADO.NET, Data Binding, and LINQ?

You rarely enter all data manually using Visual Studio. You typically let the user do it, or you do it through an application. You can also either import data from another source or create the new data using SQL scripts, but those are more advanced concepts that will not be covered in this book.

This section will focus on how to build Windows applications that can connect to and receive data from a SQL Server 2005 Express Edition database using ADO.NET and LINQ to Datasets. The following is a formal, official definition of ADO.NET from the MSDN online library:

ADO.NET provides consistent access to data sources, such as Microsoft SQL Server, as well as data sources exposed through OLE DB and XML. Data-sharing consumer applications can use ADO.NET to connect to these data sources and retrieve, manipulate, and update data.

ADO.NET cleanly factors data access from data manipulation into discrete components that can be used separately or in tandem. ADO.NET includes .NET Framework data providers for connecting to a database, executing commands, and retrieving results. Those results are either processed directly or placed in an ADO.NET DataSet object in order to be exposed to the user in an ad-hoc manner, combined with data from multiple sources, or remoted between tiers. The ADO.NET DataSet object can also be used independently of a .NET Framework data provider to manage data local to the application or sourced from XML.

SQL and T-SQL Documentation

If you want more information about SQL and T-SQL, you can read the SQL Server 2005 Express Edition documentation at http://msdn2.microsoft.com/en-us/library/ms165706.aspx. The SQL Server 2005 Express Edition documentation is designed to help you answer most questions you might have, but it might also refer you to the SQL Server 2005 documentation, which is at http://msdn2.microsoft.com/en-us/sqlserver/bb428874.aspx.

The ADO.NET classes are found in System.Data.dll and are integrated with the XML classes found in System.Xml.dll. When compiling code that uses the System.Data namespace, reference both System.Data.dll and System.Xml.dll.

I've presented the long and formal definition of ADO.NET because it contains elements you'll learn about while working with the CarTracker application. I also chose it because I want you to refer to it whenever you're working with ADO.NET. Here is a less formal definition that I think summarizes what ADO.NET is all about: ADO.NET is the .NET Framework way of accessing and programmatically manipulating databases. With ADO.NET you can also manipulate other sources of data such as XML.

With ADO.NET 2.0 came new ways of accessing data from different sources. In Visual C# 2008 Express Edition, you are limited to the following data sources: databases (SQL Server Express and Microsoft Access databases), Web services, and custom objects. It is much easier (that is, there is less code) to manipulate data in ADO.NET 2.0, especially when using all the tools included in Visual Studio 2008. Many new wizards and other tools make the experience of working with databases a pleasant one. Visual Studio 2008 covers numerous common scenarios with its tools and wizards, but it's also very powerful when used programmatically without using the visual tools. You will learn the basics in this book, but nothing is preventing you from learning more about data binding and ADO.NET and from unleashing powerful applications.

With LINQ you can create queries within your Visual C# code and query and update all kinds of data (arrays, lists, XML, Web services, SQL databases) easily. Here's a formal definition of LINQ, and then let's jump into the code:

Language-Integrated Query (LINQ) adds query capabilities to Visual C# and provides simple and powerful capabilities when you work with all kinds of data. Rather than sending a query to a database to be processed, or working with different query syntax for each type of data that you are searching, LINQ introduces queries as part of the Visual C# language. It uses a unified syntax regardless of the type of data.

LINQ enables you to query data from a SQL Server database, XML, in-memory arrays and collections, ADO.NET datasets, or any other remote or local data source that supports LINQ. You can do all this with common Visual C# language elements. Because your queries are written in the Visual C# language, your query results are returned as strongly typed objects. These objects support IntelliSense, which enables you to write code faster and catch errors in your queries at compile time instead of at run time. LINQ queries can be used as the source of additional queries to refine results. They can also be bound to controls so that users can easily view and modify your query results.

We'll return to the topic of LINQ later in the implementation of the CarTracker application, but before proceeding any further, let's talk more about CarTracker. The main goal of the application is to track car ads over the Internet. Because you now have your database ready to go, you need to consider what will be included in this application. What you need is simply a way of displaying the ads, adding new ads, modifying and deleting existing ads, and searching through the ads using a series of drop-down boxes that help you narrow your search based on certain criteria. These search criteria will come directly from the tables (in other words, separate drop-down controls for the car type, color, make, and so forth).

When using drop-down controls or any other controls with data that you know exists in your database, you don't want to populate the data by hand. You want to use the data-binding capabilities of a control. *Data binding* is an easy and transparent way to read and write data and link a control on a Windows form to a data source in your application.

NOTE
Not all Windows Forms controls are "data-binding-aware." When they are aware, they have a *DataBindings* property.

ADO.NET takes care of a great deal of activity behind the scenes (it's even better in .NET Framework 3.5), as well as managing the connection to the database. Managing the connection doesn't stop at opening and closing the connection; it also concerns itself with finding the database with which you're trying to connect. When a connection is opened, it means your application can talk to the database through ADO.NET method calls. ADO.NET manages all exchanges (send/receive) of data between your application and the database for you. ADO.NET also manages the data through diverse mechanisms: read-only forward navigation, navigation in any direction with read-write, field evaluation, and so forth. And the beauty of it is that you usually don't have to write a lot of code to enjoy those nice features.

Developing the CarTracker Application

You'll now start developing the CarTracker application. First you need to create a dataset that will provide you with all the data binding you need for the CarTracker application. Now that your tables are established, you can configure the dataset with all the elements you've just added to your database.

Before creating a dataset, though, you must learn what a dataset is. A *dataset* is an in-memory representation of one or more tables and is used to store the rows you retrieve that match the query you sent to the database. You can then add, delete, or update rows in memory. When the user is done, you can submit, save, or commit the changes to the database. In a few steps, you'll see the CarTrackerDataSet.xsd file, which is called an *XML schema definition* file. The .xsd file ensures that the data will be structured and respect the schema. You'll use this file later in the project when I discuss data binding.

To create a dataset, you'll learn to use the Data Sources window. This window gives you access to all the data sources you have configured in your application. Figure 8-16 shows where the Data Sources window is located. If you don't see the Data Sources window, you can access it by clicking the Data menu and clicking Show Data Sources. If Show Data Sources does not appear on the Data menu, be sure you have closed all the CarTracker table data grids and Form1 is visible.

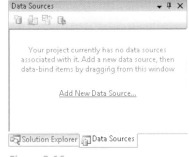

Figure 8-16
The Data Sources window

NOTE

The Data Sources window might end up somewhere else in your IDE. Because your IDE is entirely customizable to your liking, you can have your windows and tabs appear wherever you think they are most productive for you.

TO CREATE A DATASET

1. In the Data Sources window, click the Add New Data Source link, or click the Add New Data Source button in the toolbar. The Data Source Configuration Wizard appears.

    On the next page, you will choose your data connection. You should see the CarTracker connection string prepopulating the connection field. The reason is simple: When you created the CarTracker SQL Server Express database in your project, a data connection was created for you. The connection string was added to your application as an application setting, so if you right-click your project name and select Properties and then the Settings tab, you will see the connection string entry. You can also click the plus sign (+) at the bottom of the dialog box to see what the connection string looks like. This connection string defines how your application will connect to the database. Having the connection string in your application configuration file is actually a best practice. It gives you the advantage of only modifying the file and restarting the application without recompilation so as to automatically pick up the changes in your connection string and connect to that new location.

    The application configuration is stored in an XML file named using the application's executable name and adding .config at the end of the executable filename. In our application, the file is named CarTracker.exe.config, although you see only app.config while working in Visual Studio.

2. Click Next on the Choose Your Data Connection page.

   The next page in the wizard inquires whether you want to save this connection string in the application configuration file. As you saw on the previous page, you know where your database is stored. Yet you might change your mind and deploy the file somewhere else. If you do that, you don't want to modify the source code and recompile it. As I mentioned previously, putting the connection string in your application configuration file is a best practice. It gives you the advantage of only modifying the file and restarting the application without recompilation.

   If you want to save the connection string, you are also asked to provide a variable name under which it will be saved in the file.

3. Make sure the Yes, Save The Connection As check box is selected, and then click Next.

4. On the next page, you'll select all the tables from the database that will be in your dataset and name your dataset. In this case, you will need all the tables, so expand the Tables node, and select all the tables. Leave the dataset name set to CarTrackerDataSet, and then click Finish.

   The result of your dataset configuration is an XSD file, and it defines the internal structure of your dataset. Remember that a dataset is an in-memory representation of one or more tables from your database. ADO.NET uses this schema file when working with your application. When running the application, the user will be able to add, delete, or modify rows in the dataset (in the computer's memory). The changes will remain in memory until the user commits the changes to the database, which in our example is the CarTracker.mdf file.

5. In Solution Explorer, double-click the .xsd file named CarTrackerDataSet.xsd. As shown in Figure 8-17, the result of the dataset creation is similar to the database diagram you created earlier. Your diagram might be different depending on your screen resolution and how you customized your IDE.

   There are some notable differences, however. You'll see the same columns you have created in your physical database, but

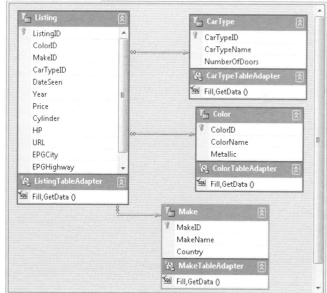

Figure 8-17
Graphical representation of the CarTracker dataset

Figure 8-18
View of the Color and Listing dataset tables in the Data Sources window

at the bottom of each table you will see some methods: *Fill* and *GetData()*. These methods are particular to the dataset, and the ADO.NET-generated code by Visual Studio will use them to bind data to your Windows Forms controls—controls that do not exist yet!

6. Return to the Data Sources window, and expand the dataset tables. You'll see the in-memory representation of your tables, and you'll also see that each column has a small icon that gives you its type. (These icons should look familiar to you because they are similar to the controls in the Toolbox.) Refer to Figure 8-18 for a quick glance at the Color and Listing dataset tables and their column types.

7. Close the graphical representation of your dataset by clicking the X in the corner of the designer surface. Depending on your screen resolution, you might have moved the boxes around; if that's the case, when you try to close this window, you'll be asked to save it. You can click Yes if you want to preserve where on the design surface the data tables are located. This is only design-time information that will be saved, though, because you didn't change anything else.

8. In Solution Explorer, double-click your Form1.cs file to open the designer surface for Form1.

9. In the Data Sources window, select the Listing node in your dataset, and click the drop-down arrow that's next to the word *Listing*. You will see with two choices: DataGridView and Details. DataGridView brings all the dataset fields into a table or grid format with multiple rows, while Details brings the dataset fields in one row at a time with all fields as individual controls. For our example, select Details.

   You'll also see that each member of the dataset has the same drop-down arrow, which means you can change which controls will be dropped onto the form when it is dragged. Choosing controls prior to dragging the dataset table onto the form prevents you from having to lay out the UI piece by piece.

10. Change ColorID, MakeID, and CarTypeID to the ComboBox type by clicking the drop-down arrow next to each column and selecting ComboBox.

11. Select the Listing node by clicking it, and then drag it near the top-left corner of the designer surface on Form1.

12. You'll now modify the form size like you did in previous chapters by modifying the form's *Size* property. Change the form size so that its width is 450 pixels and its height is 550 pixels.

13. Move all the controls so that the first label is almost in the top-left corner just beneath the tool strip. See Figure 8-19 to determine how the controls should approximately be placed.

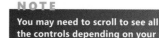
NOTE
You may need to scroll to see all the controls depending on your screen resolution.

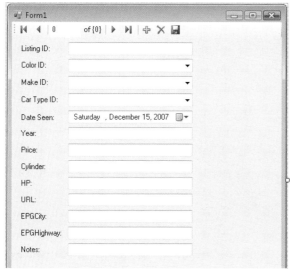

Figure 8-19
Resized CarTracker form after moving all the controls

As you can see, many things have just happened. Let's start by looking at the designer surface. All the fields from the dataset have been added as controls, and labels were also added based on the name of the field in the dataset. This feature is called Smart Captions. Visual Studio uses Pascal or camel casing as a mechanism to insert a space in labels when using smart captions. When you drop the dataset fields onto the form, the Smart Captions feature looks at each field's casing. When it finds an uppercase letter or an underscore (_) character following a lowercase letter, it inserts or replaces the underscore with a space. You can see an exception to this rule in the EPGCity and EPGHighway fields. When you use uppercase letters for an acronym, Visual Studio cannot distinguish that these are two words and therefore doesn't split them apart. You'll have to split these two fields manually.

Know Your Files

When working with local database files, understand that they are treated like any other content file. For desktop projects, this means that by default the database file will be copied to the output folder (that is, the bin folder) each time the project is built. After pressing F5, here's what your file structure will look like on disk:

CarTracker\CarTracker.mdf
CarTracker\Form1.cs
CarTracker\Bin\Debug\CarTracker.mdf
CarTracker\Bin\Debug\CarTracker.exe

At design time, the data tools and wizards use CarTracker\CarTracker.mdf. At run time, the application uses the database under the bin\debug folder. As a result of the copy operation, many people assume the application did not save the data to the database file because two copies of the data file are involved. This also happens when looking at schema/data through Database Explorer. The tools are using the copy in the project folder and not the file in the bin\debug folder.

The following are a few ways to work around this copy behavior.

First, if you select your database file in Solution Explorer, you will see a property called Copy to Output Directory *in the Properties window. By default, it is set to* Copy Always, *which means data files in the project folder will be copied to the bin\debug folder on each build, thus overwriting the existing data files, if any. You can set this property to* Do Not Copy *and then manually place a copy of the data file in the bin\debug folder. In this way, on subsequent builds, the project system leaves the database file in the bin\debug folder and doesn't try to overwrite it with the one from the project. The downside to this method is that you still have two copies. Therefore, after you modify the database file using the application, if you want to make those same changes within the project, you need to copy the changes to the project manually, and vice versa.*

Alternatively, you can leave the data file outside the project and create a connection to it in Database Explorer. When the IDE asks you to bring the file into the project, simply click No. This way, both the design time and the run time will be using the same data file. The downside to this method is that the path in the connection string will be hard-coded, and it will therefore be harder to share the project and deploy the application. Before deploying the application, make sure to replace the full path in the settings with a relative path. If you want to read more about the relative path versus the full path (plus a bit more about this copy behavior), read the article at http://blogs.msdn.com/smartclientdata/archive/2005/08/26/456886.aspx. You'll see that I took portions of that article and modified them so that they fit our application.

You will also notice that a tool strip has been added that contains almost the same buttons you used while working with the database table designer.

14. Read the "Know Your Files" sidebar on the previous page. With this copy behavior in mind, I suggest you use the first approach even though you'll have to perform some manual steps. If you want to debug your application from within Visual Studio, it's preferable to use this solution, or you will not be able to see the changes applied to your database file. The database file will always return to the initial one from your project, which is similar to resetting the whole database to what it is in Visual Studio.

15. Select the CarTracker.mdf database file in Solution Explorer, and change the *Copy to Output Directory* property to *Do Not Copy* in the Properties window.

16. Press F5 to build and run your application. You'll get an exception message because the file won't be copied in the bin\debug directory. Also, on the *Form_Load* event when your code tries to fill the dataset, it won't find the database at the place specified by the connection string. Therefore, you get an SQLException stating that it's not able to attach to the database. Click the Stop Debugging button or press Shift+F5 to stop debugging.

17. Using Windows Explorer, go into your project directory (it should be located at Documents\Visual Studio 2008\Projects\CarTracker\CarTracker\), and copy the .mdf and .ldf files into the bin\debug directory under CarTracker. If you're not able to copy the files because Visual Studio still has them open, save all your files, and then close the project. Then copy the two files mentioned earlier, and re-open your project.

18. Now press F5 to build and run your application again.

You should see the two records you've manually inserted into the Listing table. You should be able to navigate using the tool strip and also modify, insert, and delete a record. Figure 8-20 shows a snapshot of your CarTracker application at run time.

19. Change the URL of the row at position 1 to end with .net instead .com.

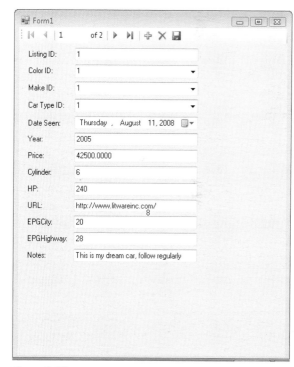

Figure 8-20
Execution of the CarTracker application

MORE INFO

If you want the same data in Visual Studio as you have when executing the application in debug mode, you must close your project completely. Using Windows Explorer, copy the .mdf and .ldf files from the bin\debug folder to the project folder. When you reopen your project, the database will now contain the same content.

Suppose you then want to modify the structure of your database, such as adding a column to a table. If you don't want to lose the data within the bin\debug database files, you must copy them to the project folder before you modify the table structure. When done with the modifications, you simply copy both the .mdf and .ldf files back to the bin\debug folder. Of course, if your application needs those new database changes, you will also have to modify the dataset, but that process is beyond the scope of this book.

20. After changing the URL for the record, click the disk icon to commit the changes to the database.

21. Close the CarTracker application, and restart it by pressing F5. You should now see the first row with the modified URL ending in .net. Close the application again.

22. To verify that you are working with design-time and run-time versions of the CarTracker database, open the Listing table, and select Show Table Data in Database Explorer. The first row should still contain an URL column ending in .com and not in .net.

Point proven! The database file in Visual Studio is now decoupled from the one your application is using at run time. Read the More Info note in the left margin to learn how to make the data the same in both the design-time and run-time versions.

Using the Component Tray

When you dragged the Listing dataset table to the designer surface, you probably saw that five items were added in the gray area below the designer surface. This section of the designer surface is called the *component tray* and is the section Visual Studio uses for nonvisual controls. In this case, it added an instance of the CarTracker dataset, a Listing table adapter, a Listing binding source, a table adapter manager, and finally a Listing binding navigator.

I'll describe several of these individually:

■ **Binding source**   You can think of a binding source as a "broker" or a layer of indirection. You can also think of it as an intermediary between a data-bound control on your form and a data source, such as a dataset. A binding source provides currency management and notification services (events). The binding source has many methods to facilitate, such as sorting, filtering, navigating, and editing of data from its data-bound controls to the data source. It's also linked tightly to the next component: the binding navigator. When you see a binding navigator, you're assured of getting a binding source.

- **Binding navigator**   The binding navigator is a means to add navigation and data manipulation. It has a UI component or, more specifically, a tool strip with buttons to facilitate the functionality provided by the binding source.

- **Typed dataset**   Although you know what a dataset is, you might not know that it's a strongly typed object. It contains data tables of the DataTable type that constitute the in-memory representation of your database tables. These data tables also have a special data adapter called the *table adapter*. There is a table adapter for each data table.

- **Table adapter**   A table adapter is a data access object. It connects to the database (for example, SQL Server 2005 Express Edition), executes the queries, and fills a data table with data when it returns from SQL Server. Therefore, it's the central point for all data access on an individual table. There is one table adapter per table in your data source. A table adapter can have more than one SELECT query.

- **Table adapter manager**   The *TableAdapterManager* class has been added in .NET 3.5 to help you to maintain referential integrity to your typed datasets. It adds logic to maintain it and lets you specify in which order the CRUD (create, read, update, delete) transactions are happening. For instance, you can say that the update order is insert-update-delete or update-insert-delete. It also helps you to have a single point of update, so instead of calling the update method on each table adapter, you just have to call the *TableAdapaterManager.UpdateAll* method to save the changes to the database.

Getting More Meaningful Information on the Form

Let's return to our CarTracker project. As you can see when you run the application, the ColorID, MakeID, and CarTypeID combo boxes are there, but they are displaying the ID and not the name associated with the ID. This is not helpful for the user because an ID doesn't have any meaning to users, and they might not be able to easily add or modify rows without having a human-readable format for those columns. Consequently, you need to make sure the data is displayed in a humanly readable way and that the ID is stored in the row whenever the user modifies the information.

There's an easy way to accomplish this, which you will do now for your three combo boxes.

TO DATA BIND WITH DOMAIN TABLES

1. In the Data Sources window, select the Color table from the dataset, and drag it to the form's designer surface over the ColorID combo box.

   Figure 8-21
   ColorID combo box Smart Tag information showing data binding mode

   You'll see that another table adapter (ColorTableAdapter) and another binding source (ColorBindingSource) were added to the component tray. If you go to the ColorID combo box and click the Smart Tag triangle, you'll see the Data Binding Mode information box appear, as shown in Figure 8-21. You'll notice that your drag-and-drop action bound the combo box control with the ColorBindingSource. Because of this action, whenever the combo box is displayed, it shows the color names instead of ColorID. When the user picks a color from the combo box, the associated value member that will be used in the row will still be the ColorID, specifically the ColorID associated with the ColorName. Wonderful, isn't it? And we didn't use any lines of code.

2. Repeat the same process for the Make and CarType dataset tables and the corresponding MakeID and CarTypeID combo boxes.

3. Build and run your application, and then look at each combo box. You now have real color names and not merely ColorIDs; the same is true for CarType and Make. The combo boxes are also populated with all the values coming from those tables and not simply the value for that specific row. Click the drop-down arrow, and you'll see all other potential values. Close the application.

4. Rename the labels to remove the *ID* part from the ColorID, MakeID, and CarTypeID labels.

5. You will now enlarge the Notes field by making it a multiline text box. Select the Notes text box, and change the *Multiline* property to *true*. Also change the *MaxLength* property to *250*, the *Size:Height* property to *50*, and the *Size:Width* property to *250*.

6. Delete the ListingID text box and its label.

7. Size and reposition the controls on the form so that the form resembles the one shown in Figure 8-22; it does not need to be an exact duplicate. It will be good practice to bring back UI design concepts from Chapter 5, "Using Rapid Application Development Tools

with Visual C# 2008," and also good preparation for Chapter 9, "Building Your Own Weather Tracker Application." Change the *Text* property of the form to *Car Tracker*.

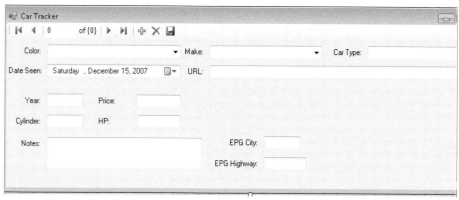

Figure 8-22
New visual aspects of the CarTracker application

8. In Solution Explorer, rename form1.cs to Main.cs. When asked whether you want to rename all references in this project, click Yes.

9. Select the form, and change the *BackColor* property to *GradientActiveCaption*.

10. Now add a tool strip container to the form like you did in Chapter 6, "Modifying Your Web Browser." Set the *Dock* property to fill the form. In the Smart Tag menu, select Re-Parent Controls to place all your tool strips on the top panel and all your other controls in your content panel. If necessary, use the Document Outline window to view and adjust the hierarchy of objects on the form.

Everything is nearly complete for this application, but the research capabilities are lacking. Currently, the only way to search is to scan through all the rows until you find the correct one. This is not difficult now because you have only two rows in your CarTracker database. Yet, if you had 500 rows, the Scan method would not be effective at all! Therefore, you'll implement search capabilities by adding queries to your application by using the Dataset Designer. That's where we will introduce the LINQ to Datasets capabilities. You will implement one search capability with plain ADO.NET and two with LINQ to Datasets. After that, you will add a bit more functionality to your application using LINQ.

TO ADD QUERIES TO YOUR APPLICATION

1. Let's start by adding the search capability to our application by using ADO.NET. In the Data Sources window, select CarTrackerDataSet. Right-click, and select Edit DataSet with Designer.

2. Select the Listing data table, and then select the ListingTableAdapter section at the bottom of the data table.

   When you look at the Properties window, you'll see that four types of queries were automatically generated by Visual Studio: SelectCommand, InsertCommand, DeleteCommand, and UpdateCommand. They are the queries that help you have a fully workable application without writing a single line of code. When you read about table adapters earlier, you learned that you can have multiple queries with a table adapter because it is the central point of data access. You will thus add search capabilities to your application by adding queries to the table adapters and by using elements from the UI as parameters to your queries. You will first add the ability to search for listings that have a certain color.

3. Right-click the ListingTableAdapter section, and select Add Query..., as shown in Figure 8-23.

   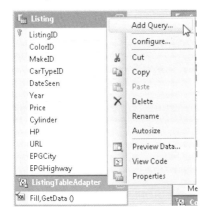

   Figure 8-23
   Adding new queries to a table adapter

   This brings you to the TableAdapter Query Configuration Wizard. This wizard will help you add another SELECT query that will use parameters to refine your search. You can also create a SELECT query and turn it into a stored procedure or use an existing stored procedure. As its name implies, a *stored procedure* is one that is stored in SQL Server and contains SQL statements, along with other programming constructs, that use T-SQL.

   A new feature in SQL Server 2005 Express Edition is that stored procedures can also be coded in managed languages, such as C# and Visual C#. Stored procedures are executed on the server. This approach is usually considered safer because no SQL code is included in your application and everything executes on a separate machine, usually in a different physical location. It used to be a bit more performant, but with the newest ADO.NET, the performance argument is not as big as the safety argument. Since you're using SQL Server 2005 Express Edition, this will be of no concern because SQL Server and the application are executed on the same machine.

4. Select Use SQL Statements, and click Next. When asked which type of SQL query you want to use, choose SELECT Which Return Rows, and then click Next. Note that you could have added any SQL query type you wanted.

5. You are now presented with an edit window in which to add the SQL statement that will perform a search for all the listings containing a particular color. Refer to Figure 8-24 to see the SQL command edit window. Click the Query Builder... button to get a visual view of the query.

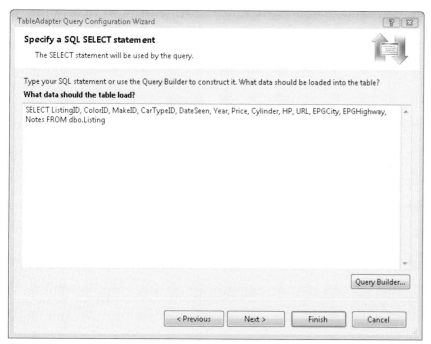

Figure 8-24
SQL command edit window ready to customize the user's search

6. You will now add the Color table to the diagram so that you'll be able to base your search on a particular color. To add the Color table, simply right-click in the diagram area, and select Add Table…. The Add Table dialog box appears, as shown in Figure 8-25. Select the Color table, and click the Add button. When the Color table has been added to the diagram, click the Close button.

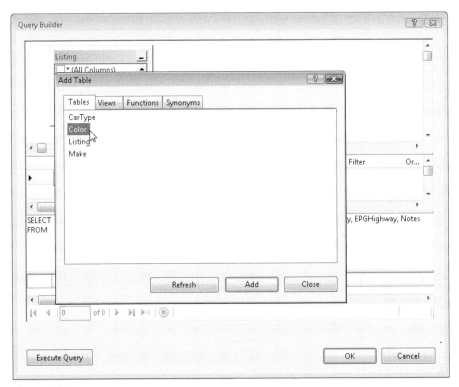

Figure 8-25
The Add Table dialog box

Microsoft Visual C# 2008 Express Edition: Build a Program Now!

7. In the SQL code pane of Query Builder, append the following SQL code that will help in the filtering process:

```
WHERE    (Color.ColorName LIKE '%' + @colorname + '%')
```

MORE INFO

The % symbol is the wildcard character in SQL, and it can mean anything. For example, in the previous WHERE clause, it means return something that has a color similar to the *ColorName* parameter.

8. Before you proceed with your new query, make sure it will give you the results you're expecting. Click the Execute Query button to display the Query Parameters dialog box, as shown in Figure 8-26.

9. Try replacing the word *NULL* with *blue*, and then click OK. The Results pane of Query Builder should display only one row. Using the word *black* should return the black car row. Simply enter **b**, and you should get both the blue and the black rows. Once you're satisfied with your query, click OK in Query Builder.

10. On the Specify a SQL SELECT Statement page of the wizard, click Next. It's time to add your query to the application.

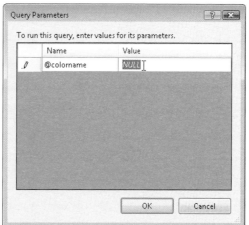

Figure 8-26
Query Parameters dialog box with prompt to enter a color name value

11. A page appears that prompts you to name the methods that your query will generate. After you create the query, those methods will be available from the Listing table adapter. Refer to Figure 8-27 to view this screen, which contains the two new method names. For both names you basically need to add what your filter is. In your case, you can add ColorName since you filtered by that name in your WHERE clause. When done, click Next.

12. After processing for a few seconds, your computer should come back with a results page informing you that your SELECT statement and your new *Fill* and *Get* methods are ready to use. Click the Finish button.

Look at the table adapter section of the Listing data table. Your new methods will be added there.

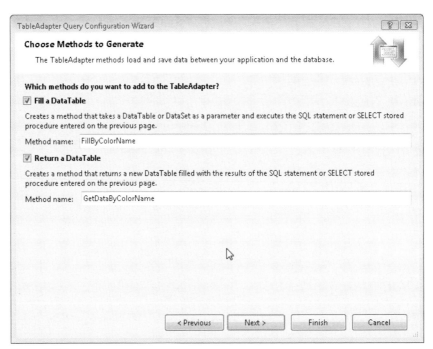

Figure 8-27
Use this page of the Query Configuration Wizard to rename the methods used to increase search capabilities.

13. Open Main.cs in Design view. Go to the component tray, click the ListingTableAdapter Smart Tag, and select Add Query.... You'll see a Search Criteria Builder dialog box that will prompt you to create a new query or pick an existing one. Since you just built a new set of methods, you merely need to select one. Select the Existing Query Name option, and then select FillByColorName, as shown in Figure 8-28.

14. Click the OK button. You'll see that a tool strip has been placed at the top of the form with a search button that will call your method when you click it, thereby giving you a way of searching by certain criteria. This was accomplished by typing only the WHERE clauses for your specific queries.

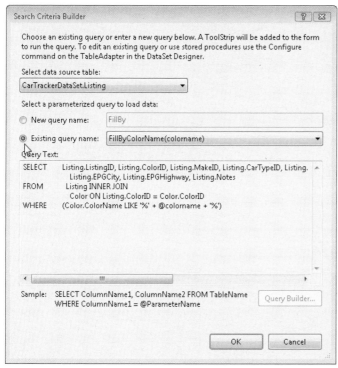

Figure 8-28
Search Criteria Builder with the FillByColorName method selected

15. When you're done moving controls, extend the top panel by clicking the grip and pulling it down so that it becomes two tool strips wide.

16. Make sure your application looks like the one shown in Figure 8-29. Press F5 to see the results of your work. Type **blue** in the ColorName tool strip, and click FillByColorName to see whether it returns blue color car listings.

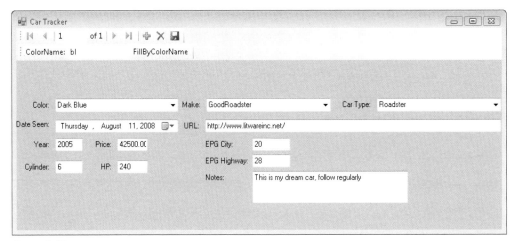

Figure 8-29
CarTracker application screen with the filter by color name

17. You will now add the two other buttons to the tool strip to narrow down the number of rows: one for the car type and one for the make. Add two tool strip labels, two tool strip text boxes, and two tool strip buttons. You can find the magnifier image in the Chapter6 folder of the companion content. Set the *Image* property to the file by browsing to the Images folder in Chapter6. Figure 8-30 shows what you should have when you're done. Make sure to name your variables appropriately because you'll need them in the event handlers in a minute.

Figure 8-30
Tool strip after you're done adding Filter By Make and Filter By CarType

Using LINQ

How you use LINQ depends on the type of data you are playing with. When used with strongly typed datasets (the ones we have), LINQ queries in code almost look like SQL. Let's look at the structure of a query using LINQ. MSDN states that a LINQ query, often referred to as a *query expression*, consists of a combination of query clauses identifying the data sources and iteration variables for the query. A query expression can also include instructions for sorting, filtering, grouping, and joining or can include calculations to apply to the source data. Query expression syntax resembles the syntax of SQL; therefore, you might find much of the syntax familiar. The following query gives us the customer names for all customers who are in the United States:

```
var queryResults = from cust in customers _
                where cust.Country = "USA"
                select cust.CompanyName, cust.Country;
```

TO ADD A LINQ QUERY

1. Double-click the tool strip button for the Make filter, and insert the following code:

```
var filterByMake = from Listing in this.carTrackerDataSet.Listing
                join Make in this.carTrackerDataSet.Make
                on Listing.MakeID equals Make.MakeID
                where (Make.MakeName.ToLower().Contains(tstbFilterByMake.
Text.ToLower()))
                select Listing;
this.listingBindingSource.DataSource = filterByMake;
```

This step is essentially the same as you performed for the color filtering, except you didn't add a query to the dataset; instead, you used LINQ to filter the results on the screen. In reality, the dataset in memory still contains all the data, but you are displaying only the rows that match one of your filters. That's nice!

I'll now explain what is happening. The LINQ query you just wrote is joining two tables in your CarTracker dataset on the MakeID column and is also using the value in the tool strip text box for comparison. Note that the use of Like is really similar to how you used LIKE for the color filter, except that the syntax is slightly different for the wildcard. Finally, you can assign the result of your query (in other words, *filteredByMake*) to the

DataSource property of your binding source because it is a collection of Listing rows. Therefore you can simply assign it to the data source in the same way you would do it without LINQ.

2. Now let's do the same for CarType by adding the following code to the *click* event of the tool strip button for the Filter By CarType text box:

```
var filterByCarType = from Listing in this.carTrackerDataSet.Listing
                      join CarType in this.carTrackerDataSet.CarType
                      on Listing.CarTypeID equals CarType.CarTypeID
                      where (CarType.CarTypeName.ToLower().
Contains(tstbFilterByCarType.Text.ToLower()))
                      select Listing;
this.listingBindingSource.DataSource = filterByCarType;
```

Figure 8-31 shows what you should have at the end of this chapter.

Figure 8-31
CarTracker application with all the filters

Test the application by adding new rows of data that have similar Make and CarType values and colors so you can validate that your application works well. Note that you could have created the same application by using LINQ to SQL. This book won't go into the details of the implementation for LINQ to SQL, but if you want to learn more about it, please take a look at the free video series at this web site: *http://www.myvbprof.com/2007_Version/LINQ_ to_SQL.aspx*. You'll see that there are many similarities to what we have done in this chapter; even though it is in Visual Basic, it will give you a great idea on what LINQ to SQL is. You'll find another use of LINQ called LINQ to XML. Just note that with LINQ you can use the query structure on many different collections of data. For example, you could do a LINQ query on strings in a dictionary and then iterate through the result with a *for each*. LINQ is a wonderful and powerful new technology that will save you time and lines of code and that will improve the readability of your code.

CarTracker is a simple application that you can probably modify to handle more information, such as pictures of the cars. But there is nothing you can't add by yourself now! Here's a list of other tasks you can perform if you want to continue to work on this application:

- Add validations for user input, such as making sure the year of the car is not greater than the current year + 2.
- Add pictures in the databases and on the form.
- Add a sold check mark.
- Add three forms to add data in the domain tables (CarType, Make, Color).
- Add more information in the listing, such as contact information.
- Make the URL clickable.
- Save an ad as a text file.

In Summary...

That was a big chapter with a lot of material! Let's review what you've learned. You were first introduced to databases and database concepts. You learned what constitutes a database and what you usually find within a database. You learned about data integrity and how it relates to primary keys and foreign keys.

You then used Visual C# 2008 Express Edition to create a database and tables and then populated them with some initial data using various tools in Visual C# 2008 Express Edition. You implemented all the foreign key relationships without leaving Visual Studio and validated them as well.

After entering your data manually, you developed a sample CarTracker application that lets a user easily enter data and that uses ADO.NET and data binding.

Lastly, you learned about the new components of ADO.NET 2.0 and how, with little or no code, you can develop a fully working data-centric application. You've been introduced only to a brief part of ADO.NET, because it's a vast subject. If you want to learn more, refer to the code or samples on MSDN. A good place to begin is the samples for Visual Studio 2008. Pay particular attention to the topic of data access with ADO.NET and LINQ. Here's the link: *http://msdn2.microsoft.com/en-us/vcsharp/bb466226.aspx?wt.slv=RightRail*. Also refer to the Windows Forms videos at the following link: *http://windowsclient.net/learn/videos.aspx*. At this location you'll find some data binding examples. Finally, look at the Learn C# Web site; this site evolves over time and will provide you with additional sources for learning data access using Visual C#: *http://msdn2.microsoft.com/en-us/vcsharp/aa336766.aspx?wt.slv=RightRail*.

In the next chapter, you will develop the final application of this book—the Weather Tracker application. You'll learn new concepts such as deployment, consuming Web services, user settings, and much more in a complete application with all of the necessary validations.

Chapter 9

Building Your Own Weather Tracker Application

Exploring the Features of the Weather Tracker Application, 196

Creating the Application User Interface, 197

Using the MSN Weather Web Service, 213

And Now, Just ClickOnce, 241

You have now reached the last chapter of the book and have learned quite a few new concepts along the way. In this chapter, you'll dot the i's and cross the t's by developing a fully functional weather-tracking application. You will be working with new processes in this chapter, but you will also draw on what you've learned in previous chapters to create the final product. In this chapter, you will put everything you've learned together to create this one application.

In this section, you'll become acquainted with the features used to create version 1.0 of the weather-tracking application, called Weather Tracker. This application contains the following features in version 1.0:

- Starts and resides as an icon in the notification area.
- Configures optional user settings from the notification area icon in the context menu.
- Refreshes all weather data on demand from the context menu in the notification area.
- Uses the MSN Weather service to provide data (weather locations, conditions, and forecasts) for cities around the world.
- Stores and persists user settings using XML.
- Minimizes but doesn't close when the user clicks the Close button in the title bar. The application will close only when the user clicks Exit on the context menu.
- Contains a splash screen on start-up.
- Contains an About box available from the context menu.
- Displays the current temperature in the system tray with a weather icon and color coding.
- Converts between metric units and English (or Imperial) units.

The application will not contain the following features in version 1.0:

- Will not work for more than one city at a time
- No graphical gauge controls for wind, pressure, temperature, and so forth

I'll now explain how the Weather Tracker application functions. First, the user will briefly see the splash screen. Then the application will go directly to the notification area in the Windows taskbar and display the current temperature. If the temperature is above 100 degrees Fahrenheit (or 38 degrees Celsius), the temperature will be displayed in red starting at 100. If the temperature is below 32 degrees Fahrenheit (or 0 degrees Celsius, which are negative degrees), the temperature will be displayed in violet. If the temperature in Fahrenheit is below

0 (or -18 degrees Celsius), the temperature will be displayed in blue. Otherwise, the temperature will be displayed in white. If the reading is not complete, a red *NA* will show up in place of the temperature reading.

If the user right-clicks the icon in the notification area, a context menu opens with choices to open the Main form and retrieve the current weather. The current weather will have an icon and provide useful weather data that comes from the MSN Weather service.

Clicking Refresh Weather Info in the context menu after clicking the notification area icon will trigger a call to the weather Web service to update weather data. This will be done asynchronously and will start by updating the current weather. If the user clicks Options in the context menu, an Options dialog box will be displayed. The user will be able to search for different cities around the world. If the user clicks About in the context menu, the application will display an About dialog box.

In this chapter, I will use a different approach than in previous chapters. Specifically, as long as you are using the same components that I specify, you can personalize your application as far as size, color, and other attributes are concerned. I will also present a great deal of code and explain the sections that are linked to the features described earlier. You can refer to the complete solution in the companion content folder for Chapter9 to copy the code for your own application.

To produce the application in this chapter, you will follow an incremental approach in which you implement one feature, integrate it with the rest of the application, and then test it. You will then move to the next feature until the application is complete.

Creating the Application User Interface

The Main form user interface (UI) will contain all the weather information you'll display to the user. Figure 9-1 shows what the Main form will look like when it is finished.

NOTE

As you learned in the previous chapter, you use data binding to bind the controls to the weather data. You'll recall that when creating the data source, you had a choice of database, Web service, and objects. In this application, you will use a Web service as a data source, and the fields you will display on the form will be data bound to the Web service's dataset.

IMPORTANT

All icons or image files in this chapter are in a folder named Images under the Chapter9 folder where you installed the companion content. The default location is Documents\Microsoft Press\ VCS 2008 Express\.

MORE INFO

DoubleBuffered helps reduce or prevent flickering when the form is redrawn. The form control is using a secondary buffer to update the form's graphics data, whereby a quick write to the displayed surface memory is then performed, reducing the chances of flickering. If *DoubleBuffered* is not enabled, then progressive redrawing of parts of the displayed form occurs, creating the flickering.

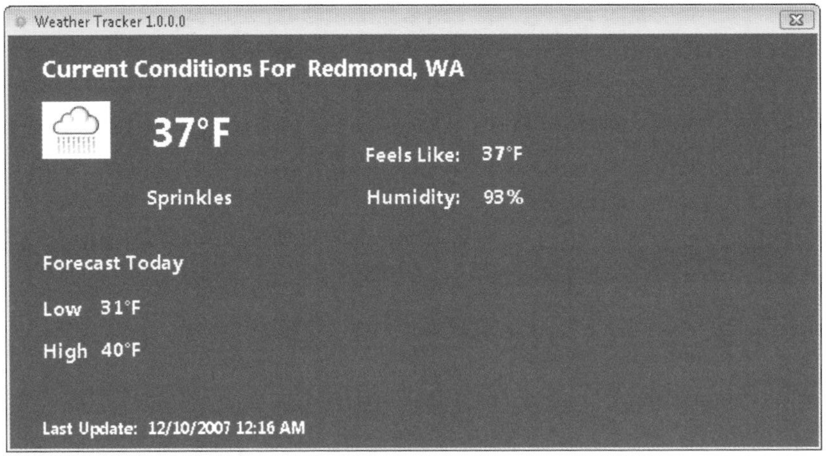

Figure 9-1
Main form in the Weather Tracker application

TO CREATE A DATA SOURCE FOR A MAIN FORM CONTROL

1. Start Microsoft Visual C# 2008 Express Edition, and create a new Windows Forms Application project. Name the application Weather Tracker.

2. In Solution Explorer, rename Form1.cs to Main.cs. When you do this, Visual C# will ask you whether you want to rename all references to Form1 in the project. Click Yes to accept.

3. Using the Properties window, change the properties for the Main form to the values in Table 9-1.

Property	Value
BackColor	System:HotTrack
DoubleBuffered	True
Font	Segoe UI 8 Bold

Table 9-1
Properties for Main.cs

Property	Value
ForeColor	Web:White
FormBorderStyle	FixedDialog
Icon	Sun.ico
MaximizeBox	False
MinimizeBox	False
ShowInTaskBar	False
Size:Height	350
Size:Width	660
StartPosition	CenterScreen
WindowState	Minimized

Table 9-1 (continued)
Properties for Main.cs

Adding Notification Area Capabilities

Now that you have established the Main form, you'll add the notification area capabilities. Let's talk about terminology. If an application uses an icon located in the notification area (the area on the Windows taskbar where the clock ordinarily appears), this icon is called a *notify icon* and is implemented with a NotifyIcon control. The icon can have a context menu with different actions. Your icon will have a context menu with the following choices: About, Refresh Weather Info, Options, Open, and Exit.

NOTE

The NotifyIcon control does not have a design representation on the form surface, so you'll add it to the component tray at the same place where you added the ADO.NET components in the previous chapter.

TO CREATE A NOTIFYICON CONTROL

1. In the Toolbox, drag a NotifyIcon control from the Common Controls group to the form. It appears in the component tray. Name the control *notifyWeather*.

2. Change its *Text* property to *Weather Tracker*.

3. In the Toolbox, drag a ContextMenuStrip control from the Menus & Toolbars group to the form, and name it *cmsNotify*.

4. Using the Smart Tag on the *cmsNotify* control in the component tray, select Edit Items.... The Items Collection Editor appears.

5. In the Items Collection Editor, change the *cmsNotify* control's properties using the values in Table 9-2.

Property	Value
BackColor	System:Gradient InactiveCaption
ShowImageMargin	False

Table 9-2
Properties for the cmsNotify Control

6. While still working in the Items Collection Editor, from the Select Item and Add to List Below drop-down list on the left, select MenuItem, and then click the Add button. Change the control's properties using the values shown in Table 9-3.

Property	Value
(Name)	tsmiAbout
ForeColor	System:HotTrack
Text	About...

Table 9-3
Properties for the About Menu Item

7. From the Select Item and Add to List Below drop-down list, select Separator, and click the Add button. Change its *ForeColor* property to *System:HotTrack*.

8. From the Select Item and Add to List Below drop-down list, select MenuItem, and click the Add button. Change the control's properties by using the values shown in Table 9-4.

Property	Value
(Name)	tsmiRefresh
ForeColor	System:HotTrack
Text	Refresh Weather Info

Table 9-4
Properties for the Refresh Menu Item

9. From the Select Item and Add to List Below drop-down list, select Separator, and click the Add button. Change its *ForeColor* property to *System:HotTrack*.

10. From the Select Item and Add to List Below drop-down list, select MenuItem, and click the Add button. Change the control's properties using the values shown in Table 9-5.

Property	Value
(Name)	tsmiOptions
ForeColor	System:HotTrack
Text	Options...

Table 9-5
Properties for the Options Menu Item

11. From the Select Item and Add to List Below drop-down list, select Separator, and click the Add button. Change its *ForeColor* property to *System:HotTrack*.

12. From the Select Item and Add to List Below drop-down list, select MenuItem, and click the Add button. Change the control's properties using the values shown in Table 9-6.

Property	Value
(Name)	tsmiOpen
ForeColor	System:HotTrack
Text	Open...

Table 9-6
Properties for the Open Menu Item

13. From the Select Item and Add to List Below drop-down list, select MenuItem, and click the Add button. Change the control's properties using the values shown in Table 9-7.

Property	Value
(Name)	tsmiExit
ForeColor	System:HotTrack
Text	Exit

Table 9-7
Properties for the Exit Menu Item

You're finished adding items to the context menu strip. The Items Collection Editor should look like Figure 9-2.

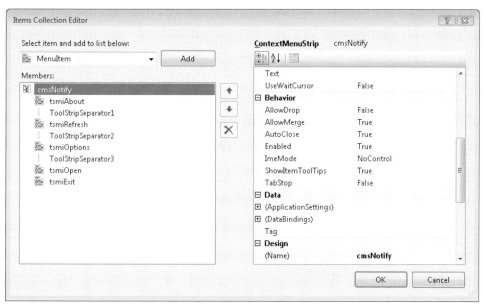

Figure 9-2
Items for the context menu

14. Click OK to close the Items Collection Editor.

You now need to associate the context menu strip with the *notifyWeather* control, which is fairly easy to do.

TO ASSOCIATE THE CONTEXT MENU STRIP WITH THE CONTROL

1. Select the *notifyWeather* control in the component tray, and in the Properties window, change the *ContextMenuStrip* property to *cmsNotify*.

You are currently acting as the user. For you to be able to click the application when it's in the notification area, your *notifyWeather* control needs an icon. The icon will later become dynamically generated by your application, and the icon will become the current temperature. Therefore, you now need to associate a temporary icon with the application; otherwise, you will not be able to select it in the notification area.

2. In the Properties window for *notifyWeather*, set the *Icon* property to *otheroptions.ico*. This file is located in a folder named Images in the Chapter9 folder where you installed the companion content.

3. Press F5 to execute the application.

   You should see this icon in your notification area:

   If you right-click this icon, you should see the context menu shown in Figure 9-3.

Figure 9-3
Context menu of the notifyWeather *control*

When you are finished, the only way to stop the application is to click the blue Stop Debugging button in the Visual Studio toolbar. You will now add another way to stop the application.

TO STOP AN APPLICATION

1. Select the *tsmiExit* control from the Properties window drop-down list.

2. Click the Events button (the yellow lightning icon) in the Properties window, and then double-click the *Click* event to open Code view.

3. Edit the *tsmiExit_Click* event handler, and add the *Shutdown* method as shown in the following code. You're adding the *Shutdown* method because you always want to make your code reusable, and a *Shutdown* method lets you do this.

```
1  private void tsmiExit_Click(object sender, EventArgs e)
2  {
3      this.Shutdown();
4  }
5
```

```
 6  private void Shutdown()
 7  {
 8      if (notifyWeather.Visible)
 9      {
10          notifyWeather.Visible = false;
11      }
12      Application.Exit();
13  }
```

The first instruction of the *Shutdown* method verifies whether the *notifyWeather* control is visible and, if it is, makes the notify icon disappear from the notification area. The last line terminates the application. You will now be able to click the Exit menu item in the context menu to terminate the application; you won't need to use the Stop Debugging button. You can try your application by pressing F5 and then verifying whether the Exit menu item works as expected.

Now you can exit from your application, but you don't have a way to open the Main form, which will have the weather information. To do this, you will want to link the double-click event of the *notifyWeather* control icon in the notification area to the action of opening the Main form in the middle of the screen.

4. In Design view, select the *notifyWeather* control in the component tray. In the events list of the Properties window, double-click the *MouseDoubleClick* event. Edit the *notify-Weather_MouseDoubleClick* event handler, and add the *Restore* method as shown in the following code:

```
14  private void notifyWeather_MouseDoubleClick(object sender,
        MouseEventArgs e)
15  {
16      this.Restore();
17  }
18
19  private void Restore()
20  {
21      if (this.WindowState == FormWindowState.Minimized)
22      {
23          this.WindowState = FormWindowState.Normal;
24      }
25      this.Visible = true;
26  }
```

Again, you created a private method called *Restore* in case you need it elsewhere for your Main form.

The first line of code in the *Restore* method is there because it is impossible to know in which context your method will be called. In this case, when you created the form, you set the *WindowState* property to *minimized* and *ShowInTaskbar* to *false* so that the form starts minimized and the user doesn't see it. When you start the application, the first time the user clicks the Open... menu choice (you'll code this soon) or double-clicks the *notifyWeather* control, the user won't be able to see the form if you have set only its *Visible* property to *true*. Therefore, you need to verify in which window state the form appears. If it's still minimized, you need to set it to *Normal* so that the focus is on the Main form.

5. Press F5 to test the changes. Double-click the *notifyWeather* icon in the notification area, and the Main form should appear.

Now let's see what happens if the user clicks the Close button (the red X). If you close the application by clicking the Close button, it closes permanently. Yet, our design requirements state that the application should simply minimize to the notification area when the user clicks the Close button. Therefore, you'll now intercept an event that occurs just before the form is closed and just before the form object is deleted, which is an event called *FormClosing*. By using a *FormClosing* event, you can extract the reason for the form's closing and in this way intercept the event when the user clicks the Close button.

6. In Design view, select the Main form. Go to the events list in the Properties window, and double-click the *FormClosing* event. Add the following code to the *Main_FormClosing* event handler:

```
27 private void Main_FormClosing(object sender, FormClosingEventArgs e)
28 {
29     if (e.CloseReason == CloseReason.UserClosing)
30     {
31         e.Cancel = true;
32         this.Hide();
33     }
34 }
```

MORE INFO
If you want to learn more about why a form is closing, you can search the Help system for *CloseReason enumeration*.

Part of the event is *FormClosingEventArgs*, which contains the arguments that accompany the event notification as well as the reason why the form is closing.

If the user is closing the form, setting the *Cancel* property to *true* will stop the closing process and prevent the form from closing. The next instruction is a call to the *Hide* method. The *Hide* method is simply a synonym for setting the *Visible* property to *false*. The form will simply be hidden.

When the user clicks the Exit item in the context menu, the *FormClosing* event will be raised; however, the reason given will not be *UserClosing*. Instead, it will be *Application-ExitCall*, and therefore the application will continue the closing process.

MORE INFO
The *UserClosing* event will also be called whenever the user presses Alt+F4 or whenever the user clicks Close in the form control menu (the menu that appears when you click the left corner where the icon is usually located).

7. You'll now add the code for the Open... menu choice. To write the code for this event, click *cmsNotify* in the component tray, and then double-click the Open... menu choice on the content menu strip. The *Click* event handler will be created, and you'll call the *Restore* method to handle the form's visibility, which is done by the *Restore* code. You will write code to make sure the form has the focus so that it ends up on top of any other windows that are displayed. Add the following code to the *tsmiOpen_Click* event handler:

```
35 private void tsmiOpen_Click(object sender, EventArgs e)
36 {
37     this.Restore();
38     this.Focus();
39 }
```

Now, test the application with the following test scenario.

Start the application by pressing F5. Right-click the notify icon, and select Open.... The Main form should appear in the middle of your screen. Minimize the Main form by clicking the Close button. Once it is minimized, double-click the notify icon. You should see the Main form again. Terminate the application by clicking the Exit menu item.

Adding the Splash Screen and About Dialog Box

Because you created a splash screen and dialog box in Chapter 6, "Modifying Your Web Browser," I won't spend too much time on those topics in this section. You'll just add forms that are almost finished from the companion content. Follow these steps to add the Splash-WeatherTracker.cs form and the AboutWeatherTracker.cs form to your Main.cs file.

TO ADD A SPLASH SCREEN AND ABOUT DIALOG BOX

1. In Solution Explorer, right-click the Weather Tracker project, click Add, and then click Existing Item. The Add Existing Item dialog box apears.

2. Browse to the SplashAbout folder under the Chapter9 companion content. By default, the companion content is located at Documents\Microsoft Press\VCS 2008 Express.

3. Select the AboutWeatherTracker.cs file, and while pressing the Ctrl key, select the SplashWeatherTracker.cs file.

4. Click Add to add the AboutWeatherTracker and SplashWeatherTracker forms to your project in Solution Explorer.

   Using the values in Table 9-8, set the specified properties for the SplashWeatherTracker form. The location of your labels doesn't matter; place them wherever you want. Any images are located in the Images folder under Chapter9 where you installed the companion content.

Control Name	Control Type	Property	Value
SplashWeather	Form	BackgroundImage	Mountain.jpg
SplashWeather	Form	BackgroundImageLayout	Stretch

Table 9-8
Properties for SplashWeatherTracker.cs

Using the values in Table 9-9, set the specified properties on the AboutWeatherTracker form. The images are located in the Images folder under Chapter 9 of the companion content.

Component	Property	Value
LogoPictureBox	Image	Sunset.jpg

Table 9-9
Properties for AboutWeatherTracker.cs

Now you need to attach these two forms to the rest of the application.

TO ATTACH FORMS TO AN APPLICATION

1. To attach the splash screen, begin by opening the code for Main.cs and modifying the constructor so that it looks like the following:

```
1 public partial class Main : Form
2 {
3   SplashWeatherTracker splashScreen = new SplashWeatherTracker();
4   public Main()
5   {
6       InitializeComponent();
7       splashScreen.Show();
8       Application.DoEvents();
9   }
```

2. The previous step will display the splash screen, but you also need to close it. Open the Main.cs form in design mode, and select the form. Click the Events button (yellow lightning) at the top of the Properties window, and double-click the *Load* event.

3. Add the following code to the *Main_Load* event handler:

```
10 private void Main_Load(object sender, EventArgs e)
11 {
12     //Splash screen business.
13     Thread.Sleep(2000);
14     splashScreen.Close();
15 }
```

4. Place your mouse pointer within the "Thread" text. You should see a familiar yellow and red Smart Tag. This Smart Tag is there to let you know that the *Thread* class is in the *System.Threading* namespace and that you don't have a reference to it in your *using* directives at the top of Main.cs. Move your mouse pointer over the Smart Tag, click the down arrow, and then select the *using System.Threading;* option to add it to your list of *using* directives.

5. To attach the About dialog box, you need to tie it to the context menu's About... choice. At the top of Main.cs, just below the line *SplashWeatherTracker splashScreen = new SplashWeatherTracker();*, add the following line of code:

```
AboutWeatherTracker aboutScreen = new AboutWeatherTracker();
```

6. Go to your Main.cs form in design mode, select *cmsNotify* in the component tray, and double-click the About... menu choice in the context menu strip. Add the following code to the *tsmiAbout_Click* event hander:

```
16 private void tsmiAbout_Click(object sender, EventArgs e)
17 {
18     aboutScreen.ShowDialog();
19 }
```

7. In Solution Explorer, right-click the Weather Tracker project, and select Properties to open the Project Designer.

8. On the Application tab, click Assembly Information, and set the assembly information for the project. This information will fill the splash screen and About dialog box fields.

9. On the Application tab, change the application icon to Sun.ico. Click the ellipsis (...) button next to the .cslcon drop-down list. Select the Sun.ico file in the Chapter9 Images folder.

Adding the Options Dialog Box

You now have three forms. You will add the final Options dialog box form that will appear when the user clicks the Options... menu item in the context menu after clicking the notify icon.

TO ADD THE OPTIONS DIALOG BOX FORM

1. In Solution Explorer, right-click Weather Tracker, select Add, and then click Windows Form in the context menu.

2. From the templates, select Windows Form, name the form Options.cs, and then click Add.

3. Using the values in Table 9-10, set properties and add controls to the Options form so that it looks like the form shown in Figure 9-4.

Control Name	Control Type	Property	Value
Options	Form	Font	Segoe UI 8 Regular
Options	Form	BackColor	System:HotTrack
Options	Form	StartPosition	CenterScreen
Options	Form	ForeColor	Web:White
Options	Form	ControlBox	False
Options	Form	FormBorderStyle	FixedDialog
Option	Form	MaximizeBox	False
Options	Form	MinimizeBox	False
Options	Form	Text	Options
Options	Form	Size:Width	295
Options	Form	Size:Height	295
txtCurrentCity	Textbox	AcceptReturn	False
txtCurrentCity	Textbox	BackColor	System:InactiveCaption
lblCurrentCity	Label	Text	Location:
lbPossibleCities	ListBox	BackColor	System:InactiveCaption
lbPossibleCities	ListBox	Cursor	Hand
lbPossibleCities	ListBox	SelectionMode	One
lbPossibleCities	ListBox	ForeColor	Web:White
btnOk	Button	BackColor	System:InactiveCaption

Table 9-10
Properties and Controls for the Options Dialog Box

Figure 9-4
The Options form

Control Name	Control Type	Property	Value
btnOk	Button	FlatStyle	Popup
btnOk	Button	Text	Ok
btnCancel	Button	BackColor	System:InactiveCaption
btnCancel	Button	Text	Cancel
btnCancel	Button	FlatStyle	Popup
Options	Form	CancelButton	btnCancel
rbCelsius	Radio Button	BackColor	System:HotTrack
rbFahrenheit	RadioButton	BackColor	System:HotTrack
rbFahrenheit	RadioButton	Checked	True
lblUnit	Label	Text	Unit

Table 9-10 (continued)
Properties and Controls for the Options Dialog Box

TO HOOK UP THE FORM TO THE CONTEXT MENU

1. Display the Main form in design mode.

2. Select *cmsNotify* in the component tray, and double-click the Options... menu choice in the context menu.

3. At the top of Main.cs, just below the line *AboutWeatherTracker aboutScreen = new AboutWeatherTracker();*, add the following line of code:

```
Options optionsForm = new Options();
```

4. Add the following line of code to the *tsmiOptions_Click* event handler:

```
private void tsmiOptions_Click(object sender, EventArgs e)
{
    optionsForm.ShowDialog();
// The next line below should be commented out because it's not
// implemented yet.
```

```
        // this.UpdateWeather();
    }
```

5. Press F5 to run the application. You should see your splash screen. Use the context menu
   on the notify icon to open the About dialog box and the Options dialog box. When finished, exit the application.

   You are now finished with this part of the project. Be sure to save your project. It is time
   to add the meat of the project: using the MSN Weather service.

Using the MSN Weather Web Service

You have constructed a nice shell, but the shell is rather empty at this moment. You need
to access weather data in order to populate the shell. To accomplish this, you will learn to
consume Web services. But first, what is a Web service?

A *Web service* is an application that runs on a Web server such as Internet Information
Services (IIS). A Web service has a series of exposed public methods that an application can
call. You'll find numerous examples of Web services on the Internet. You can use Web services that perform a variety of operations, such as finding a ZIP code, viewing a map, buying
movie tickets, looking for information on search engines such as MSN or Google, and accessing weather information like your application will soon do. In the .NET world, classes and
wizards are available to help you consume Web services. There are two popular implementa-
tions of Web services in use on the Web: SOAP and REST.

SOAP Web services use XML to send messages and return results. All objects are serial-
ized (the messages are sent as a series of bits and pieces over the Internet) and are then
deserialized on the other side into objects. The beauty of XML Web services is that they can
be hosted and consumed on any operating system and developed in any language. Because
they use a series of standardized protocols and rules, XML Web services promote interoper-
ability and efficiency. The future of the transacted world over the Internet lies in big part
with the success of Web services.

REST Web services use HTTP to make calls to services and receive XML data. They are lighter to use and implement, and you call them just as you would type a URL in a browser. For instance, *http://www.foobar.com/parts/111* will call a Web service and get you the details about a part with the part number 111. The XML coming back to your browser would be the details of that part. REST stands for Representational State Transfer. It's not a standard like SOAP is; it is simply an architectural style. However, although it's not a standard, it does prescribe the use of many standards such as XML, HTTP, URL, HTML, and so on.

In this project, you will use REST Web services as offered by MSN.

Connecting to MSN Weather Web Services

You will now build a business logic DLL to get the data and then display the object returned by the different methods in that DLL.

First you will create a .NET assembly that will contain the information used to communicate with MSN and to map to items in the user interface you'll define later.

Trying a Web Service

You can use your regular Web browser to try a SOAP or REST Web service without writing a line of code. You can usually point your Web browser to the Web service address and invoke its methods. This is an excellent way to learn what a Web method needs and what its output looks like. (Please note that it's not possible to talk to all of them in this way.) As an example, try a SOAP Web service that returns a currency conversion rate between two currencies: http://www.webservicex.com/CurrencyConvertor.asmx. *Click the* ConversionRate *method, scroll down until you see two text boxes, type* **CAD** *and* **USD** *in the two text boxes, and then click Invoke. In a separate browser window, you will obtain XML and the conversion rate (as of today).*

To test a REST Web service, you can use the same URL that you will use in code later in this chapter. In your browser, type the following: http://weather.service.msn.com/data.aspx?src=vista&wealocations=wc:USWA0367. *In the same browser tab or window, you'll see the XML containing weather information for the city of Redmond, Washington.*

TO CONNECT TO A WEB SERVICE

1. Click File, Add, New Project, and then select the Class Library template. Type **WeatherReport** for the class library name.

2. In your class library, rename class1.cs to WeatherReport.cs.

3. You will need the *Bitmap* class for an image representing the weather, so add a reference to the *System.Drawing* namespace. While you're in Solution Explorer, add a reference to your newly created class library in your WeatherTracker project.

4. To use the bitmap, you'll have to add a *using* statement to your code. To do this, open the WeatherReport.cs file, and add the following:

```
using System.Drawing
```

5. This time, instead of binding the data to a database as you did in Chapter 8, you'll bind the Web service data to an object that will then be bound to items on your form. Now add the fields and properties in Table 9-11 to your WeatherReport.cs file. To add a field and a property quickly and correctly, you will use a snippet. Open the WeatherReport.cs file, and then for each field listed in the table, right-click in the editor, and select Insert Snippet…/Visual C#/prop. (Refer to WeatherReport.cs in the companion content folder for examples of how these field and properties are implemented.)

Field	Property	Type
currentTemperatureValue	CurrentTemperature	Integer
feelsLikeTemperatureValue	FeelsLikeTemperature	Integer
humidityValue	Humidity	Integer
lastUpdateValue	LastUpdate	DateTime
locationValue	Location	String
minTemperatureForecastValue	MinTemperatureForecast	Integer

Table 9-11
Fields and Properties for WeatherReport.cs

Field	Property	Type
maxTemperatureForecastValue	MaxTemperatureForecast	Integer
skyCodeValue	SkyCode	Integer
skyTextValue	SkyText	String
skyImageValue	SkyImage	Bitmap
locationCodeValue	LocationCode	String

Table 9-11 (continued)
Fields and Properties for WeatherReport.cs

6. Save your file after adding all the fields and properties.

7. Build your solution by pressing Ctrl+Shift+B.

Now you'll add the weather information to your form.

TO ADD WEATHER INFORMATION TO YOUR FORM

1. Make sure you are viewing the Main form on the designer surface.

2. Go to the Data Sources window, and then select Add New Data Source....

3. You will see the familiar Data Source Configuration Wizard, but this time select Object instead of Database, and then click Next.

4. You'll add a reference to your newly created class library since this object will be the one you'll use to map the data from the Web service and the data displayed on your form. Click the Add Reference... button, and on the Projects tab select your WeatherReport class library. Your screen should display the wizard with the WeatherReport assembly added, as shown in Figure 9-5. Click Next to continue and then the Finish button.

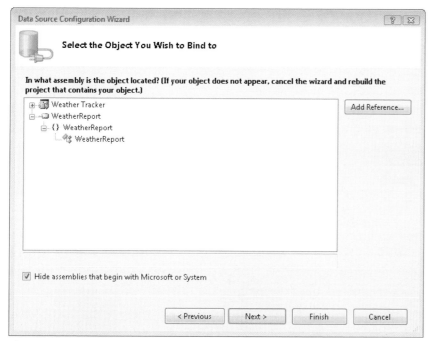

Figure 9-5
Data Source Configuration Wizard with the WeatherReport assembly selected

You should see the WeatherReport data source on the Data Sources tab beside Solution Explorer. Refer to Figure 9-6 to make sure you're at the right place.

5. As you can see in Figure 9-6, the data source name is actually also a drop-down control. Click it, and select Details. Then click the plus sign to expand it and see the details of your data source that was created from your WeatherReport class library assembly. You'll see that all the properties you created are represented in the data source.

6. With the WeatherReport node expanded, change all the element types (except SkyImage) from TextBox to Label by clicking the down arrow on each element and selecting Label from the drop-down list.

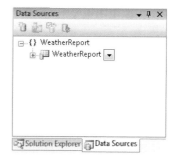

Figure 9-6
Data Sources tab with the newly created WeatherReport data source

7. Drag WeatherReport to the Main form design surface. This creates all the fields and labels for you. In the sample code I present later in the chapter in the section "Adding Unit Labels and a Conversion Utility," the labels have been renamed to something more meaningful. Look at the code, and rename the labels to match the code. If you don't, you will get compiler errors at compile/build time.

The design might not be what you want, but at least it's partially done for you. You'll fix this design in a minute. Note that two new controls have been added to the component tray: *weatherReportBindingSource* and *weatherReportBindingNavigator*.

8. Click *weatherReportBindingNavigator* in the component tray, and change its *Visible* property to *false*. (You might need to click the Properties button at the top of the Properties window to see the list of properties.)

9. You can't see the boundaries of all the controls on the form. To help with layout, select all the controls on the form by dragging a large selection rectangle around them with your mouse pointer. In the Properties window, change *BorderStyle* from *None* to *FixedSingle*. Black borders should appear around all controls. Once the form is done, you'll reset *BorderStyle* to *None*.

10. Now you can start modifying the layout and look and feel of your form. For the PictureBox control, set the *Name* property to *pbSkyImage*, set the *BackColor* property to *Web:White*, set the *Size.Width* property to *55*, and set the *Size.Height* property to *45*.

11. Delete the Sky Image: label.

12. Add a Label control, and set the *Text* property to *Current Weather*.

13. Add a Label control, and set the *Text* property to *Contacting MSN Weather Service* and the *Visible* property to *False*. Name the label lblProgress.

14. Add a PictureBox control, and set *Visible* to *False* and *Image* to *progressbar_green.gif* from the Images folder. Name the PictureBox control PictureBoxProgress.

15. Using Figure 9-7 as a proposed guide (you can have something different, it's your application in this chapter), size and position the controls on the form. If you want, adjust the font size and style of the labels.

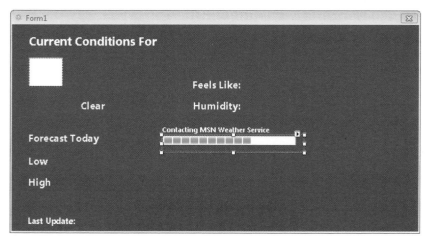

Figure 9-7
Layout of the current weather information

Setting User and Application Preferences

The application settings are stored in an XML file and persist from one execution to another. The current location code will be saved here so that a user doesn't have to re-enter the location every time your application starts.

TO CREATE USER SETTING ENTRIES

1. In Solution Explorer, right-click the Weather Tracker project, and select Properties. The Project Designer appears.

2. On the Settings tab, add entries for CurrentLocation, CurrentLocationCode, and CurrentUnit, as shown in Figure 9-8.

Name	Type	Scope	Value
CurrentLocationCode	string	User	wc:USWA0367
CurrentUnit	string	User	F
CurrentLocation	string	User	Redmond, Washington

Figure 9-8
Application settings in the Project Designer

All entries are strongly typed (that is, a real .NET type) and set to type *String*. The scope field is set to User, which means this setting is related to user preferences and the user can change it during execution. This type of setting will be persisted from one execution to another. The other possible setting is Application-scoped, which is usually associated with an application that uses a database connection string. Users can't change those settings at execution time.

3. Save your project, and close the Project Designer.

Working in the Background

If you try to run your form now, you won't get anything from the Web service; you'll get only the default text you might have entered. This process differs from your work with databases, in which a great deal of code was completed for you so you could retrieve the data and populate the fields. When dealing with a Web service, you must do more actual coding to get the data into the form. Let's talk about how you'll do this.

First, talking to a Web service can be a long process. This typically means only a few seconds (perhaps up to 30 seconds), but you can't leave the user with a blocked UI while your application is retrieving information. You therefore need a way of saying to your application: "Go get this information, and let me know when you have it." This programming technique is called *multithreaded* or *asynchronous programming with callbacks*. Since .NET Framework 2.0, this type of programming has been simplified by a new class called *BackgroundWorker*. As its name implies, it works in the background on a task; what's not implied is that it will let you know when it has completed the task.

TO ADD THE MSN WEATHER DATA CLASS

To communicate and retrieve the data from the MSN Weather service, you'll create a new class called MSNWeatherData.cs and add it to your WeatherTracker project. This class will insulate you from the service and its technicalities; it's an OOP technique called *abstraction*, which enables you (or somebody else using your class) to just say, "Give me the weather report for a location. I know it returns a *WeatherReport* object, and that's all I need in order to integrate the weather report into my application." In addition, you can use the *MSNWeather-Data* class in other applications. Isn't that cool?

To talk to the MSN Weather service and return the data from the MSN *WeatherReport* class, you've already created a DLL to handle the mapping between the form and the code; you also enabled the data binding on an object. In the following code, you'll see that to connect to the MSN Web service and read the data, you have to use a simple *XMLTextReader* to connect to the server and open the resulting XML. In the following steps, we'll add the code for the two methods in this class. The code is not really difficult to understand because it is repetitive, but essentially it's just a task of mapping the correct XML file and mapping the methods to the appropriate fields in the *WeatherReport* class.

1. Create a new class in your WeatherTracker project, and call it MSNWeatherData.cs. Add the following code:

```
using System;
using System.Collections.Generic;
using System.Drawing;
using System.Linq;
using System.Text;
using WeatherReport;
using System.Xml;

namespace WeatherTracker
{
    class MSNWeatherData
    {
        public WeatherReport.WeatherReport GetWeatherReport(string location)
        {
            WeatherReport.WeatherReport currentWeatherReport = new
                WeatherReport.WeatherReport();

            // URL corresponding to the MSN REST Web Service - see how the
            // locationCodeis passed in parameter to this URL.
            // The XMLTextReader opens up the URL and receives the XML
            // returned by the server
            // http://weather.service.msn.com/
            // data.aspx?src=vista&wealocations=wc:USWA0367
            string feedUrl =
```

```
"http://weather.service.msn.com/data.aspx?src=vista&wealocations="
+ location;
            XmlTextReader reader = new XmlTextReader(feedUrl);
            bool firstForecastDone = false;
            string skyImagesRelativeUrl = "Images/";
            int MaxTemp, MinTemp, CurrentTemp, FeelsLike, Humidity, SkyCode;

            try
            {
                while (reader.Read())
                {
                    if ((reader.NodeType == XmlNodeType.Element) &&
                        (reader.Name == "weather"))
                    {
                        reader.MoveToAttribute("weatherlocationname");
                        currentWeatherReport.Location = reader.Value;
                    }
                    else if ((reader.NodeType == XmlNodeType.Element) &&
                        ((reader.Name == "forecast")
                        && (firstForecastDone == false)))
                    {
                        firstForecastDone = true;
                        reader.MoveToAttribute("high");
                        int.TryParse(reader.Value, out MaxTemp);
                        currentWeatherReport.MaxTemperatureForecast = MaxTemp;
                        reader.MoveToAttribute("low");
                        int.TryParse(reader.Value, out MinTemp);
                        currentWeatherReport.MinTemperatureForecast = MinTemp;
                    }
                    else if ((reader.NodeType == XmlNodeType.Element) &&
                        (reader.Name == "current"))
                    {
                        reader.MoveToAttribute("temperature");
                        int.TryParse(reader.Value, out CurrentTemp);
                        currentWeatherReport.CurrentTemperature = CurrentTemp;

                        reader.MoveToAttribute("feelslike");
                        int.TryParse(reader.Value, out FeelsLike);
                        currentWeatherReport.FeelsLikeTemperature = FeelsLike;

                        reader.MoveToAttribute("humidity");
                        int.TryParse(reader.Value, out Humidity);
```

```
                    currentWeatherReport.Humidity = Humidity;

                    reader.MoveToAttribute("skytext");
                    currentWeatherReport.SkyText = reader.Value;

                    reader.MoveToAttribute("skycode");
                    int.TryParse(reader.Value, out SkyCode);
                    currentWeatherReport.SkyCode = SkyCode;
                    string fileName = skyImagesRelativeUrl +
                        currentWeatherReport.SkyCode + ".gif";
                    currentWeatherReport.SkyImage = new Bitmap(fileName);

                    reader.MoveToAttribute("observationtime");
                    char[] splitter = ":".ToCharArray();
                    string[] hourMinuteSecond =
                        reader.Value.Split(splitter);
                    int hour, minute, second;
                    int.TryParse(hourMinuteSecond[0], out hour);
                    int.TryParse(hourMinuteSecond[1], out minute);
                    int.TryParse(hourMinuteSecond[2], out second);

                    reader.MoveToAttribute("date");
                    splitter = "-".ToCharArray();
                    string[] yearMonthDay = reader.Value.Split(splitter);
                    int year, month, day;
                    int.TryParse(yearMonthDay[0], out year);
                    int.TryParse(yearMonthDay[1], out month);
                    int.TryParse(yearMonthDay[2], out day);
                    currentWeatherReport.LastUpdate = new
                        DateTime(year, month, day, hour, minute,
                        second);
                }
            }
            // We return a valid weather report.
            return currentWeatherReport;
        }
        catch (Exception ex)
        {
            throw ex;
        }
    }
```

```csharp
public List<KeyValuePair<string, string>> GetLocations(string Query)
{
    if ((Query == "") || (Query.Length < 2))
    {
        return null;
    }
    else
    {
        // Because the ListBox in the Options UI can't bind with a
        // generic collection that doesn't support IList or
        // IListSource, hence why you use a generic List(Of Items
        // you really need) you are able to load
        List<KeyValuePair<string, string>> results = new
            List<KeyValuePair<string, string>>();
        string searchUrl =
"http://weather.service.msn.com/find.aspx?outputview=search&src=vista&wease
archstr=" + Query;
        XmlTextReader reader = new XmlTextReader(searchUrl);
        string locationCode;
        string locationFullName;

        while (reader.Read())
        {
            if ((reader.NodeType == XmlNodeType.Element) &&
                (reader.Name == "weather"))
            {

                reader.MoveToAttribute("weatherfullname");
                locationFullName = reader.Value;
                reader.MoveToAttribute("weatherlocationcode");
                locationCode = reader.Value;
                KeyValuePair<string, string> pair = new
                    KeyValuePair<string, string>(locationCode,
                    locationFullName);
                results.Add(pair);
            }
        }
        return results;
    }
}
```

Now that you've created the two methods required to obtain information from the MSN REST Weather service, you'll add the code to do it asynchronously.

TO PERFORM A TASK IN THE BACKGROUND

1. Open the Main form in Design view.

2. Go to the Toolbox. In the Components section, select the BackgroundWorker control, and drag it to your form. It doesn't have a design-time portion, so it will be added to the component tray. Rename it *BackgroundCurrentWorker*.

3. At the top of the Properties window for *BackgroundCurrentWorker*, click the Events button (the yellow lightning icon), and then double-click the *DoWork* event.

4. At the top of Main.cs, add the following *using* statement to the existing *using* statements:

```
using Weather_Tracker.Properties;
```

5. Add the following code to the *BackgroundCurrentWorker_DoWork* event handler:

```
private void BackgroundCurrentWorker_DoWork(object sender, DoWorkEventArgs e)
{
    // This method will execute in the background thread created
    // by the BackgroundWorker component
    string desiredLocationCode = e.Argument.ToString();
    MSNWeatherData myMSNWeather = new MSNWeatherData();
    e.Result = myMSNWeather.GetWeatherReport(desiredLocationCode);
}
```

The *DoWork* event handler is where the call to the MSN Weather service takes place. You will start by calling the *GetWeatherReport* method. When you invoke the *GetWeatherReport* method, it runs in a separate context so that it doesn't block the application UI. Otherwise, the application could appear to be in a "frozen" state. The *GetWeatherReport* method takes one parameter and returns a *WeatherReport* result.

6. Add the following *startBackgroundTaskGetCurrentWeather* method:

```
private void startBackgroungGetCurrentWeather()
{
    // Execute the Background Task only if it's not already working
```

```
if (!(BackgroundCurrentWorker.IsBusy))
{
    this.UseWaitCursor = true;
    this.lblProgress.Visible = true;
    this.PictureBoxProgress.Visible = true;

    BackgroundCurrentWorker.RunWorkerAsync(currentLocationCode);
}
}
```

The *startBackgroundTaskGetCurrentWeather* method starts the *BackgroundWorker* component. You first need to verify whether *BackgroundWorker* is already busy with a previous call; if you don't do this, you'll end up with an *InvalidOperationException*. Simply verifying whether *BackgroundWorker* is busy ensures that you won't get that exception when calling the *RunWorkerAsync* method. In fact, this is the only exception that this method can raise. A quick look at the documentation can confirm this.

Executing the *RunWorkerAsync* method means submitting a request to start an operation asynchronously, which raises the *DoWork* event. An event handler with the following name format is invoked: *<your backgroundworker variable>_DoWork*. In this case, the *BackgroundCurrentWorker_DoWork* method is executed when the *DoWork* event is raised.

7. Switch to Design view, and click *BackgroundCurrentWorker* in the component tray.

8. In the events list in the Properties window, double-click the *RunWorkerCompleted* event.

9. Add the following code to the *BackgroundCurrentWorker_RunWorkerCompleted* event handler:

```
Control.CheckForIllegalCrossThreadCalls = false;
if (e.Error == null)
{

    WeatherReport.WeatherReport currentWeatherReport;
    // This event fires when the DoWork event completes
    currentWeatherReport = (WeatherReport.WeatherReport)e.Result;

    UseWaitCursor = false;
    lblProgress.Visible = false;
    PictureBoxProgress.Visible = false;
```

```
        if (currentUnit == "C")
        {
            this.ConvertToMetric(ref currentWeatherReport);
        }
        weatherReportBindingSource.DataSource = currentWeatherReport;
        // Refresh the display based on the new data binding and
        // update the labels with the proper temperature unit.
        weatherReportBindingSource.ResetBindings(false);
        UpdateUnitLabels();

        // If Web service returned weather info, then
        // update notify icon
        this.CreateIcon(currentWeatherReport.CurrentTemperature);
    }
    else
    {
        MessageBox.Show("Problem with the MSN Weather Web service! Error
            message:\n" + e.Error.Message + "\nRetry Later!", "Weather Web
            service problem");
    }
```

If the MSN Web service is available, the method you invoked is working in a different context and on its own. When it is finished with its business, you will be notified that the method has completed, because a *RunWorkerCompleted* event will be raised.

To retrieve the results, you must have an event handler with the following name: *<your backgroundworker variable>_RunWorkerCompleted*. In this method, you have a parameter of type *RunWorkerCompletedEventArgs* that contains everything you need to obtain the results. If an exception was raised in the *DoWork* event handler, you'll be able to retrieve it by checking the *Error* property, which is of type *Exception*. If there is no error, you must retrieve the results yourself. Remember that the *Results* property will give you an element of type *Object*, which by itself will not help you. You need to assign it a variable with the same type as the binding class you created (that is, *WeatherReport*) to pass data back and forth between the Web service and the form.

If you recall, when you dragged the *WeatherReport* object to the designer surface, you automatically created data-bound controls for all of those fields. Thus, you simply need to assign that *currentWeatherReport* variable as the data source for *BindingSource*, and you will have a link between what's coming from the Web service and the controls on your form. In addition, you have to make a call to *ResetBindings(False)*, which will enable *BindingSource* to refresh the form and therefore display the new content for that location. After that, the method called simply adds the proper unit to the different temperatures, that is, Celsius or Fahrenheit. What happens next is the creation of the icon that will appear in the notification area representing the current temperature.

TO ADD SUPPORTING BACKGROUND CODE

1. At the very top of Main.cs, add the following *using* statements:

```
using System.Runtime.InteropServices;
using System.Net
```

2. At the top of the class, add the following lines just below *Options optionsForm = new Options();*:

```
public static double currentTemperature;
public static string currentLocationCode = Settings.Default.CurrentLocationCode;
public static string currentLocation = Settings.Default.CurrentLocation;
public static string currentUnit = Settings.Default.CurrentUnit;
```

The first line of code is declared as a public static field named *currentTemperature*. A static field simply means that it doesn't belong to any particular instance of that class but that there is only one for the entire class. The *currentLocationCode*, *currentLocation*, and *currentUnit* fields found in the next lines are also shared fields. They are initialized from the user settings, but they will change once you complete the Options form. They are also used to carry the changes made in the Options form back to the Main form.

3. Add the following *UpdateWeather* method, and remember to remove the comment in the *tsmi_Options_Click* method as well as the comment characters from the method call.

```
public void UpdateWeather()
{
    try
    {
        this.tsmiRefresh.Enabled = false;
        this.tsmiOptions.Enabled = false;
        this.startBackgroungGetCurrentWeather();
```

```
            this.tsmiRefresh.Enabled = true;
            this.tsmiOptions.Enabled = true;
        }
        catch (WebException)
        {
            MessageBox.Show(
                    "MSN Web service currently unavailable.\n" +
                    "Retry later using the Refresh Weather Info menu.",
                    "Web Exception");
                    this.tsmiRefresh.Enabled = true;
        }
        catch (Exception ex)
        {
            MessageBox.Show(
                    "Unknown problem. Error message:\n" +
                    ex.Message + "please, retry later!", "Unknown error");
                    this.tsmiRefresh.Enabled = true;
        }
    }
}
```

The *UpdateWeather* method initiates the update of the weather data by calling the *start-BackgroundGetCurrentWeather* method you added earlier. The weather data needs to be updated when the location is changed or when the Refresh Weather Info menu choice is clicked in the context menu of the notify icon. The *UpdateWeather* method also enables or disables menu choices on the context menu as appropriate.

Completing the Core Weather Tracker Functionality

In the next sections, you will add more code to set up a working version of the Weather Tracker application. This includes creating the icon, verifying connectivity, verifying weather Web service availability, and performing other tasks.

First you will add code to create and destroy the icon in the notification area. You can review the code, but I won't discuss it in much detail because GDI+ and COM "interop" are subjects that are too advanced for this book. However, you can refer to the comments within the code to learn more.

1. In Main.cs, add the following *CreateIcon* method:

```
private void CreateIcon(int temperature)
{
    string displayString;
    Bitmap drawnIcon;
    SolidBrush brushToDrawString;
    Color iconColor;
    Graphics iconGraphic;
    FontFamily fontFamily = new FontFamily("Arial");
    Font IconFont = new Font(fontFamily, 11,
    FontStyle.Regular, GraphicsUnit.Pixel);

    if (currentUnit == "F")
    {
        if (temperature == int.MinValue)
        {
            displayString = "NA";
            iconColor = Color.Red;
        }
        else if (temperature > 100)
        {
            iconColor = Color.Red;
            displayString = (temperature - 100).ToString();
        }
        else if ((temperature < 32) && (temperature > 0))
        {
            iconColor = Color.Violet;
            displayString = temperature.ToString();
        }
        else if (temperature < 0)
        {
            iconColor = Color.Blue;
            displayString = (temperature * -1).ToString();
        }
        else
        {
            iconColor = Color.White;
            displayString = temperature.ToString();
        }
```

```
        }
        else
        {
            if (temperature == int.MinValue)
            {
                displayString = "NA";
                iconColor = Color.Red;
            }
            else if (temperature > 38)
            {
                iconColor = Color.Red;
                displayString = (temperature).ToString();
            }
            else if (temperature < 0)
            {
                iconColor = Color.Violet;
                displayString = (temperature * -1).ToString();
            }
            else if (temperature < -18)
            {
                iconColor = Color.Blue;
                displayString = (temperature * -1).ToString();
            }
            else
            {
                iconColor = Color.White;
                displayString = temperature.ToString();
            }
        }

        // Start by creating a new bitmap the size of an icon
        drawnIcon = new Bitmap(16, 16);

        // To draw the string we need a brush
        brushToDrawString = new SolidBrush(iconColor);

        //  Creating a new graphic object so that we
        //  can call the drawstring method with our
        //  temperature or NA if there is no temp.
        iconGraphic = Graphics.FromImage(drawnIcon);

        //  Now we are drawing the temperature string onto
```

```
        //   graphic and therefore on the bitmap.
        iconGraphic.DrawString(displayString, IconFont,
                brushToDrawString, 0, 0);

        //   We are getting ready to convert the bitmap into
        //   an icon and to set the notifyWeather.Icon with
        //   this newly created icon
        IntPtr hIcon = drawnIcon.GetHicon();
        Icon customMadeIcon = System.Drawing.Icon.FromHandle(hIcon);
        notifyWeather.Icon = customMadeIcon;

        // Now that we're done manipulating the new icon
        // we need to destroy the unmanaged resource,
        // otherwise we'll have a handle leak.
        DestroyIcon(hIcon);
    }
```

2. Add the following *DestroyIcon* method:

```
// The GetIcon method generated an unmanaged handle
// that we need to take care of otherwise there
// will be a handle leak.
[DllImport("User32.dll")]
public static extern bool DestroyIcon(IntPtr hIcon);
```

TO FINISH THE MAIN FORM

1. In Main.cs, locate the existing *Main_Load* event handler.

2. Modify *Main_Load* to look like the following:

```
private void Main_Load(object sender, EventArgs e)
{
    // Splash Screen business
    Thread.Sleep(2000);
    splashScreen.Close();
    // Changing the title of our main form with the
    // application name and the version
    this.Text = aboutScreen.AssemblyTitle + " " +
            aboutScreen.AssemblyVersion;
```

```
    //Creating temporarily the NA icon.
    this.CreateIcon(int.MinValue);
    tsmiRefresh.Enabled = false;
    this.UpdateWeather();
}
```

The *Main_Load* event handler is the starting point for Weather Tracker. In this code, you build the title of the application by using its name and the version stored in the assembly parameters in the same manner that the About box uses this information. Next, a red *NA* (meaning not available) icon is drawn in the notification area and remains there until the Web service returns with positive results, in which case the temperature will be drawn as an icon. If everything is working as expected, the process for obtaining the weather data starts.

3. In Design view, click *cmsNotify* in the component tray. In the context menu strip, double-click the Refresh Weather Info menu item.

4. Add the following code to the *tsmiRefresh_Click* event handler. This code initiates an update of the weather data when the Refresh Weather Info menu item in the context menu is clicked.

```
private void tsmiRefresh_Click(object sender, EventArgs e)
{
    this.tsmiRefresh.Enabled = false;
    this.UpdateWeather();
}
```

5. In Design view, select all the controls on the Main form. Set the *BorderStyle* property to *None*. (You might need to click the Properties button at the top of the Properties window to see the list of properties.)

You need to copy all the weather forecast images from your companion content folder to the same folder where the Weather Tracker application is located. Specifically, you need to create an Images folder and copy all of the *.gif weather image files into this folder. You'll do this next.

Weather Links

You might be wondering what the link is between the index and the filename and who is creating that link. This is a convention used by many weather providers on the Internet; therefore, this is something that will work with many services if you want to add some later.

TO ADD WEATHER ICONS

1. In Solution Explorer, right-click the Weather Tracker project, select Add, and then select New Folder. Name the folder Images.

2. Using Windows Explorer, copy the *.gif images (1.gif through 47.gif) from the companion content to the Images folder you just created. (The default location for the companion content is Documents\Microsoft Press\VCS 2008\Chapter9\Images.)

3. In Solution Explorer, right-click the Images folder, select Add, and then select Existing Item. The Add Existing Item dialog box appears.

4. In the Files of Type drop-down list, select Image Files.

5. Make sure you are looking in the Images folder, and select all the .gif files. To select all the files, you can press Ctrl+A, or you can Shift-click.

6. When all the .gif files have been selected, click the Add button to add the images to the Weather Tracker project.

7. In Solution Explorer, select all the .gif files. First, select 1.gif, and then while pressing the Shift key, select the last .gif file.

8. With all the .gif files selected, in the Properties window, set the *Copy to Output Directory* property to *Copy Always*, as shown in Figure 9-9. Make sure the *Build Action* property is set to *Content*.

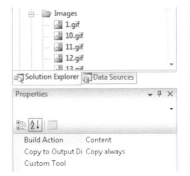

Figure 9-9
Weather icons added to the project

ADDING UNIT LABELS AND A CONVERSION UTILITY

The data that comes back from the MSN Weather service is always in Fahrenheit, and if the user wants to have the information in Celsius, you'll need to provide a small tool to do that. The Main form doesn't contain any indication about whether the data points are in Fahrenheit or Celsius, which is why you need a conversion tool to give the application time to add the degree symbol and the unit.

1. Add the following code to Main.cs to do both:

```
public void ConvertToMetric(ref WeatherReport.WeatherReport report)
{
```

```
        report.CurrentTemperature = (int)(5.0 / 9.0 *
            (report.CurrentTemperature - 32));
        report.FeelsLikeTemperature = (int)(5.0 / 9.0 *
            (report.FeelsLikeTemperature - 32));
        report.MaxTemperatureForecast = (int)(5.0 / 9.0 *
            (report.MaxTemperatureForecast - 32));
        report.MinTemperatureForecast = (int)(5.0 / 9.0 *
            (report.MinTemperatureForecast - 32));
    }

    public void UpdateUnitLabels()
    {
        lblTemperatureCurrent.Text = lblTemperatureCurrent.Text + "¬∞" +
            currentUnit;
        lblFeelsLikeTemperature.Text = lblFeelsLikeTemperature.Text + "¬∞" +
            currentUnit;
        lblMinTemperatureForecast.Text = lblMinTemperatureForecast.Text + "¬∞" +
            currentUnit;
        lblMaxTemperatureForecast.Text = lblMaxTemperatureForecast.Text + "¬∞" +
            currentUnit;
        lblHumidity.Text = lblHumidity.Text + "%";
    }
```

Testing Weather Tracker

Before running the Weather Tracker application, verify that you are connected to the Internet. Now you will see whether your application works. Press F5 to run Weather Tracker. If you have any build errors, review the errors on the Error List tab, and fix them. If necessary, you can review the completed application in the Complete folder. When you run the application, you should see your splash screen and then see a red *NA* in the notification area indicating that the current temperature has not been retrieved. Right-click the NA icon in the notification area, and select Refresh Weather Info in the context menu. If the weather Web service is available, you should see the current temperature for the Redmond, Washington, area in the notification area. (Be patient. Depending on the current Web service load, you might have to wait a few moments.) If you have to wait, you'll see that a little animated image displays while the data is coming back from the MSN server. You just have to enable it! When you double-click the temperature in the notification area, you should see detailed weather information, as shown in Figure 9-10. Right-click the temperature to see the context menu. When you have finished, exit the application.

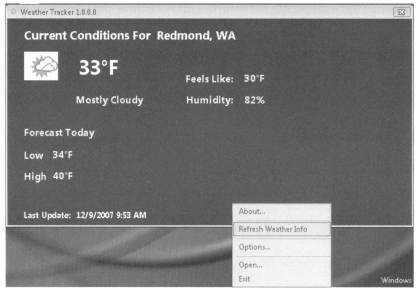

Figure 9-10
The Weather Tracker application displaying weather data from a Web service

Working with the Options Dialog Box

Currently, the location is set to a particular value, and that really isn't our intent. Therefore, you will use the Options dialog box and let users search for the city they want to monitor. Once the location code is selected, it will be persisted to disk, and whenever users restart the application, it will be restored to the last location they specified. Remembering users' settings from one execution to another will provide them with a better experience.

You will use the error provider control to display appropriate text if no city is found.

The error provider control displays error information. For example, if the user enters invalid information in a text box, an error icon is displayed next to the control indicating that an error has occurred. By default, the error icon is a small red circle with an exclamation point. When the user clicks the error icon, an error description is displayed to explain what is wrong to the user. You can change how the error is presented. For example, you can use a different error icon, or you can make the error icon blink. Once a user addresses the error, you set the error description to an empty string to make the error icon disappear.

TO VALIDATE USER INPUT

1. Open the Options form in Design view.

2. In the Toolbox, drag an ErrorProvider control from the Components group to the form. The control appears in the component tray.

3. Name the control ErrorProviderCurrentLocation.

4. Double-click the OK button.

5. Add the following code to the *btnOk_Click* event handler:

```
private void btnOk_Click(object sender, EventArgs e)
{
    UpdateCurrentInfo();
    this.DialogResult = DialogResult.OK;
    this.Close();
}
```

6. Switch back to the Options form in Design view. Select the txtCurrentCity text box, and then in the Properties window, click the Events button (yellow lightning) to display the events list.

7. Double-click the *KeyDown* event.

   Now you'll add some code to support when the user presses Enter in the current city text box. You can see that you have to launch the search if something appears in the text box. To capture the individual keys, you implement the *KeyDown* event handler. It fires as soon as the user presses a key. When the Enter key is pressed, you'll make a call to another MSN Web service to get the list of cities that have keywords in their metadata that matches your query. It's also here that you'll set the error provider to alert a user that the search didn't make any progress.

8. Add the following code to the *txtCurrentCity_KeyDown* event handler:

```csharp
private void txtCurrentCity_KeyDown(object sender, KeyEventArgs e)
{
    if (e.KeyCode == Keys.Enter)
    {
        this.Cursor = Cursors.WaitCursor;
        UpdateListBox();
        if (lbPossibleCities.Items.Count == 0)
        {
            ErrorProviderCurrentLocation.SetError(txtCurrentCity,
                                                 "No results for: " +
                                                 txtCurrentCity.Text);
        }
        else
        {
            ErrorProviderCurrentLocation.SetError(txtCurrentCity, "");
        }
    }
    this.Cursor = Cursors.Default;
}
```

9. The *UpdateListBox* method says it all; this method will contact the MSN Weather service for the currently entered city, country, or other information and bind this list of *KeyValuePair* classes to the list box *Items* collection. The reason the *KeyValuePair* class has been used here is simple: you need *locationCode* to make the call to the MSN Web service, and you need the other one to display on the form as the current monitored location.

```csharp
private void UpdateListBox()
{
    List<KeyValuePair<string, string>> Locations = new
        List<KeyValuePair<string, string>>();
    MSNWeatherData myMSNWeather = new MSNWeatherData();
    Locations = myMSNWeather.GetLocations(txtCurrentCity.Text);
    lbPossibleCities.DataSource = Locations;
    lbPossibleCities.DisplayMember = "Value";
    lbPossibleCities.ValueMember = "Key";
}
```

TO SAVE SETTINGS AND UPDATE WEATHER DATA

1. At the bottom of the Options.cs file, add the following *UpdateCurrentInfo* method:

```
private void UpdateCurrentInfo()
{
 if ((txtCurrentCity.Text != String.Empty) &&
     (lbPossibleCities.Items.Count != 0))
 {
     if (this.lbPossibleCities.SelectedValue.ToString() !=
         Settings.Default.CurrentLocationCode)
     {
         Settings.Default.CurrentLocationCode =
             this.lbPossibleCities.SelectedValue.ToString();
         Settings.Default.CurrentLocation =
             this.lbPossibleCities.SelectedItem.ToString();
         Main.currentLocation =
             this.lbPossibleCities.SelectedItem.ToString();
         Main.currentLocationCode =
             this.lbPossibleCities.SelectedValue.ToString();
     }
 }

 if (rbCelsius.Checked == true)
 {
     Settings.Default.CurrentUnit = "C";
     Main.currentUnit = "C";
 }
 else
 {
     Settings.Default.CurrentUnit = "F";
     Main.currentUnit = "F";
 }

 Settings.Default.Save();
}
```

2. Place your cursor within the "Settings" text. You should see a familiar yellow and red Smart Tag. This Smart Tag is there to let you know that the *Settings* class isn't listed in your *using* directives at the top of Options.cs. Move your mouse pointer over the Smart

Tag, click the down arrow, and then select *using Weather_Tracker.Properties;* to add it to your list of *using* directives.

The *UpdateCurrrentInfo* method saves the user's location code and location, as well as the unit selected to display the temperature, and stores those values with the application settings. It also calls the *UpdateWeather* method in the code for the Main form to update the weather data for the new location code. The *UpdateCurrentInfo* method is called when the user clicks OK in the Options dialog box.

To get the temperature unit the user selected after using the application for a while, you must load it when you open the Options form:

1. Select the Options form in the Design view by clicking the form's title bar.

2. In the Properties window, click the Events button (yellow lightning icon) to get the events list, and double-click the *Load* event.

3. In the *Options_Load* event handler, add the following code:

```
private void Options_Load(object sender, EventArgs e)
{
    if (Settings.Default.CurrentUnit == "F")
    {
        rbFahrenheit.Checked = true;
    }
    else
    {
        rbCelsius.Checked = true;
    }
}
```

Testing Weather Tracker Options

Now you will test the Options dialog box. Press F5 to run Weather Tracker. Once the splash screen disappears, right-click the icon in the notification area, and click Options. In the Options dialog box, test the location name. For example, try typing some garbage, and press Enter. In this case, you should get the error provider to the left of the text box, as shown in Figure 9-11, letting you know that there were no results for the search query you made!

Figure 9-11
The error provider control indicating an error

When you have finished, type a valid location name, and click OK. Select the city from the list that matches the one you'd like to monitor. It is quite fast, and you should see weather data for the new location code.

You should be proud of yourself. You've developed an application with numerous complex features, and it works! The Weather Tracker application accomplishes the basic features established at the beginning of the chapter. There is plenty of room for enhancement. Now it's time to learn how to distribute Weather Tracker or another application.

And Now, Just ClickOnce

The ClickOnce technology has been available since .NET Framework 2.0. It's a fantastic feature that lets you customize how your applications and tools get onto other people's machines. It's very easy—almost as easy as deploying Web applications, which often entails merely copying files onto a server. With ClickOnce, you, the developer, can distribute your application via a robust and reliable mechanism. You can deploy on Web servers, on file servers, or on CDs/DVDs. In addition, you can add the .NET Framework to your distribution package along with SQL Server 2005 Express Edition if your application needs it. ClickOnce handles rollback and uninstall well, and it's a charm for pushing new updates. In this case, you'll deploy to a CD/DVD.

TO PACKAGE AND PUBLISH YOUR APPLICATION

1. To ensure that all the *.gif files representing the weather icons are included with the installation, make sure the *Build Action* property is set to *Content* for all the *.gif images in Solution Explorer. (This process was described earlier in the chapter.)

2. Rebuild the application by clicking Build Solution on the Build menu.

3. In Solution Explorer, right-click the Weather Tracker project, and select Properties to open the Project Designer.

4. Click the Publish tab. You should see a screen that looks like the one shown in Figure 9-12.

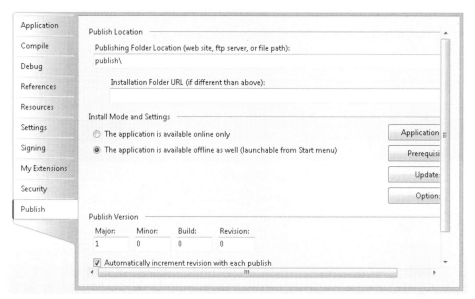

Figure 9-12
Publish tab in the Project Designer

5. Click the Application Files button to see the list of files that will be included in the installation. All the *.gif files (as well as the .exe and other files) should be listed. Click OK.

You now want to select the prerequisites for your application. When the installer runs on the user's machine, it will check for the presence of these items. If they are not present, the installer will by default download them from Microsoft.com or another source that you have configured.

6. Click the Prerequisites button. In the Prerequisites dialog box, select the .NET Framework 3.5 and Windows Installer 3.1 check boxes. Make sure the Download Prerequisites from the Component Vendor's Web Site option is selected. Click OK.

You can also set the Updates settings, which basically help you decide how your users will update their application and how frequently you want your application to automatically check for new updates. You won't do it here, but it's really trivial; take a look by clicking the Updates... button.

7. Click the Publish Wizard button.

The first page of the wizard appears, as shown in Figure 9-13, asking you to specify a location to publish the application.

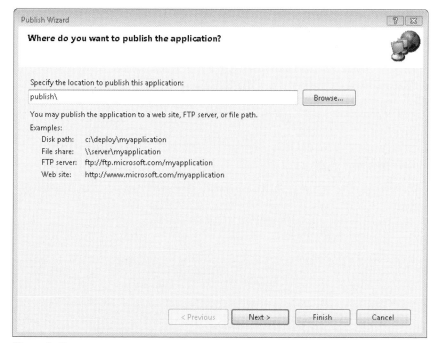

Figure 9-13
Publish Wizard's first page

8. Click the Browse button. In the Open Web Site dialog box, select File System on the left, and then select a location on your computer where you want to publish your application. I suggest you create a new folder named WeatherTracker. You can use the Create New

Folder icon at the upper left to create a new folder. When finished, click the Open button, and then click Next.

9. On the next page, select how the user will install the application. It could be a Web site, a UNC share on a network, or a CD or DVD. Select the From a CD-ROM or DVD-ROM choice, and click Next.

10. The next page asks whether you want your application to look for updates every time it starts. Because you are deploying on a CD or DVD, you won't have your application check for updates. Select the default The Application Will Not Check for Updates choice, and click Next to continue.

11. Click Finish to publish your application.

After a few moments, setup files will be created at the folder location you selected earlier. To test the installation, double-click the Setup.exe file. During the installation, a shortcut will be added to the Programs menu. (To uninstall the application, use Control Panel.)

Once the installation works as expected, you can deploy your application by simply burning the installation files onto a CD or DVD.

ClickOnce has more features, but this short demonstration will get you started creating your own installations.

NOTE
Every time you publish your application, the published version number (not the application version number) will be incremented—that is, it will become version 1.0.0.0, 1.0.0.1, and so on.

NOTE
During the installation, if you get an error message that the application validation did not succeed or you receive another error message, try republishing your application and testing again.

In Summary...

Congratulations on getting this far! You've learned a lot, and I hope you've had some fun developing applications using Visual C# 2008 Express Edition. If you like what you've learned (and I certainly hope so), then your education is just beginning. There's so much more to see and try. This book has provided a small sample of the types of applications you can create. My advice to you is to continue thinking of fun projects you can create! You'll be surprised at how much you can accomplish. In my opinion, developing an application is one of the greatest feelings of accomplishment. People are proud of their applications, and you will be too!

If you happen to create an application that's useful to you, chances are it could be useful for others as well. In the end, you might be helping people by providing them with the fruits of your labor. You can also join development projects for fun and help others in the process while learning a great deal. Visit Codeplex (*http://www.codeplex.com/*) for a sample of cool project examples. Look also at Coding4Fun (*http://blogs.msdn.com/coding4fun/*), where you'll find plenty of interesting and new ways of using your new programming skills.

You can also visit my blog at *http://blogs.msdn.com/ppelland/*. I haven't updated my blog for a while because I've been busy writing this book, but my newest endeavor at Microsoft will enable me to blog about supercool technologies and talk about my new baby. It's still under wraps, but stay alert and come to my blog from time to time to see the news about the new project. Until then, happy developing!

Glossary

A

argument A variable that is passed to a subprogram

B

black box testing Functional testing of a computer program to ensure it performs correctly

breakpoint A pause or stopping place in a program, intentionally inserted to help with debugging

C

class The basic building block of object-oriented programming; it defines the fields, properties, methods, and events of an object

compiler A computer program that translates the instructions written in one computer language into output in another computer language; compilers translate source code into some type of machine language that can be executed by a computer

console application An application that is run from a command prompt with no Windows or Web interface

context-sensitive menu A menu that provides different choices to the user depending on when it is accessed

controls Components of a graphical user interface, such as text boxes or buttons

D

data member Data encapsulated within a class or an object

database A collection of data that is stored in files using a systematic structure

data binding An easy and transparent way to create a link between a control on a Windows form and a data source from your application

debugger A computer program used to find the defects in another program

DLL (Dynamic Link Library) A binary application library file format in Microsoft Windows

E

encapsulation Hides private methods of a class or object; ensures that an object cannot be changed

event A software message that indicates something has happened in the program

execution engine Development tool for executing programs

F

FCL (Framework Class Libraries) A set of code libraries for common programming tasks

H

hyperlink A reference in a hypertext document to another document or location

I

icon A small image or picture used to represent a program, file, or other object

IDE (Integrated Development Environment) Computer software tools that help developers write computer programs

inheritance The ability to create specialized types from existing objects that can share and extend the existing object's behavior without having to re-implement it.

instance A manifestation of a class

J

Jscript An Active Scripting Engine; the Microsoft version of JavaScript

L

Language Integrated Query (LINQ) Adds query capabilities to .NET programming languages (such as Visual Basic), enabling you to query data from a SQL Server database, XML, in-memory arrays and collections, ADO.NET datasets, or any other remote or local data source that supports LINQ

M

method Procedure or function; a piece of code associated with a class or object

Microsoft .NET A software development platform developed by Microsoft

O

override A class or object can replace a behavior it has inherited

P

Perl A programming language that supports both procedural and object-oriented programming

programming language A method for providing instructions to a computer

property A quality of an object

Python An object-oriented computer programming language

R

reference The address of the memory space used to store information about a variable

S

splash screen An image that appears on the screen while a program is loading; it provides information to the user about the loading process and disappears once the program is loaded

SQL Server 2005 Express Edition A version of SQL Server 2005 designed to help developers build applications by providing a powerful database that is also free and easy to use

string A sequence of characters or words

T

toolbar A row or section of clickable icons that activate different functions of a program

tooltip Short, context-sensitive information provided at the point where the mouse pointer is held

U

user interface (UI) The means by which users interact with a computer program

V

variable A structure that holds information temporarily for use later in a program

Visual C# 2008 Express Edition A streamlined version of Visual C# that provides hobbyists, students, and novices with an easy-to-use Windows programming and development tool

W

Windows application Computer software that provides various functions for the user, such as word processing, database queries, or spreadsheet calculations

Windows Presentation Foundation (WPF) Provides a framework for building applications for Windows Vista and blends together the application's user interface, documents, and media content

Index

A

About dialog box, 100–102, 208, 210
abstraction, 220
Add Table dialog box, 186
ADO.NET
 adding queries to application, 184–90
 creating dataset, 174–80
 data binding with domain tables, 182–83
 definition of, 172–73
 developing CarTracker application, 173–74
 getting meaningful information on form, 181–90
 using component tray, 180–81
AJAX (Asynchronous JavaScript and XML), 3
alignment, label, 65
ANSIO/ISO standard, SQL, 157
antispyware applications, 18, 24
antivirus applications, 18, 24
Application-scoped settings, 220
applications, creating first, 27–49
 coding console application, 40–42
 console application, 33–40
 customizing IDE, 42–44
 types of applications, 28
 using IDE, 30–33
 Windows application, 45–48
arguments, 114, 247
Asynchronous JavaScript and XML (AJAX), 3
asynchronous programming with callbacks, 220

B

BackgroundWorker class, 220, 225–28
binding navigator, 181
binding source, 180
black box testing, 105, 247
breakpoints, 136–41, 247
browsers. See Web browsers
Build Action property, 234, 241
button controls, 57–60, 80, 112–15

C

camel casing, 177
CardSpace, 3
car-tracking application. See databases
case-sensitivity, Visual C#, 59
CheckBox control, 81
classes
 creating namespaces, 52–53
 defined, 247
 OOP, 5–9
ClickOnce, 13, 241–44
Close button, 206
CLR (Common Language Runtime)
 foundation role in .NET Framework, 4
 as .NET execution engine, 2
 unhandled exceptions and, 134
code
 console application, 40–42
 demos and samples in book, 33
 executing when event is triggered, 59–60
 learning to read, 42
 regaining current view in test project, 65

renaming controls directly in, 77–78
supporting background tasks, 228
testing own, 105
using comments in, 41, 84
using Track Changes, 66
wiring to events, 83–86
code snippets, 12, 69–72, 86
Codezone Community Web sites, 38–39
columns, database, 161–63, 169
ComboBox control, 81
comments, 41, 84
Community Access pages, 14
compiler
 .NET Framework, 2
 adding reference to application, 135
 defined, 247
 errors at build time, 146
 identifying comments, 84
 naming collisions involving, 53
 working with Immediate window, 146
component tray, 180–81
composite keys, 154
connecting, to Web service, 215–16
console application, 28, 33–42, 247
Console.WriteLine method, 68
ContextMenuStrip control, 199–204, 212–13
context-sensitive menu, 13, 31, 247
controls
 adding to browser application, 56–58
 adding tool strip container, 106–07
 adding to splash screen, 91–92

adding to tsNavigation tool strip, 115–16
associating context menu strips with, 203–04
common Windows, 80–82
defined, 247
layout on forms, 218–19
Navigate dialog box, 102–04
populating with information, 109–11
rearranging order of, 107
snapping and aligning, 64–65
wiring click action to button, 58–60
wiring source code to events, 84–86
working with component tray for non-visual, 180–81
conversion utility, MSN weather Web service, 234–35
copy operation, database files, 177–78
copyrights, viewing, 94–96
C# programming language, 4–9
Ctrl+Spacebar, IntelliSense, 66–67

D

database diagrams, 163–67
Database Explorer, 159–60, 163–71
database management system (DBMS), 150
databases, 149–94
 contents of, 150
 data normalization and integrity, 151–53
 defined, 247
 foreign keys, 156

interacting with relational,
157–58
managing data with, 149–50
null and, 154
primary keys, 154–55
using ADO.NET. see ADO.NET
using LINQ, 190–92
using SQL Server 2005 Express
Edition. see SQL Server 2005
Express Edition
data binding
connecting to Web service using,
215–16
creating dataset for, 173–80
defined, 173, 247
with domain tables, 182–83
data-enabled applications, 12
data, entering into SQL Server
tables, 167–71
data integrity
null and, 154
overview of, 157–58
using foreign key constraints,
156, 169–70
data management. See databases
data members, 5–9, 247
data normalization, 151–53
datasets, 173–81
Data Source Configuration Wizard,
174–80, 216–19
data sources, 198–99, 216–19
Data Sources window, 174, 176, 216
DBMS (database management
system), 150
debugger, 247
debugging, 133–47
breakpoints, 136–37
DLLs and, 134–36
Edit and Continue, 138–39
fixing out-of-range problem,
143–45
handling exceptions with code,
145–46
Immediate window, 146–47
overview of, 134

stepping out of code, 140–42
stop mode, 145
tabs, 137–38
visualizers, 14
declarative programming, 119
deleting a breakpoint, 140
design layout, 53
dialog boxes, interacting through,
100–105
DirectX, 119, 123–24
DLL (Dynamic Link Library), 134–36,
214–16, 247
documentation, Help system, 36–40
Document Outline window, 107

E

Edit and Continue, 13, 138–39, 143
encapsulation, 58, 247
error messages, 59, 170, 244
ErrorProvider control, 236–38
event-based programming, 83–86
events, defined, 247
Exception Assistant, 142–43
execution engine, 2, 15, 247
Extensible Application Markup
Language (XAML), 119–30
Extract Method command,
refactoring, 79

F

FCLs (Framework Class Libraries),
2, 247
fields, OOP, 5–9
files, database, 177
filters, IntelliSense, 69
folders, default location for
software, 22
foreign keys, 156, 164–66, 169–71
FormClosing event, 206–07
forms
adding information to, 216–19
adding Options dialog box,
210–12

attaching to application, 209–10
hooking up to context menu,
212–13
framework. See .NET Framework
Framework Class Libraries (FCLs),
2, 247

G

Getting Started pane, Start page, 31
GetWeatherReport method, 225
glossary, 247–248
GPUs (graphical processing units),
WPF using, 119
graphical processing units (GPUs),
WPF using, 119
Grid.Resources element, 128

H

Help system, 36–40, 100–102, 138.
See also MSDN Online, Help
system
Hide method, 207
hyperlinks, 31–32, 247

I

icons
adding CreateIcon method,
230–32
adding DestroyIcon method, 232
adding weather, 234
associating with controls, 203–04
defined, 247
entering data into SQL Server
tables using, 167
modifying browser forms, 117–18
personalizing with Windows,
111–18
IDE (Integrated Development
Environment), 30–33, 42–44,
247
identity, SQL Server 2005, 154–55,
161, 169

Immediate window, 146
inheritance, 247
instance, defined, 248
Integrated Development
Environment. See IDE
(Integrated Development
Environment)
IntelliSense, 11, 66–74
Items Collection Editor, 200–203

J

JScript, 28, 248

K

KeyDown event, 237–38
KeyUp event, 115–16
KeyValuePair class, 238

L

labels, 65, 81, 177, 234–35
layout, design, 53, 218–19
License Terms, Visual C# 2008
installation, 20–21
LINQ (Language Integrated Query)
queries, 3, 172, 190–92, 248
LINQ to SQL, 192–93
LINQ to XML, 193
ListBox control, 82
ListingTableAdapter, Listing data
table, 184, 187–88
Local Help, Help system, 38
Locals tab, debugging, 138

M

Main form, 198–99, 206, 216–19,
232–33
Main_Load event handler, 209,
232–33
Main toolbar, 32
managed applications, of .NET
Framework, 2

managing data. See databases
ManipulateStrings method, 141–44
.mdf file extension, 159
Menu bar, 32
menu strip, 108
methods
  defined, 248
  OOP, 5–9
  Web service exposed, 213
  wiring source code to events
    using, 84–86
method stubs, IntelliSense, 73
Microsoft.NET, 248
Microsoft SQL Server Compact 3.5,
  23
modal forms, 102
MSDN Express Library, 21, 23
MSDN feeds, Start page, 32
MSDN Online, Help system, 38–40,
  48, 61, 86
MsnWeatherData class, adding,
  220–25
MSN weather Web service, 213–41
  adding MSN weather data class,
    220–25
  adding weather information,
    216–19
  completing functionality, 229–35
  connecting to Web service,
    215–16
  Options dialog box, 236–40
  overview of, 213–14
  performing task in background,
    220, 225–28
  supporting background code,
    228–29
  testing Weather Tracker, 235–36,
    240–41
  user setting entries, 219–20
multitargeting, 19
multithreaded programming, 220

N

namespaces, creating, 52–53
naming collisions, 53

naming conventions, 52–53, 60,
  75–78
Navigate dialog box, 102–04
Navigate menu, 104–05
Navigate method, WebBrowser
  class, 58–60
NavigateToUrl method, 116–17, 129
.NET Framework, 2–3
New Project dialog box, 34, 45–48
normalization, 151–53
notification area, 199–203, 205–07
NotifyIcon control, 199–200
notifyWeather control. See UI (user
  interface)
null, 154
NumericUpDown control, 82

O

objects, OOP, 5–9
Online Help Settings dialog box,
  36–37
OOPLs (object-oriented
  programming languages), 4–5
OOP (object-oriented
  programming), 4–9
Options dialog box, 210–13, 236–41
Options_Load event handler, 240
Organize Usings command, 73
override, 7–9, 248

P

packaging applications, 241–43
Pascal casing, 177
Perl, 28, 248
prerequisites, setting application,
  242–43
primary keys, 154–55
programming languages, 248
progress bar, 108–11
Project Designer, 94, 219–20,
  241–44
Projects, 52–53
properties
  control, 56–58

defined, 248
modifying, 55
Navigate dialog box, 102–04
relationship, 166
renaming controls, 75–77
setting in Properties window,
  54–55
splash screen, 91
viewing title, version and
  copyright, 94–96
publishing applications, 243–44
Python, 28, 248
queries, 184–90

Q

Query Builder, 185–87
query expression, 191
Query Parameters dialog box, 187
Questions, Help system, 39–40

R

RadioButton control, 81
RAD (rapid application
  development) tools, 63–87
  common Windows controls,
    80–82
  event-based programming, 83–86
  IntelliSense. see IntelliSense
  refactoring, 79
  renaming, 74–78
  snap lines, 64–65
rapid application development.
  See RAD (rapid application
  development) tools
RDBMS (relational database
  management system), 150,
  154–55, 157–58
ReadFile method, 141
ReadToEnd method, 141
Recent Projects pane, Start page, 31
refactoring feature, 13, 79
references, 135–36, 215, 248

relational database management
  system (RDBMS), 150, 154–55,
  157–58
relationships, between database
  tables, 163–67
renaming feature, 74–78
Restore method, 206–07
REST (Representational State
  Transfer), 3, 214
RSS feeds, 14
RunWorkerAsync method, 226

S

SaveFileDialog control, 84–86
saving
  changing default project location,
    34
  console applications, 41
  database files, 160
  Weather tracker application
    settings, 239
SDK (software development kit),
  SQL Server, 158
SELECT query, 184–87
Show All Files button, 75
Shutdown method, 204–05
side-by-side installation, 18
Silverlight, 22
Smart Captions, 177
smart tags, 12–13, 56
snap lines, 64–65
SOAP Web services, 213, 214
software development kit (SDK),
  SQL Server, 158
Solution Explorer
  creating WPF version of browser,
    123
  defined, 32
  regaining current view in test
    project, 65
  renaming controls in, 78
  Show All Files button, 75
  working with, 34–35
sorting, in Properties window, 55
splash screens, 90–96, 208–09, 248

SQL Command edit window, 185
SQL Server 2005 Express Edition,
　158–71
　creating database, 159–60
　creating relationships between
　　tables, 163–67
　creating tables in database, 161–63
　defined, 248
　entering data in tables using
　　Visual Studio, 167–71
　interacting with relational
　　database, 157–58
　overview of, 158
　as Visual C# 2008 installation
　　component, 21, 23
SQL (Structured Query Language),
　157, 171
Starter Kits, 11
Start page, 14, 31–32
status bar, 33
StatusStrip control, 108–11
Step Into function, 138–39
Step Out button, 140–42
stored procedures, 184–85
string, 248
Structured Query Language (SQL),
　157, 171
surrogate key, 154
Surround With...option, IntelliSense,
　69–71

T

Tab key, IntelliSense, 67
TableAdapter Query Configuration
　Wizard, 184
table adapters, 181, 184–90
Table Designer toolbar, 161
tables
　creating, 161–63
　creating relationships between,
　　163–67
　data binding with, 182–83
　dataset, 174–75
　entering data into, 167–71

tabs, debugger, 138
testing
　black box, 105
　REST Web service, 214
　Test Connection button, 160
　Weather tracker application,
　　235–36, 240–41
TextBox control, 57, 80
.tif files, 234, 241–42
titles, viewing application
　properties, 94
Toggle Breakpoint, 140
toolbar, 42–44
　adding buttons to, 83
　adding icon to, 42–44
　clicking icon on, 31
　commenting code using buttons
　　from, 84
　defined, 248
　Help, 38
　Main, 32
　Solution Explorer, 35, 65, 75
　Table Designer, 161
　Toolbox, 32
Toolbox, 32
ToolStripButton control, 112–13
tool strip container, adding, 106–07
ToolStrip control, 84–86
tool strips, adding to browser,
　112–13
tooltip, 82, 248
Track Changes feature, 66
tsNavigation tool strip, 115–16
T-SQL, 171
typed datasets, 181
types, OOP, 5–9

U

UI (user interface), 197–213
　adding notification area
　　capabilities, 199–203
　adding Options dialog box,
　　210–12

adding splash screen and About
　dialog box, 208
associating context menu strip
　with control, 203–04
attaching forms to application,
　209–10
creating data source for a Main
　form control, 198–99
defined, 248
hooking up form to context
　menu, 212–13
overview of, 197–98
stopping application, 204–07
UpdateCurrentInfo method, 239–40
UpdateListBox method, 238
updates, setting for application, 243
updates, Visual C# 2008 installation,
　18, 24
UpdateWeather method, 228–29,
　240
URL, configuring browser to
　navigate to, 116–17
UserClosing event, 207
user interface. See UI (user
　interface)
users, creating application settings,
　219–20
using directive, 135–36
using statements, 13, 72–73, 228–29

V

variables
　changing value of, 139
　defined, 248
　entering in Watch tab, 146
　naming, 13, 60, 75–78, 112
　refactoring, 79
versions, viewing properties, 94–96
View Code button, 65, 76
View Designer button, 65
Visual C# 2008 Express Edition,
　10–14, 18–24, 248
Visual C# Express Headlines page,
　Start page, 31

visualizers, debugging, 14
Visual Studio 2008, 3–4

W

Watch tab, 146
WCF (Windows Communication
　Foundation), 3
Weather Tracker application,
　195–245
　features/functions of, 196–97
　user interface. see UI (user
　　interface)
　using MSN weather Web service.
　　see MSN weather Web
　　service
WebBrowser control, 56
Web browsers
　adding professional touches,
　　106–18
　creating simple, 54–58
　creating splash screen, 90–94
　creating WPF version of, 120–30
　defining projects, 52–53
　design layout, 53
　experimenting, 60–61
　interacting through dialog boxes,
　　100–105
　viewing application title, version
　　and copyright, 94–99
　wiring click action to button,
　　58–60
Web service, 213. See also MSN
　weather Web service
WF (Windows Workflow
　Foundation), 3
Windows applications, 30, 45–48,
　248
Windows Communication
　Foundation (WCF), 3
Windows Forms applications
　creating simple Web browser,
　　54–58
　creating using snap lines, 64–65

developing with SQL Server. see
SQL Server 2005 Express
Edition
Weather Tracker. see Weather
Tracker application
Windows Forms controls
adding to browser, 56–57
data binding, 173

defined, 12
list of common, 80–82
Windows Forms Designer, 12, 45–48
WindowsFormsHost class, 128, 130
Windows Vista, 3, 20, 119
Windows Workflow Foundation
(WF), 3
WPF Designer, 12

WPF (Windows Presentation
Foundation), 3, 30, 119–30,
248

X

XAML editor, 12

XAML (Extensible Application
Markup Language), 119–30
XML schema definition (.xsd) file,
174, 175
XMLTextReader, 221–24
XML Web services, 12, 213